D0459329

Diana & Jackie

Also by Jay Mulvaney

Jackie: The Clothes of Camelot

Kennedy Weddings: A Family Album

Diana & Jackie

Maidens, Mothers, Myths

JAY MULVANEY

St. Martin's Press ❧ New York

www.stmartins.com

"Ithaka" by C. P. Cavafy. From *C. P. Cavafy: Collected Poems*, translated by Edmund Keeley and Philip Sherrard and edited by George Savidis. Copyright © 1992 by Princeton University Press.

"A Class Act" by Linda Kline and Lonny Prince quoted with the gracious permission of the authors.

ISBN 0-312-28204-4

To Dick Duane and Bob Thixton

I count myself in nothing else so happy
as in a soul remembering my good friends.
                    —William Shakespeare, *Richard II*

Contents

Introduction

They were two of the saddest rituals of the modern age, the funerals of a president and a princess, and at the emotional core of each event were two women.

They were two women who stilled the world's heartbeat for a moment, one walking majestically behind the caisson of her slain husband, the second's flag-draped coffin rumbling over the cobblestone streets of an ancient city, bearing a floral tribute hand addressed to "Mummy."

They were two women who took center stage at these rare moments of global communion—that exhilarating experience of sharing a sense of purpose and desire with millions of faceless others.

Diana, Princess of Wales, and Jacqueline Kennedy Onassis. Two women who have been subject to intense public scrutiny for many years—each in turn enchanted and reviled.

There have been women throughout history who have captured the imagination of their times and retain a vivid presence to this day—Cleopatra and Joan of Arc are two—but their lives were separated by centuries. It's rare when two such women share the world stage. Diana and Jackie were two very different women, yet they led two very similar lives.

From their youth as daughters whose lives were shattered by divorce, to their marriages to complex men, then their lives as unmarried women, to their untimely deaths, Diana and Jackie were kept in the public eye by an omnipresent media that made us feel we knew them as we have never known public figures before.

Jacqueline Kennedy entered the public arena just as television was coming of age as a means of communication with an instantaneous global reach. She was the first First Lady of TV and as much a master of the medium as that other TV first lady, Lucille Ball. Jackie used the medium to draw attention to those of her interests that she deemed important and worthy of public notice, most famously the restoration of the White House. Jackie also used television to project the image of herself that she wanted her audience to see—rarely speaking in public, moving through life with an air of mystery, like a great silent-film star.

Twenty years later, when Diana Spencer arrived on the scene, television had matured and spawned an insatiable appetite for celebrity gossip. Where once there was restraint, there was now unending revelation. What had once been kept quiet—the sexual peccadilloes of the President of the United States—was now fodder for round-the-clock media exploitation, from the breakfast news shows to late-night comic monologues. It wasn't until the last months of her life that Diana began to use her hard-won knowledge of the media for the selfless promotion of a worthy cause—the anti-land-mine campaign. (An example of her power: the white-hot media glow she brought to the campaign focused the world's attention on the land-mine issue, winning the Nobel Peace Prize for Jody Williams.) For most of her life, Diana didn't use the media to project the image of herself she wished us to see. Instead she searched through their lenses on a quest for a self she could identify with.

Despite their differences, Diana and Jackie found themselves living oddly parallel lives. Their stories have been told many times, but never before compared. On a surface level, the comparisons are easy and have a tabloid sheen: they both had husbands who cheated on them, they both were fashion icons, they both were good mothers, etc. On closer inspection, similarities become apparent that illuminate a distinct parallel between their two lives:

Diana and Jackie were both daughters of acrimonious divorce. They each married men twelve years their senior; Charles Windsor and Jack Kennedy were both resilient bachelors who needed "trophy brides" to advance their career. Both women married into tub-thumping families who tried to force them to suppress their individuality for the common family good. Each gained official roles through marriage. Both were shrewd manipulators of their public image, evoking a style and glamour that seduced the world, continuing even after their deaths. Lastly, they shattered forever the archetypes of "First Lady" and "Royal Princess."

For all the similarities, there were many ways in which they were completely different: Jackie's father adored her and fed her a steady diet of "Vitamin P" (for Praise). Diana, as the third daughter to an heirless British peer, was considered a disappointment at birth. Jackie was superbly educated, well prepared to take her place on the world stage. Diana was the equivalent of a high-school dropout, relying on instinct, not intellect. England's Diana operated with an American "quivering lower lip," opening her heart to the world, in comparison to Jackie's very British "stiff upper lip" and strict adherence to the adage "Never complain, never explain."

The one basic role they shared, of course, was that of woman. Both Diana and Jackie were women of their times. Adapting the archetypal three stages of women—Virgin, Mother, Crone—to Maiden, Mother, and Myth offers a prism through which to tell their stories. This framework also provides a look at the evolving role of women in society over the past two generations. What was impossible for one became a standard way of behavior for the other. There's an odd symbiosis between Jackie and Diana, as if the elder paved the way for the younger's journey. When Diana's marriage began to unravel, for example, the truth about JFK's infidelities was well known. It was impossible to try to pull the wool over our eyes. Diana could express the outrage and betrayal she felt, whereas Jackie was forced by the conventions of the time, and her upbringing, to mask her true feelings.

Diana entered our lives as the maiden, the nursery-school teacher with a beguiling blush and virginal reputation. To reinforce the archaic notion that the role of the monarchy was to be the moral bedrock of British society, Prince Charles had to find a bride whose white wedding gown was an honest talisman of her "purity." Diana lived up to her part of the bargain. Charles, and by extension, the royal family, did not live up to his. But the royal wedding took place; the maiden became a princess before the eyes of millions. Diana would change during her years on the public stage, but it is "Shy

Di"—the innocent virgin seduced and betrayed—that is her enduring legacy.

Diana came to us a maiden; Jackie came to us a mother. Indeed, her first accomplishment after the 1960 election was to give birth to a son, the presumed heir to the Kennedy political legacy. Motherhood was the leitmotiv of the early years of Jackie's public life: placing a kitchen and dining room in the family quarters of the White House so the Kennedys could eat together; sharply curtailing her official schedule to allow maximum time with her two children; fiercely protecting them from fawning servants, photo-snapping tourists, and inquisitive reporters.

Being a mother was what made Jackie happiest, and her happiness was hard-earned. She had had a miscarriage during the second year of her marriage, in 1955, and then a year later had carried almost to term, enduring the tragedy of a stillborn child. The birth of their daughter, Caroline, in 1957 and that of John F. Kennedy Jr. three years later brought both of the Kennedys great joy. In 1963 Jackie's second son, Patrick Bouvier Kennedy, died of a respiratory ailment two days after his birth. The infant's death brought Jack and Jackie closer than they had ever been during their ten-year marriage. Then came Dallas.

Jacqueline Kennedy became a single mother at thirty-four. Despite a second marriage and a long-term romantic relationship in her later years, she essentially remained a single mother for the rest of her life.

It would be impossible to label either Diana or Jackie a crone. Jackie came into her own in the last years of her life, enjoying a fulfilling career and a warm and loving relationship. Diana was laying the foundation for a life revolving around the substantial issues she considered important. The circumstances of their lives have created a third archetypal role for them: Myth.

Jacqueline Kennedy Onassis wore no crown. But her thousand days as First Lady created a myth out of a bookish Vassar girl. She nurtured her country's aesthetic growth, fostering an appreciation for our cultural heritage. She created an identity as First Lady completely separate from that of the president. For four days in November 1963, she held her country's soul in her heart.

Diana seemed too perfect to be true in those early days when she first came into our lives during the fall of 1980. We were captivated by this charming young girl, her head habitually tucked down, eyes trained firmly on the pavement when walking from her car to the nursery school where she taught and was famously photographed in that diaphanous skirt.

Diana's life was a fairy tale for a very short time, with a happy prince and princess and two baby princes. But then the fairy tale imploded, and what was once whispered was now shouted—and the shouts rocked the royal family to its very core. The princess spoke openly about things that princesses shouldn't even know about. Part of Diana's myth was that this storybook princess—tall, blond, thin, beautiful, wealthy—spoke out about subjects that are usually cloaked in shame: bulimia, betrayal, adultery, depression, divorce. In showing us that she was not immune to the pressures and destructive behaviors inherent in modern-day life, she opened the door for women around the world to address these problems free of shame and condescension.

Both Diana and Jackie tapped into our subconscious desire. We responded to Jackie's innate nobility and to Diana's neediness. Jackie was a victor in the game of life. Diana was its victim. They were England's princess and America's queen. This is the story of their two lives, compared.

Diana & Jackie

Prologue

Two Weddings

Here is the stuff of which fairy tales are made.
—Robert Runcie, archbishop of Canterbury, July 29, 1981

Indeed, the day began like a fairy tale, with the morning sun dancing and dappling through the trees as the majestic old house came alive with excitement and anticipation. The house itself enjoyed historic ties to its community and had witnessed many celebrations, but that day would be special. That day's wedding would become one of the signature events in the house's long history. It was a big house, if not palatial, with sitting rooms and drawing rooms and reception rooms, two dining rooms and a separate wing for servants, and bedrooms for close to two dozen people.

The house had rarely been so busy. Servants and staff members scurried up and down the back stairs, bringing tea and fetching breakfast trays; the laughter of young children wafted through the hallways, carried along by the slight warm breeze. Even those whose responsibilities were crucial to the day's success—dressmakers, hairdressers, and makeup artists—were caught up in the glittering romance of the moment. Their task was important, to transform the young girl who stood there in her third-floor bedroom into something more than just a pretty bride. They had to create a symbol, a consort, a princess. Many eyes would be focused on their result, and they went about their work with a sense of calm efficiency.

The object of their attention, the central figure of the day, stood in the center of the yellow-walled bedroom, wrapped her dressing gown tightly around her slender waist, and began to prepare for the most important moment of her life. One day she would be the most famous woman in the world, but that day she was just a young woman preparing for her wedding. One day her life would be under public scrutiny, revered by some, reviled by others, but on that morning, she was concentrating on the elaborate festivities that would consume so much of her energy. One day she would draw the attention of literally the entire globe as it stopped to watch her procession through the streets of the capital city. But that day she was filled with hope and promise and dreams, utterly unaware of the magnitude that life had in store for her. She was a bride, a young girl about to marry the man she loved, and in that moment she shared with women around the globe and throughout history the sense of joy and communion that takes place in the preparation for one of society's oldest rituals, the marriage ceremony.

Tall, taller than average, and slim, she exuded health and vitality. It was to be the happiest day of her life, one that she had dreamed about since she was a young girl, and one that she had been planning for months. Surrounded by her sisters, family, and friends, she was able to concentrate on the task at hand. Taking a deep breath and sneaking a quick look outside her bedroom window, she sat on a white wicker stool as her hairdresser began brushing her thick, short hair, preparing it for the elaborate headdress she would wear, a family heirloom. It was fragile, difficult to wear, and her hairdresser had to make certain that it could be securely fastened to her head.

When her hair was done, she stood and removed her dressing gown. Assisted by the dressmakers and her mother's ladies' maid, and being careful not to leave a trace of her subtle makeup on the silk, she stepped into her wedding dress and stood patiently as it was buttoned and zipped and smoothed in place. The dress was a masterpiece, a luxuriant creation, with a tight bodice and a very full skirt made of acres of silk and tulle. It was a spectacular dress, a dress that said, "This is a *bride*," a dress that had little relation to contemporary fashion but spoke volumes about romance and history. You could see Scarlett O'Hara wearing such a dress, or the Empress Eugénie. If it was a little too fussy for its wearer's taste, she understood that it fit the occasion perfectly, that she would walk down the aisle and cause people to gasp in admiration. She looked very much like a fairy-tale heroine about to marry the prince.

In a very real sense, that is just what Jackie was about to do.

Newport, 1953

It was September 12, 1953, and twenty-four-year-old Jacqueline Lee Bouvier was about to become the bride of John F. Kennedy, the recently elected senator from the Commonwealth of Massachusetts. His political star had long been on the rise, thanks to the drive, power, and wealth of his father, the former American ambassador to the Court of St. James. But his elevation to the U.S. Senate, and his astonishing electoral victory over Henry Cabot Lodge Jr., had given the thirty-six-year-old Jack Kennedy a stature and position on the American political landscape that few enjoyed and many envied. He was certainly the most eligible bachelor in the country, and great things were planned for him. But for him to succeed, he needed, above all else, a wife. A wife to stand by his side, a wife to provide him with the children and family that would reassure the country that he possessed all the qualities required to lead them. Leadership ability, heroism, charisma, *and* a healthy family life—they were what the country wanted, and Jack Kennedy was blessed with all of them, except for the latter. So his mission was to be married, and a suitable bride had to be found.

Friends had introduced them ("*Shamelessly* matchmaking," Jackie would later recall), realizing that their two quicksilver minds and rapier wits would appeal to each other. Jack's friends knew that in addition to being Catholic and from the right social background, any woman whom he might marry had to be someone who could cap-tivate his intellect. And in Jackie Bouvier, they found his perfect match. She had been born to a socially prominent French Catholic family, and yet she had solid connections, through second marriages and step-relations, to the great WASP establishment. She was beautiful and well read and had the kind of humor that appealed to him: ironic, slightly detached, and razor sharp.

Yes, she was a perfect bride for Jack Kennedy, as perfect as any storyteller could have created. As she gazed out the windows of Hammersmith Farm, her view extending down over the rolling fields toward the frothy whitecapped waves of Narragansett Bay, she knew that her wedding was symbolic of much more than just marrying the man she loved. She was providing a key dynastic link in the Kennedy family saga, and as she looked in the mirror to fasten a single strand of pearls around her neck, she readied herself to being the focus of the hundreds and hundreds of people who would gaze on her that day.

London, 1981

Nearly twenty-eight years after that September morning, Diana Frances Spencer stood in front of the full-length gilt-framed looking glass in her borrowed bedroom at Clarence House, the Queen Mother's London home, and faced a strikingly similar situation, although there would be hundreds and hundreds of *millions* of people around the globe focusing on her that day. Diana, too, was about to marry her prince. But her prince, unlike Jackie's, was *literally* a prince, possessor of the most exalted princely title the world could offer— Charles Philip Arthur George, Prince of Wales and Earl of Chester, Duke of Cornwall and Rothesay, Earl of Carrick and Baron Renfrew, Lord of the Isles and Great Steward of Scotland. He was heir to the throne of the United Kingdom and Northern Ireland, and in marrying him, she would become his consort and the future queen.

For the past decade, there had been endless speculation on whom Charles would pick as his bride. Every date, every time he smiled in public at a woman, was an invitation for the media to start guessing when the engagement would be announced. Over the past two or three years, the media frenzy had escalated, in part because of Charles's own pronouncement that "thirty seemed a good age to be married." Not only were the press and public eager for him to marry at age thirty-two, so was his own family. His father, Prince Philip, duke of Edinburgh, was impatient for him to perform his duty, which was to marry and produce an heir. Charles had had many and varied girlfriends, from all walks of life, but in the end he chose, in both a literal and figurative sense, the girl next door.

Throughout history, the Spencer family had had a long and rich association with the monarchy. Diana's father, the eighth Earl Spencer, had served as an equerry to both the queen and her father, George VI, in the early 1950s. When he left royal service, he moved into a house next door to the queen's private estate at Sandringham, where Diana was born. But the close association with the royal family continued. Diana's younger brother, Charles, who counted the queen as one of his godparents, had served as a page of honor to Her Majesty in 1977. Her sister Jane was married to the queen's assistant private secretary, and her maternal grandmother, Ruth, Lady Fermoy, was a lady-in-waiting and close friend to Queen Elizabeth, the Queen Mother.

It was these two grannies who had first thought of Diana as an appropriate bride for the Prince of Wales. Well born and beautiful, she seemed to be a pleasant and docile young woman. Diana was the perfect choice. Her young age (she was nineteen when she became engaged) largely precluded her from having had any prior romantic excursions, which, as odd as it may seem to modern eyes, would have tainted her reputation and been viewed as unseemly by the royal establishment. On the surface, it all appeared to be perfect.

And yet...

Diana was barely twenty years old as she looked out the window of Clarence House on that warm July morning, looking at the hundreds of people who had slept on the street for two or three days to ensure a prime viewing location. At her wedding Jackie had stood on familiar ground, Hammersmith Farm having been her summer home for ten years. Clarence House was alien territory for the soft-spoken Lady Diana. She had spent a few nights there after her engagement, when it was thought that, for both security's and propriety's sake, she should move from her bachelor girl's apartment in the raffish London neighborhood called Earls Court. Years later she would remember that on that morning she "was very calm . . . when we were getting up at Clarence House. Must have been awake at five A.M." As she moved from the window and gazed at her reflection in the looking glass, the image reflected was that of a picture-perfect bride—in her case, literally a fairy-tale princess. Tall as an Amazon, blond and slim, she was almost overwhelmed by her voluminous gown. Her great height and aristocratic bearing saved her, though, and she looked, in the words of the Queen Mother, "simply enchanting."

Diana's dress was similar in silhouette to Jackie's, featuring a tight bodice and very full skirt. It was the creation of a pair of designers, the husband-and-wife team of David and Elizabeth Emanuel. Diana chose them after wearing some of their clothes during a photo shoot early in her engagement. The Emanuels were fully aware of the importance of their design. They looked at the design history of royal wedding dresses, sat in St. Paul's Cathedral to gauge the proportions and colors, consulted with other designers on the specific requirements of royal dressing. Yet the gown they designed was more romantic, more ethereal than any royal wedding dress in recent history.

Whereas Jackie's dress was elaborate, it was also sophisticated. The effect of Diana's gown, which was even more elaborate than Jackie's, was younger, more girlish, more storybook pretty. Whereas Jackie's bodice had tiny capped sleeves and intricate tucking and banding, almost like a cummerbund, the bodice of Diana's gown embraced a more romantic fantasy, with its piecrust lace ruffles, full sleeves adorned with bows, ruffles, and lace and incorporating a piece of Carrickmacross lace, worked by her husband-to-be's great-grandmother Queen Mary. On Diana's head she wore the Spencer family tiara, with its waves and bowknots of diamonds complemented by the shimmering mother-of-pearl sequins dotting her silk tulle veil. Jackie's headdress was also a family heirloom, her maternal grandmother's lace cap and billowing veil, whose crisp whiteness had yellowed slightly with age, dictating the use of ivory silk taffeta for her wedding gown, so the slight impurities of the whites would complement each other.

Diana dressed with the help of her sister Sarah, who had spent the night with her, and laughed and teased with the others present. "Diana was joking around," reminisces Elizabeth Emanuel, "singing [the commercial ditty] 'Just on cornetto!' ... She was in top form. She was really excited." Gathered around her were her bridesmaids. When Princess Elizabeth, the last heir to the throne to be married in England, wed the Greek prince Philip in 1947, her bridesmaids had all been contemporaries, eight young women from aristocratic families, including her sister, Princess Margaret, and her cousin Princess Alexandra. But over the years, the traditions had changed in England, and it was now considered fashionable for young brides to be surrounded by children as they walked down the aisle. Often nieces and nephews, godchildren, or the offspring of close friends are pressed into service. This tradition may have started in 1960, about the time of the wedding of Princess Margaret, who was almost thirty on the day of her wedding. Most of her contemporary female friends had been married for several years and may have been deemed too matronly to serve as bridesmaids. Ever since then, children have been used as bridesmaids and pages.

Diana's chief bridesmaid was Princess Margaret's daughter, Lady Sarah Armstrong-Jones. Sarah, who had previous experience in this role, having been a bridesmaid to her cousin Princess Anne at her 1973 wedding to Captain Mark Phillips, was joined by her cousin India Hicks; two daughters of friends of Prince Charles, Sarah Jane Gaselee and Catherine Cameron; and one of Diana's nursery-school charges, Clementine Hambro, the great-granddaughter of Winston Churchill, as bridesmaids. Charles's cousin Lord Nicholas Windsor and another child of one of his friends, Edward van Cutsem, were the pages. As they stood in the main entranceway of Clarence House, waiting for Diana and her father to arrange themselves in the glass coach that would take them through London to St. Paul's Cathedral, the group was a picture of perfect happiness.

And yet ...

As Diana settled into the confined space of the tiny carriage, engulfed by her voluminous skirts and crinolines and her twenty-five-foot-long train, she thought of the daunting task that was now only a few minutes away, that long, long walk up the aisle of St. Paul's.

She would be walking on the arm of her father, but it's hard to say who would be offering whom the most support, as Johnnie Spencer had only recently recovered from a massive stroke that almost killed him. He would need Diana's strength as much as she needed his.

What none of the hundreds of people in the cathedral nor the millions watching on television were aware of was that as she took that long walk up the aisle, she had a secret dread in her heart. Much as she was completely in love with Prince Charles, the love he returned to her was a half love, a love tempered by a sense of duty and obligation. Try as she might to suppress her doubts and fears, they were with her as she began the procession down the red carpet, accompanied by the stately cadence of Jeremiah Clarke's "Trumpet Voluntary."

"As I walked up the aisle, I was looking for her," Diana later remembered, speaking of her husband-to-be's inamorata, Camilla Parker Bowles. "I knew she was there, of course." For Diana, a month out of her teens, marrying the most exalted bachelor in the world was intimidating enough. To walk down the aisle nursing the fear that it was all a charade, that her prince was in love with another woman, made the feeling far worse.

As Diana recalled years later, "Walking down the aisle, I spotted Camilla, pale gray, veiled pillbox hat, her son Tom standing on a chair. To this day, you know—vivid memory."

Reaching the end of the aisle and turning toward Prince Charles, she tucked away the doubt and fear that lurked in her heart. One can't help but wonder if she surrendered to the fairy tale, sharing with millions of others the fantasy that everything was perfect.

And yet, and yet . . .

Newport, 1953

The perfect-picture facade began to crack in the big house on Harrison Avenue late on Saturday morning. What should have been Jackie's day was close to spinning out of control. Most of the details of the wedding, decisions that by right belonged to her, had been wrenched away from her, from the size of the wedding itself to the design of her gown to the baker of the wedding cake. And now the single most important piece of the day to her—having her adored father escort her down the aisle toward the new chapter in her life—was being taken away from her as well. It was a sad episode on what should have been a gloriously happy day. It forever altered her relationship with her mother, Janet Lee Auchincloss, tingeing the proceedings with a bittersweet mélange of shame, recrimination, and regret.

As Jackie attended to her final preparations, pinning to her bodice the diamond clip that was a gift from Joe Kennedy and slipping on the diamond bracelet that her fiancé had casually dropped in her lap at the rehearsal dinner, Janet was working ferociously behind the scenes to control the one wild-card appearance of the day . . . that of Jackie's father. Black Jack Bouvier was scheduled to arrive at Hammersmith Farm to take Jackie to St. Mary's Church and escort her down the aisle. He had performed this duty with dash and aplomb five months earlier at the wedding of his younger daughter, Lee, and was looking forward with particular relish to taking his beloved "Jacque-leen" on his arm in front of the seven hundred invited guests arriving in Newport that morning.

But Janet had conspired to have her former husband excluded from all of the pre-wedding parties and dinners and made it clear, in no uncertain terms, that he would not be welcome at Hammersmith Farm for the reception. Bouvier, a proud man and an alcoholic, started drinking, and although not falling-down drunk, he was deemed by Janet to be in no shape to do his fatherly duty. Janet forbade him to appear and threatened to cause a scene if he arrived at the church.

"Janet was a vindictive woman," her stepson Yusha Auchincloss would say years later, "and Jackie never forgave her for what she did to Jack Bouvier that day."

Janet in turn blamed Jackie. "I knew your father would do something like this to ruin the day. I just knew it. Why you insisted he be here to do this to us, I'll never know." Jackie fled to her room in tears, but she soon composed herself and was driven to the church with her mother and stepfather, Hugh D. Auchincloss II, who stood in for the disgraced Jack Bouvier.

Looking at a photograph of Jackie entering St. Mary's on the arm of her "Uncle Hughdie," one of her closest friends pointed to her seemingly serene face and recalled that "this is a look of absolute fury. . . . When you saw this look on her face, this set jaw and those laser-beam eyes, the best thing you could do was to run . . . fast . . . and in the opposite direction."

But no one who wasn't an intimate of Jacqueline Bouvier would have had the slightest idea that anything was amiss. Her father, it was announced, had, alas, come down with the flu. She carried on, in the very best tradition of the "stiff upper lip." Jackie acted her role brilliantly, with a grace and courage that would one day impress the world, just as Diana would nearly thirty years later. These two young women shared more than a tight grip of the brass ring on their respective wedding days. Each woman was being married under intense public scrutiny and had to mask bitter personal disappointment and put her personal feelings of despair on hold as she walked down the aisle toward her new life.

And as they did so, they entered our lives and began an intensely symbiotic relationship with a public that could never seem to get enough of either of them, a relationship that altered the delicate balance of public and private boundaries in the lives of celebrated people.

And yet . . .

On those two mornings, in 1953 and 1981, they were simply two young women walking down the aisle to join the men they loved. As they took the hands of their respective spouses, they pushed the disappointments and doubts aside and joyfully recited the sacred vows. Neither had any idea of what life had in store for her.

Chapter One

Gilded Daughters of Privilege

*I've known two great decades in my life, the twenties and the sixties,
and I'm always comparing them. . . . In those two decades you got
something so sharp, so new.*

—Diana Vreeland, DV

Both Diana and Jackie were born on the cusp of great social change.
They entered worlds that seemed secure and prosperous, but very
early on in their lives, seismic shifts radically altered the tenor of
those worlds. July babies, Diana a Cancer and Jackie a Leo, they
were very much daughters of their place and time. Jackie was born
three months before the October 1929 stock market crash that heralded the Great Depression; that event would rock the foundations
of her family life, leading to her father's financial decline and ultimately to the divorce of her parents.

The England of Diana's birth in 1961 was to alter dramatically in
the ensuing decade, a social revolution set on Carnaby Street with a
soundtrack by the Beatles and the Rolling Stones. The relaxation of
social standards would result in a devastating scandal that tore Diana's family apart.

Born into the highest levels of society, Diana and Jackie grew up
in a rarefied world of privilege and insulation that is one of the
advantages of great wealth. But the old adage "Money doesn't buy
happiness," often doled out like a bitter-tasting medicine, certainly
rings true in the tale of these two golden daughters of privilege.

New York, 1929

Seven-forty Park Avenue is the type of building that comes to mind when people talk about "a Park Avenue apartment." With its gleaming limestone facade and Art Deco detailing, it's the kind of building that Hollywood movies and smart novels set in the 1930s and 1940s would use to glorify the American essence of luxury, comfort, and success. It's easy, for example, to imagine the snooty Vassar society girl from Mary McCarthy's *The Group* living at 740, or to hear an Irving Berlin song and picture Fred Astaire and Ginger Rogers dancing through the gray marble lobby, or to suppose that apartment 12B, a fourteen-room duplex, was home to Carole Lombard and her madcap family in the screwball comedy movie *My Man Godfrey*.

But the little girl who lived in 12B at 740 Park Avenue was no fictional heroine. She went to Vassar, but she wasn't a society snob. She never appeared in a Hollywood movie, but she would become the greatest star in the world (*Variety,* the show-business bible, once hailed her as the "world's top B.O. [box office] femme"). Her life's narrative is unique in the annals of American history, but no one knew what life had in store for her; at the time of her birth, Jacqueline Lee Bouvier was the daughter of the uniquely American trilogy of success, ingenuity, and reinvention.

Her first husband, when asked at a press conference during his 1960 presidential campaign whether the most beautiful women came from his state, Massachusetts, or from Texas, the home of his running mate, laughed and replied, "Well, my wife comes from New York, so . . . ," and crinkled his eyes in glee as the room erupted in laughter.

Jackie was a daughter of New York, born in Southampton, then a quiet resort town for the rich and socially prominent; raised in New York City until she was thirteen; and returning to spend the last thirty years of her life a few blocks away from her girlhood home. Seven-forty sits atop a low rising knoll on the northwest corner of Park Avenue and East Seventy-first Street, commanding, like some preening dowager in her box at the Metropolitan Opera, a spectacular view up and down the broad boulevard. The address is proudly carved in the dove gray marble that surrounds the entranceway, whose columns are decorated with stylized flowers in carved bas-relief. The building's limestone facade, rising eighteen stories from the ground, is decorous in comparison with the entrance, relieved from starkness by subtle fluted pilasters and restrained ornamental decorations around the upper floors. It is a supremely elegant building and yet possesses, thanks to its Art Deco detailing, an undeniably insouciant charm.

Jackie's parents, Janet Norton Lee and John Vernou "Black Jack" Bouvier III, possessed much the same sort of charm; they were the darlings of their age, characters out of an F. Scott Fitzgerald story. She was an accomplished horsewoman, he a dashing rake with a wandering eye for fillies of the two-legged variety. They had been married in July 1928, slightly more than a year before the birth of their elder daughter. Their wedding, with more than five hundred guests in attendance, was gushingly reported in the society pages. Janet was "a stately bride bedecked in satin, lace and silver," and her bridesmaids called to mind "green and gold jonquils nodding in the sunshine."

The marriage, while on a personal level tumultuous and ultimately a failure, was on a certain plane a successful pairing. Jack and Janet represented two immigrant families, both Catholic, both of whom had fulfilled the promise of their adopted homeland and become successful, wealthy, and, to different degrees, socially prominent and influential members of their community.

In the baby Jacqueline, born on July 28, 1929, and christened with a feminized French version of her father's name, the coupling of the two disparate sides of the immigrants' dream became complete. The more settled Bouviers, whose family came from France to the United States in the early days of the republic, had made their fortune and acquired social prominence. The Irish Lees, more rough-and-tumble recent arrivals whose money was still new, were, in the parlance of the times, marrying "up," a great American tradition and one in which the Bouviers themselves were well practiced.

The Bouvier Chapel, tucked away in a corner of St. Patrick's Cathedral in New York City, is a memorial to the founding member of the American Bouvier family. Dedicated to Saint Michael and

Saint Louis, the two warrior saints (one celestial, the other terrestrial), the chapel was a gift of Michel C. Bouvier, given in memory of his parents, Louise Vernou and Michel Bouvier. The chapel was designed by Charles T. Matthews and built by Tiffany and Co., and its design was influenced by thirteenth-century French Gothic architecture; its decorations include marble fleur-de-lis, the lilies of France. Its position, next to the Lady Chapel behind the main altar, and its exquisite jewel-box design easily signify the prominence of the Bouvier family in the social life of New York City in post–Civil War society. The family's American story had started in Philadelphia in the early 1800s, moved to Nutley, New Jersey (later home to another renowned tastemaker, Martha Stewart), and, through marriage and hard work, had culminated with acceptance in the original ranks of the Four Hundred— Mrs. Astor's list that separated the haves from the have-nots. The Bouviers were definitely among the haves. That their status was embellished with the 1940 publication of a private family genealogy, *Our Forebears*, which presented the family as descendants of French nobility, was a source of bemusement for the adult Jacqueline Kennedy. The truth was quite different, and the family's origins more humble, but this little exercise in reinvention, an American pastime, was widely accepted as fact during the most important part of the Bouviers' impact on the national scene, the early 1960s.

Black Jack was a charmer, a dashing and handsome man. The son of a millionaire, he possessed a devil-may-care attitude that conventional men found corrupt and impressionable young women found irresistible. A stockbroker by trade, his main avocation in life was the pursuit of pleasure. Black Jack's vanity was legendary. Tall and well built, he continually worked on his physique, using the facilities at the Yale Club and even going so far as installing a private gym in one of the six bedrooms at 740 Park. He kept a perpetual tan, sunbathing at every opportunity, in the nude if possible; the tan, coupled with an odd pigmentation condition, gave his skin the color of warm walnut oil, hence the nickname Black Jack. He enjoyed the name, just as he enjoyed the frequent comparisons to movie stars and matinee idols, first, in the 1920s, to Rudolph Valentino and later to Clark Gable. "He was this Clark Gable character," a friend was later to reflect, "with the mustache and the sexy gleam in his eye."

It was that sexy glint, and the dangerous air that came with it, that first caught the attention of Janet Lee, a friend of Black Jack's younger twin sisters, Maude and Michelle. That Janet was sixteen years younger than he made no difference; indeed, it added to the air of excitement, as there was something vaguely pedophilic about the disparity in ages. Their wedding was the perfect culmination of the Jazz Age. Taking place in East Hampton, at the quaint white clapboard St. Philomena's Church, it was a scene out of a summer garden, with the bridesmaids' wide-brimmed hats nodding up and down in the warm salty air like buttercups blowing in a field. The reception was held at Janet's parents summer home on Lily Pond Lane.

There has never been much publicity about Jackie's maternal family, the Lees. There have been those who cynically claim that Jackie deliberately soft-pedaled them in an effort to downplay her Irish ancestry when courting John F. Kennedy, appealing to his internalized snobbish instinct that French Catholics were a rung up the social ladder from Irish Catholics. Then there have been those, the writer Gore Vidal leading the pack, who have hinted with splenetic glee that Lee is an Americanized version of Levy and that the family was of Jewish origin. Vidal and writer John Davis, a Bouvier cousin of Jackie's, both merrily report that Janet herself repeatedly tried to pass herself off as a "Lee of Virginia," a descendant of the Civil War general Robert E. Lee. Vidal and Davis each had an ax to grind with Janet Lee, as her divorce and remarriage would affect each of their lives, at least peripherally, but it is true that very little was ever mentioned in print about the Lees until well after the Camelot years had passed into history.

James T. Lee, Jackie's maternal grandfather, was a self-made man. A lawyer, banker, and real-estate developer, he built more than two hundred buildings in New York City, among them luxurious apartment houses on Fifth and Park Avenues. He had a cantankerous relationship with his wife, Margaret Merritt; their three daughters—

Janet and her sisters, Winifred and Marion—were accustomed to emotionally strained family dinners at which their father would not speak directly to his wife but would relay requests through his daughters. Jackie's younger sister, Lee Radziwill, remembers him with a shudder: "We were never close, to say the least, to my grandfather Lee. He was a very severe man, a miser and a terribly successful businessman. He didn't have much warmth or charm."

James T. Lee showed no warmth or charm to his son-in-law—he actively disliked Black Jack to the point where he excluded his two Bouvier granddaughters from his will—and did not celebrate his daughter's wedding with joy. Nonetheless, the newlywed Bouviers quickly settled into the life of prominent New York society figures. Their fourteen-room duplex at 740 was provided to them rent-free begrudgingly as a gift from the bride's father, who owned the building. The apartment's formal layout of public rooms (reception room, living room, dining room, and library, each with a working fireplace), centered on a twenty-five-by-twelve-foot entrance gallery with a sweeping curved staircase leading upstairs to six bedrooms plus servants' quarters, gave them an extravagant base of operations that few in their social circle could equal. Summers were spent at a rented home on Egypt Lane, close to the hub of East Hampton social activity, the Maidstone Club, where the Bouviers maintained a cabana.

Janet became pregnant in September, two months after her wedding, and Jackie was born the following July, six weeks late. In an effort to forge a better relationship with "Old Man Lee" (Black Jack's name for his wife's father), the baby was given the middle name of Lee and wore his christening dress at her baptism in December 1929. By then, of course, the stock market had crashed and the Bouviers' carefree existence started to careen out of control. The family's financial situation became perilous, and with the birth of a second child in 1933 (a second daughter, named Caroline Lee, again in honor of James T.), Black Jack found himself in the humiliating position of having to seek the largesse of his father-in-law, turning up, hat in hand, for handouts on a luxurious scale: the free apartment, the staff salaries, loans to pay living expenses. He was forced to seek financial assistance from a man who came close to despising him.

Another problem between Jack and Janet was his rampant philandering. He had been a bachelor for so long that perhaps he was incapable of changing his ways. However, there is no evidence that he wanted to, or even tried. There was society gossip at the time of their wedding that, on their honeymoon cruise aboard the *Aquitania,* Jack had deserted his young bride for a rendezvous with the tobacco heiress Doris Duke. The honeymoon also highlighted his careless attitude with money. According to a story Jackie would tell her friends years later, "On their honeymoon . . . he went to the casino and came back very depressed because he had lost everything. . . . He gambled away all the money."

Black Jack's cavalier attitude toward money, whether it was the cash in his pocket or the profits of his work, would be a source of long-lasting tensions within the family. The fear of economic insecurity found outside the Bouvier household with the malaise of the Great Depression was also firmly lodged inside the luxurious rooms at 740 Park Avenue. Black Jack's casual approach to his marriage vows would also register heavily on the impressionable mind of his elder daughter. Jackie's absorption and acceptance of these two character traits would manifest itself in actions large and small throughout her life, demonstrated in her behavior, attitude, and deeds that the world would observe with voyeuristic delight.

England, 1961

The baby was born at "magic time" on a warm midsummer's night, just as the sun was dipping behind the trees on the western edge of the pastures and fields surrounding the manor house, its rays filtering a golden yellow light over the warm bricks and through the windows to the first-floor bedroom where the child's parents were full of anticipation and great excitement.

The sense of excitement was not for the impending birth of just any baby; *this* baby, born under *these* circumstances, engendered a special cause for celebration. Several bonfires had been assembled throughout the property, waiting to be lit by the proud father, signaling to all the countryside the joyful birth of a son and heir. For this was no ordinary child, and the father was no ordinary father. Johnnie Spencer was the only son and heir to the seventh Earl Spencer, head of one of the most illustrious of English aristocratic families. Johnnie was a nervous blend of excitement and anxiety as he waited for his young wife, Frances, to complete her labor and present him with a son.

A son is of paramount importance in the world of the British aristocracy. The entire social, political, and financial structure of that world revolves around the concept of primogeniture—whereby the titles, estates, and fortunes of the ruling class have been handed down from father to son over the course of centuries. When there is no son to inherit, then the fortunes go to brother, or to nephew, or to cousin. This is the way that world works, and though hardly fair, it is a system that is rarely questioned and, indeed, is credited for being the mechanism that kept in place the great collections of art, furnishings, and estates that add such richness to England's cultural heritage.

Johnnie Spencer was anxious because he was already a father twice over, to two daughters, Sarah and Jane. Frances had borne him a son, John, who had died less than twelve hours after his birth a year and a half earlier. The tragedy of an infant's death, the awful pain, both physical and emotional, was compounded by the additional pressure of providing a male heir. "It was a dreadful time for my parents," the current Earl Spencer remembers. "I don't think they ever got over it." So much of the pressure was placed on Frances. That this baby be a son was of supreme importance to her. It was the duty of the aristocratic bride to continue the male line and was actually understood, in a tacit way, to be her primary responsibility. That thought was famously expressed by the American-born Consuelo Vanderbilt, duchess of Marlborough, who, after giving birth to Lords John and Ivor Spencer-Churchill, said that she could now relax, having provided "the heir and the spare."

So, in the few moments after the baby was born, at quarter to eight in the evening on July 1, 1961, the first words Frances Spencer uttered were to query, "Is it a boy?" When told that she had a healthy, seven-pound baby girl, the first words ever spoken about Diana Frances Spencer were her mother's plaintive lament, "Oh, Johnnie will be so disappointed."

Those were the first words Diana was ever to hear.

The bonfires went unlit, and nearly a week passed before the baby girl even had a name. She was called Diana Frances Spencer and was given the courtesy title of Honorable, or Hon., as her parents were styled Viscount and Viscountess Althorp. They would be called Lord and Lady Althorp until the day that the seventh Earl Spencer, Diana's grandfather, died, when they would assume the titles Earl and Countess Spencer.

The Honorable Diana Frances Spencer was born into a family with a distinguished heritage. The Spencers were one of the grandest families in England, their history rich with associations with the royal family spanning two centuries. The earldom, conferred by King George III in 1765 to an earlier John Spencer, is considered especially fine, as it predates the great industrial age and the Victorian era, when elevation to the nobility was much more common and the great wealth of a "self-made man" could purchase a title.

The Spencers were one of the great landowner families, and their fortune dates back over five centuries to the 1500s. The fortune had its roots in the sheep trade of the sixteenth and seventeenth centuries, and as it grew, it allowed for the family to maintain two magnificent houses, the stately Spencer House in London and a country seat, Althorp, in Northamptonshire.

The Spencers were great accumulators, of both people and possessions. Through judicious marriages over the centuries, they were related to most of the noblest families in the land, counting as cousins the dukes of Devonshire, Abercorn, and Marlborough, the earls of Sunderland and Dorset, and such noble families as Churchill, Seymour, Suffolk, Halifax, and Baring. The Spencer family tradition of providing brides to the aristocracy would, of course, reach its apex with the marriage of Lady Diana Spencer to the Prince of Wales in 1981, forever tying the Spencers to the royal family that they had served so nobly for over two hundred years. The fourth, fifth, and sixth earls Spencer had all been conferred the honor Knight of the Garter, the highest honor the monarch can convey. An intimate connection with the royal family was part of Diana's birthright. Diana's great-grandfather had been the Lord Chamberlain to King George V; her paternal grandmother had been a lady-in-waiting to Queen Elizabeth II; her maternal grandmother, a lady-in-waiting to Queen Elizabeth, the Queen Mother; and her father, an equerry to both King George VI and Queen Elizabeth II.

As they had collected a rich association with royalty, the Spencers over the centuries had also amassed a great collection of treasures. Spencer House, in the heart of St. James, facing London's Green Park, is one of the few remaining great town houses of the eighteenth and nineteenth centuries and among the last still in private ownership. Every nobleman once owned an imposing London edifice, but most of them, over the years, have given way to apartment buildings, government offices, and department stores. Spencer House is an ambitious neo-Palladian structure, but as striking as the exterior facade presents itself to passersby walking through Green Park, the house was more renowned for its interiors, which were hailed as "the most magnificent interiors of eighteenth-century London." The large house was rented out as offices in 1926 and, unscathed by war or commercial use, survives in its splendor, its public rooms recently restored to their former glory and the rest of the house rented out as offices. It is, in fact, still owned by the Spencer family, just as Apsley House, the London home of the fabled duke of Wellington, is still owned by the Wellesley family, with the duke and duchess still living in a suite of rooms on the first floor and the rest of the house open as a museum to the great war hero.

Althorp, in Northamptonshire, has been the seat of the Spencer family since 1586, although Spencers had owned the property for almost a century before that. The house that was first built in the 1500s was made of red brick, and as the family's fortunes and ambitions grew, Althorp was modernized, first in 1660 and then again in 1780. The facade was covered in Weldon stone, with Corinthian columns, pediments, and a classical balustrade added to the main structure. As was the case with Spencer House, the exterior splendor of Althorp was matched by its interior contents. Generations of discriminating collectors had filled the house with an impressive array of artwork, chiefly family portraits by Van Dyck, Reynolds, Gainsborough, and Rubens, magnificent gold plate, porcelain, and china collections and fine furniture. The Spencer family collections were testament to the family's leading position in the social, political, and financial arenas of British history from the time of the Tudors, and despite a controversial "distress sale" period during the 1980s, when Raine Spencer, stepmother to Diana and her three siblings, sold off perhaps 20 percent of the family's treasures, the collections today are as outstanding as any to be found in private hands.

If Diana's paternal heritage was exalted, her mother's family, the Fermoys, was also quite aristocratic, if on a significantly lesser scale. Diana's mother, Frances Roche, was the daughter of the fourth Baron Fermoy, Maurice Burke Roche. Fermoy had an American mother, the heiress Fanny Work, who had married the third Baron Fermoy in one of those advantageous nineteenth-century marriages between impoverished European titleholders and wealthy American girls.

Fanny Work was a childhood friend of Jennie Jerome, the famous American beauty who was Winston Churchill's mother. In 1879, during a four-month "grand tour" of Europe, Jennie introduced her friend to the charming and roguish James Burke Roche, heir to the Fermoy barony. Their courtship was swift and the subsequent marriage short, for Fermoy was a scoundrel who cheated on Fanny and spent most of her money. Fanny took her young son, Maurice, divorced Fermoy, and returned to the United States. When, at forty-four, Maurice Roche inherited the title upon the death of his father, he moved back to England and quickly ingratiated himself with the shy duke of York and his wife, the future George VI and Elizabeth. He married Ruth Gill, the daughter of an Aberdeenshire farmer, who gave up a promising career as a concert pianist to become Lady Fermoy. So close was the friendship between the Yorks and the

Fermoys that the duke of York arranged through his father, George V, for the Fermoys to lease Park House, a property on the private royal estate at Sandringham. This was to be their home for the rest of their married life. When Lord Fermoy died in the mid-1950s, his widow became a lady-in-waiting to the Queen Mother; finding Park House too large for her needs, she turned the lease over to her daughter and son-in-law, Frances and Johnnie Spencer.

Ruth, Lady Fermoy, had been thrilled when her seventeen-year-old daughter caught the eye of Johnnie Spencer, Viscount Althorp, in 1953. Tall, red-haired, and handsome, Spencer was considered one of the finest catches in Britain. He had just left royal service, after serving a tour of duty with the queen and the Duke of Edinburgh.

Frances Roche and Johnnie Spencer were married on June 1, 1954, at Westminster Abbey in London. The site of the wedding indicated both the high position and high esteem in which the young couple was held, as the abbey was the special preserve of the royal family. The Queen, Prince Philip, and the Queen Mother led the seventeen hundred guests, and the list included all the senior members of the royal family and a dazzling array of aristocrats, society figures, and politicians. They seemed destined to have a remarkable future.

Alas, it was not to be the case. There was a twelve-year age difference between Frances and Johnnie (as, interestingly, there would be between Diana and Charles), and they quickly discovered that they shared few interests and had little in common. Whereas Frances was young, impetuous, and eager to try new things, Johnnie was stolid, set in his ways, and perfectly content with the status quo. Their first child, a daughter, Sarah, was born the year after their wedding, in 1955. A second child, daughter Jane, was born in 1957. There were tensions in the marriage, and drink and the lack of an heir exacerbated them. Frances was sent to doctors and fertility specialists, a humiliating and degrading experience. The joy that accompanied the birth of their son, John, was tragically short-lived, as he died ten hours after his birth in the winter of 1959. Back to the doctors and the specialists and the humiliation and the disabling sense of failure.

Waiting for the birth of Frances's baby that summer was a period filled with both joy and not a little tension, thanks to the unseemly quest for a child of specific gender. That the baby girl went a week without a name is only one indication of the kind of welcome accorded the Spencers' third daughter. Both Sarah and Jane Spencer had a member of the royal family for a godparent, the Queen Mother for Sarah and the Duke of Kent for Jane. There was to be no royal godparent for Diana. It was understood that Johnnie would call in his greatest chip, that of Her Majesty, the queen, to be the godmother of his son. But there were any number of royals who would happily had filled the role: Princess Margaret; the duke or duchess of Gloucester; or Princess Mary, the Princess Royal.

This is not to say that Diana was banished to the attic, like a modern-day Cinderella. Not at all. Her childhood was fairly normal, as a matter of fact. Normal, that is, in the world of privilege and gilt furniture. Diana and her sisters were under the care of a nanny, and her parents, because of their wealth and position, were freed from many of the duties and responsibilities that most parents perform on a daily basis. Johnnie Spencer did not go to an office, and Frances never pushed a supermarket cart down the produce aisle. Their lives were not bound up by two-week vacations every August and mowing the lawn. There was staff to do the housekeeping work, and trust funds to provide a steady income.

Frances Spencer suffered from postpartum depression after the birth of Diana, and much of the responsibility for raising the youngest Spencer girl fell to the care of a governess, Gertrude Allen, called Ally. A spinster of the type who devoted herself to the care of small children, Ally had taken care of Frances as a young girl, and Frances trusted her with the care of her children. Ally remembers the young Diana as "a serious little girl who tried hard."

Finally, in 1964, Frances gave birth to a son, named Charles Edward Maurice. The queen agreed to Johnnie's request and became godmother to the boy. Now that she had "done her duty" and provided an heir, Frances could fully have expected the tensions in her marriage to ease, and they did, but not for long. Frances was just twenty-eight, the mother of four, and she found herself trapped in a marriage to a man completely unsuited to her temperamentally and emotionally. Something was bound to crack, and when it did, there would be painful ramifications for all concerned.

Chapter Two

Darling Daddy
(and Mummy Dearest)

My father always said: "Treat everybody as an individual and never throw your weight around."

—Diana, Princess of Wales, 1991

"Jackie, you never have to worry about keeping up with the Joneses, because we are the Joneses. Everyone has to keep up with us."

—Jack Bouvier, to his elder daughter

They shared the name John but had little else, if anything, in common. John Vernou Bouvier III and Edward John, eighth Earl Spencer: known as Black Jack and Johnnie, they were perfect, if distinctly different, specimens of a "gentleman." One dashing and urbane, out of the pages of the old *Esquire* or *Vanity Fair*, the other lumbering and tweedy, the classic country squire. One was a dashing rake, avid sportsman, and ardent hedonist, the other a dutiful caretaker of a five-hundred-year-old heritage. Jack Bouvier was born the son of a millionaire and died in painfully (relatively speaking) reduced circumstances, the seaside mansion replaced by a two-bedroom apartment. Johnnie Spencer was born the son of a millionaire and died the multimillionaire owner of an enormous estate that included prized collections of art, furnishings, and precious objets d'art. One died alone and largely forgotten, the other's death was remembered around the world and honored by the sovereign whom he had once served.

But it is in their relationships with their celebrated daughters that Jack Bouvier and Johnnie Spencer differed the most. It is in these father-daughter bonds that the nuclei of both Jackie's and Diana's personalities were formed. It is possible to look through every major event in their lives and trace it back to the psychological underpinnings of their relationships with their fathers.

Jack Bouvier worshiped his elder daughter, calling her "all things holy," and from him she learned the skills of seduction that would, in her later years, be compared with those of the most accomplished geisha. From her father, Jackie inherited a strong sense of self and an understanding of the power that she could wield over men. These two attributes, coupled with an exquisite courtesy that would bear the stamp of her mother's tutelage, enabled Jackie to survive the indignities, horrors, and misplaced adulation that would be heaped upon her. The unconditional adoration she got from Black Jack from the moment of her birth was as solid a piece of armor as any that would grace the Medieval Hall in the Metropolitan Museum of Art across the street from her longtime home on New York's Fifth Avenue.

Diana had no such armor to protect her from either of the worlds that would come crashing down around her—the insular, inbred world of the royal family into which she would marry, or the insane world of the media celebrity, which she was at the center of for nearly half her life. She felt superfluous to life. "I was the girl who was supposed to be a boy," she would confide to a friend, and she knew that had her elder brother survived or had one of her two sisters been born male, there was every likelihood that she would never have been conceived at all. Whether or not that is true, it is what she believed. It would be unfair to say that Johnnie Spencer didn't love Diana; he did, but the residue of disappointment in her gender is something that she desperately clung to as a means of explaining her later unhappiness. She did not enjoy that bedrock of solid, unquestioning love that Jackie did. For a variety of reasons, Diana was denied that anchor from her earliest days, and so when adoration would later come her way, she was ill prepared to cope with it. When the adoration vanished, she was incapable of understanding just where it had gone or what had happened.

Diana's need for external approbation ("I *love* it," she famously said on the Squidgy-gate tape) was as much a part of her being as Jackie's disdain for the unwanted nuisance of her own "celebrity" was integral to her persona.

Diana Spencer's "darling daddy" was the first in a long line of men who would betray her. Father, husband, brother, lover, practically every man in her life betrayed her terribly, feeding her feelings of insecurity and lack of self-worth and causing her to pursue one frantic attempt after another to regain the elusive unconditional affection she craved. Diana's compulsive need to please others in her quest for love reached its apex with her marriage to the Prince of Wales. What better example of "people pleasing" a father who was disappointed that you were not born a boy to inherit his title than to rise to a level even greater than that of a mere earldom? An earl, after all, is only halfway up the aristocratic scale of baron, viscount, earl, marquess, and duke.

In becoming a royal bride, the wife to the heir to the throne, Diana trumped Johnnie Spencer. In walking down the aisle with Charles, her inner child was calling out, "I'm sorry I disappointed you by being born a girl, but look here, I'm making you the grandfather of a king!" It is a classic example of the underdog as overachiever, taken to the extreme edges of romantic glory.

Jackie, too, would suffer betrayals and humiliations, but because she had a secure foundation, she had a psychic security blanket that she could draw around her, forever protecting her calm and reserved facade. If her husband cheated on her, it was something that happened because "all men are rats," as she once noted to a female relative. If her father's absence from her wedding marred the day's happiness for her, she didn't let anyone know it. She didn't blame herself for others' shortcomings. It was never "I am not worthy of this or that" but "This or that is not worthy of me." She enjoyed a more balanced sense of self than Diana ever did, even though they had similarly turbulent childhoods.

Their mothers were significantly younger than their husbands (Janet Lee by sixteen years, Frances Roche by twelve) and played vital, but less important, roles in shaping Diana's and Jackie's characters. Janet resented the imbalance: it was Jack who spoiled the girls and she who disciplined them. It was left to both mothers to instill in their daughters manners, courtesy, and politesse.

Jackie's rapport with her mother was part of an incredibly complex relationship. It was also the longest relationship in Jackie's life, lasting over sixty years. As a child, Jackie was often the victim of Janet's high-strung anxiety as her marriage unraveled. Jack and Janet would use Jackie as a pawn in their increasingly acrimonious relationship. The feelings between mother and daughter reached their nadir on Jackie's wedding day, when she blamed her mother for her role in preventing Jack Bouvier from participating in the ceremonies. "I don't think Jackie ever forgave Janet for what happened that morning," Jackie's stepbrother Yusha Auchincloss would say, "although she took care of her when Janet became ill at the end of her life."

Diana's relationship with her mother was strained during most of her adulthood. In the last few months of her life, she seemed particularly fierce in her estrangement, telling one visitor to Kensington Palace, "I don't tell her anything—ever!" The pain of childhood had roiled inside her for many years, and though in her marital situation she shared much with her mother, there was too much hurt for her to reconcile. Like Diana, in her mid-twenties Frances found herself trapped in an unhappy marriage and, having discharged her responsibility to produce an heir, looked for fulfillment through independence. Frances left the family's Norfolk home to spend more time in London, much like the heroine in *A Handful of Dust*, Evelyn Waugh's biting comic novel of the British landed gentry. The adventures on which she embarked in London would rip her family apart.

Every child who grows up with two parents is, of course, the result of a joint effort. Such was the case with both Diana and Jackie. Often it is one parent, in this case the mother, who creates the backbone, the infrastructure of a child's character. Then there is the parent who is the architect of a child's spirit. For Diana and Jackie, this was the contribution made by their fathers. Their relationships with their fathers forged their individual sense of self. One daughter was brought up to feel that she was an exceptional child, the other that she was unwanted. This relationship between father and daughter shaped their lives forever.

England, 1960s

The England of Diana's childhood was a curious place, a dichotomy of old traditions and new values, rather like a graceful dowager gamely trying to dance the Watusi. The class structure that separated the populace almost as rigidly as a caste system (royalty, aristocracy, gentry, and the masses) had been challenged by the two World Wars. If World War I caused faint rumblings of dissatisfaction, then World War II began its active deconstruction. The social changes installed by the postwar Labour government were an active assault on a system that allowed the haves to get more and the have-nots to never get any at all.

The lifestyle of the aristocracy and landed gentry, steeped in tradition and sentiment, was the world into which Diana and her siblings were born and, at the time of her birth, one that she could expect to inhabit for the rest of her life. There were no undue demands upon or even expectations of the children of that class. First sons and heirs were in a tougher spot. They were expected to spend their formative years preparing to inherit the estate, accumulating a working knowledge of their heritage, and devising a means to make it pay, by becoming great showmen (in the case of the duke of Bedford, who pioneered the stately home as a tourist-attraction business) or clever businessmen (as the dukes of Westminster, with their vast real-estate holdings) or successful husbands (like the current crown prince of the Hellenes, married to a duty-free-shop heiress). Younger sons could expect a proper education and then a pat on the back as they were pushed out the door to find their own way (witness Prince Edward, earl of Wessex and ex–television documentary producer). Daughters weren't even given a proper education. In the 1960s there was little more expected of them than to make a good marriage to another member of their class. The skills needed to succeed in that endeavor—charm, the ability to manage a household, a smattering of French, perfect manners, and such—could be easily attained by a decent boarding school and perhaps a year in Switzerland or France.

Diana had exquisite manners and a keen sense of understanding that enabled her to be comfortable with anyone from any walk of life. More important, she could make people comfortable when talking with her. She would credit her father for this, saying, "I always got on very well with everybody. Whether it be the gardener, or the local police, or whoever, I went over to talk with them. My father always said: 'Treat a duke like a dustman and a dustman like a duke.' "

Diana's childhood home, Park House, was a delightful place for young children, and her early days were filled with outdoor activities: fishing, riding, games, and spending time with animals. There were herds of cattle, as well as rabbits, foxes, hedgehogs, and deer. The indoor menagerie included dogs and cats and goldfish and hamsters and guinea pigs, and their deaths were the cause for Diana to create elaborate funeral celebrations, complete with shoe-box coffins and garden burials with small white cross markers (though the goldfish were just flushed down the toilet).

Even though the house was less than five miles from the beach, where the family owned a small private hut on the shore, Johnnie Spencer installed a heated swimming pool, a novelty that made the house a popular destination. During the summers the house teemed with neighborhood children. The young royal cousins, Princes Andrew and Edward and Lord Linley, Princess Margaret's son, were frequent visitors, and at Christmas the Spencer children would be invited over to Sandringham house for a special showing of the movie *Chitty Chitty Bang Bang*. After the third consecutive year's viewing, however, Diana remembered how she "used to kick and fight anyone who tried to make us go over there." In the end, because her father insisted that they could not be rude to the queen, she went but found the atmosphere "strange."

As with most children born into similar circumstances, Diana's young life was managed by nurses, nannies, and tutors. Her parents played important, but essentially supporting, roles in her day-to-day life. She didn't see as much of her mother as she would have liked, and saw even less of her father. It was the nanny she would run to when she skinned a knee, when one of her hamsters escaped its cage, or when she had a question that needed an immediate answer. Visits with Mummy and Daddy were more formally orchestrated, and as Charles Spencer, Diana's brother and the current earl, remembers, he was seven years old before he sat down to dinner with his father in the family's formal dining room. Up till then, children ate with the nanny in their nursery quarters.

It seems inconceivable to many that this was, and in some rare cases still is, the way children were brought up. But as Charles Spencer notes: "We had no idea that we were privileged. As children we accepted our circumstances as normal. . . . It was a privileged upbringing out of a different age, a distant way of living from your parents. I don't know anyone who brings up children like that anymore. It certainly lacked a mother figure."

By the mid-1960s Frances Althorp found herself reaching her thirtieth birthday with an increasing sense of despair, and it's not hard to surmise why her youngest child recalls her absence from his childhood. Charles's birth, in 1964, came at a huge cost to Frances's dignity and self-esteem. Shortly after Diana's birth there were more humiliating consultations with gynecological specialists, all conducted amid the gossip of the aristos. With the birth of the precious heir, and the completion of her duty, Frances began to realize just how little she had in common with her husband. He was dull and stolid and—not surprisingly, given his stature in their world—lacked ambition. She was a lively and engaging young woman who enjoyed urban life as much as she did country life, and she realized that she was married to an older, settled, and uninspiring man. The tensions that had plagued their marriage during the quest for a male child returned now, stronger, because their marriage had not been built on a very durable foundation of mutual interests and enthusiasms.

The tensions led to alcohol-fueled fights, and Diana had many painful memories of what she would later term "a very unhappy childhood . . . always seeing my mother crying. Daddy never spoke to us about it. We never asked questions." There were violent arguments between the couple, and Diana was often a silent witness, hiding behind doors and curtains and then running frightened to her governess.

Two things happened in 1966 that would have a profound effect on Diana's young life. The first was when her two elder sisters, Sarah and Jane, went off to boarding school at West Heath in Kent. Diana said she "idolized" her eldest sister, and splitting up the four Spencer children, who had been schooled at home in a big old-fashioned parlor, presaged the disintegration of her family. The second event, the one that sparked the eventual breakup of Johnnie and Frances's marriage, happened at a Christmas party in London, where they met Peter and Janet Shand Kydd. Peter, heir to a wallpaper fortune, was charming, tall, and handsome, with an easygoing manner that contrasted sharply with Johnnie's dark moods. The two couples became friends, and even took a Swiss skiing holiday together.

Frances was drawn to Peter's lighthearted charm and began to go up to London, alone, for "shopping visits" but in reality to conduct an affair with him in a South Kensington apartment loaned by friends. Eventually, using her own money, she took an apartment in Cadogan Place, a short distance from Sloane Square. Although it was confusing for the younger children, tensions between their parents actually eased a bit, as Frances was noticeably happier. The incessant bickering stopped, and the children thought that, perhaps, things were back to normal. Even Johnnie was pleased, thinking that Frances was merely spreading her wings and, after exhibiting a little freedom, would come home. He told a friend, "How many of those fourteen years were happy? I thought all of them." But, of course, they weren't. As 1967 progressed, Lady Althorp asked for a trial separation. Frances left Park House and moved into the apartment in Cadogan Place. She registered Diana and Charles for school in London. As disruptive to their young lives as it must have been, the two children gamely went with their mother and began what would be years of traveling between parents, Frances during the week and Johnnie on weekends.

The entire family was reunited at Christmas 1967, but Frances realized that the end was near, later recalling, "It was my last Christmas there, for by now it had become apparent that the marriage had completely broken down." As the holiday came to a close, Johnnie put his foot down. "He refused to let [Diana and Charles] return in the New Year to London." With this line drawn boldly in the sand, Johnnie had taken the first step in what would become a shockingly scandalous divorce that pitted not only husband against wife but mother against child. It would be the emotional hallmark of Diana's early life.

New York, 1930s

The birth of Caroline Lee Bouvier in 1933 completed the Bouvier family—father, mother, and, as it turned out, a girl for him and a girl for her.

Both sisters revered their father. His unrelenting pursuit of pleasure was an ideal source of entertainment for two young girls. Their early lives, spent between New York City and East Hampton, were full of ponies and dogs, Sunday lunches at Schraffts, and trips to the circus. In an authorized biography of her early life, heavily edited and sanitized by Jackie just before she entered the White House, she remembered that her father "encouraged the girls to climb trees, learn to ride no hands on a bicycle and was the despair of their nurses because he let them eat sweets too soon before dinner." When in the country, they attended summer-league baseball games, rooting for Bouvier's Black Ducks, the team Jack sponsored. Weekends in the city, in the fall and spring, meant trips to Columbia University's sporting fields, where they would play in the outdoor stationary sculls set up for rowing practice. There were trips in Jack's maroon Stutz town car to Belmont Park, where they would be taken down to the paddocks to visit and pet the horses and meet the jockeys.

It was the good life, and Jackie would recall, "All my friends loved Daddy. He'd take batches of us out to lunch. . . . We must have eaten him broke." Jack shared with her his passion for the most exclusive of sports, and young Jacqueline became an expert equestrienne. The Bouviers kept half a dozen horses at the family's fourteen-acre East Hampton estate. Danseuse (or Donny) was Jackie's favorite, but there was also Gandhi, Arnoldean, Stepaside, Clearanfast, and Pas d'Or. She would spend hours in the stables, helping the grooms feed the horses and braid their manes, while her Bouvier and Beale and Davis cousins were playing games or swimming.

As much as Jack Bouvier loved being a father, he didn't much enjoy being a husband. The sixteen-year difference between Janet and him didn't help, as he had firmly settled into his bachelor life by the time he wed. A few years into his marriage, he began to admit to friends that married life was something he was "not cut out for." Jack's flirtatious manner was a key ingredient to his charm, and his infidelities became legendary. During the summers, when Janet and the girls would stay in the country for four or five months, Jack would be seen regularly in the Westbury Hotel's Polo Bar, zeroing in on a pretty young thing, unconcerned by the presence of his family (his sister's husband would often see him there, with "stunningly beautiful women"). He was sometimes brazen about his affairs and was once famously photographed holding hands with a pretty young woman while Janet, seated inches away, was caught unaware. Humiliated when the photograph was published, Janet lit into her husband.

Her aggrandized sense of propriety (the markings of an Irish Catholic upstart in a WASP world) accounted for a serene face in public, but in private Janet was furious with her husband's behavior and was continually in a rage. It wasn't just his infidelities that irked her; there were also problems with finances. In her authorized biography, whose main purpose was to present a "rose-colored glasses" version of her early years, Jackie went so far as to say, "He was a stockbroker like his grandfather and great-uncle, but, being younger and less well established, suffered more from the up and down quirks of the market." The truth is that Jack was quickly going broke, and his laissez-faire attitude infuriated both Janet and her father. This caused loud scenes at home, witnessed by the couple's servants and, of course, the children. As their parents' relationship began to deteriorate, the Bouvier sisters began to pick up some of the tensions, and the often ugly scenes began to have ramifications in the relationships between Jackie and Lee and their parents.

It's not surprising that there was trouble in the marriage. They were very dissimilar types and poorly suited to each other from the beginning. Jack was a man born for the easy life; when life got rough, as it did during the early years of his marriage, with the Great Depression and the teetering stock market, he was ill prepared to understand what to do and how to behave. He was a forty-five-year-old Peter Pan. He did not want to grow up, and marriage wasn't going to change him. But bad times forced a change in his lifestyle, and he was forced to go hat in hand to his relatives, including his uncle and father-in-law, to bail him out with loans and free rent. The humiliation he suffered in the "grown-up" world only stiffened his resolve to become more of a bon vivant and to seek, within his own family, a kindred spirit.

He found that kindred spirit in Jackie. Jack Bouvier had always had a special relationship with his elder daughter, as Janet would come in time to favor her younger daughter. In her adult life Lee would ruefully acknowledge that she took second place in her father's affections. "That was very clear to me . . . but if I didn't come in for as much praise as Jackie, I also didn't receive the same amount of criticism as she did. He was so vulnerable to any imagined slight or neglect on her part that reproach upon reproach was directed at my sister."

Jack Bouvier wasn't so much a father to Jackie as he was a chaste suitor, and his lifelong obsession with her bordered on the inappropriate. There are plenty of fathers who adore their children, but few do so with the hedonistic delight that Jack Bouvier showered on his daughter. He started early, introducing her to the gourmet tastes of pistachio ice cream. One of Jackie's most vivid memories of her youth revolves around a 1930s version of "bring-your-daughter-to-work day," a very special occasion when Jack took her downtown to the stock exchange, where she sat, transfixed in the gallery, watching the shouting and jostling brokers below her. Later they had lunch on Wall Street, passing the bustling Fulton Fish Market. Jackie fondly recalled the "imaginative, mischievous side to his nature, which made him the greatest companion to the young" and how her friends "simply ate him up."

Jack taught her the art of seduction. She was distinctive even among her Bouvier cousins, who remember a combination of fun and earnestness in her, how she was perfectly happy with her own company, and how dedicated she was to the singular pursuits of horseback riding and writing poetry and stories. As she grew older, Jack would teach her how to maximize her femininity to lure men into her orbit, always projecting a sense of mystery, of allure. Jackie could fairly claim ownership to the plaintive lament of the femme fatale in the Marlene Dietrich song: "Men cluster to me / Like moths around a flame / And if their wings burn / I know I'm not to blame."

Janet rarely gets credit for her part in raising the woman Jackie became. She was the disciplinarian, the one who got Jackie and Lee to brush their teeth and write thank-you notes. But it must be noted that she provided the foundation that Jack built this fantastic creature on top of. Even Lee Radziwill would discount her mother's contribution to Jackie's exceptional character. Lee analyzed her sister's personality once, and commented, "I think that if it hadn't been for this exceptional bond she had with my grandfather Bouvier and my father that she never would have gained the particular strength and independence and individuality she had."

An example of her independence comes in an oft-told story of how, in the spring of 1934, Janet Bouvier, returning home from a lunch party, answered the telephone to find a police lieutenant on the line.

"We have a little girl here. We can't understand her name, but she knows her telephone number. Could she be yours?"

An anxious Janet scurried over to the Central Park police station and discovered four-year-old Jackie chatting away with some amused policemen. "Hello, Mummy" was her self-assured response. The lieutenant told Janet how he had come across the little girl while walking his beat in the park. She came up to him and announced, "My nurse is lost." The nurse, Bertha Kimmerle, had been attending to the infant Lee when Jackie, engrossed by some butterfly or bird, had wandered off.

The story speaks not only of a simpler time but also of a remarkable personality, unencumbered by fear or anxiety. This was a little girl who behaved like a princess because she was treated like a princess, at least by her father. A girl whose birthday parties were noted in the society pages and whose equestrian accomplishments were noted in the sports pages, both before the time she entered kindergarten. Both Jackie and her younger sister seemed destined to lead charmed lives, a picture-perfect existence.

Such, of course, was not to be, for, as Lee was to note, "we didn't have a very normal family." The tensions inside the Bouvier household, always simmering, came to a boil in the mid-1930s, just as three decades later the Spencer family drama would turn into a crisis. Ominous change was in the air for both families, and the early promise of a happy couple and a glorious future would fade, turn brittle, and finally crack into thousands of little pieces.

Chapter Three

Separation Anxiety:
Children of Divorce

The biggest disruption [in my childhood] was when Mummy de-cided to leg it. For my brother and I it was a very painful expe-rience.

—Diana, 1991

*There have been so many marriages in every part of the family . . .
it's a shambles . . . you don't know who your relatives really are.*

—Jackie, 1962

Divorce is such a commonplace occurrence these days that it's al-most hard to believe that the unceremonious discarding of the sacred bond of matrimony ("What God has put together, let no man put asunder") was, until relatively recently, a source of private shame and public disapproval. Although divorce may still wreak havoc on the personal lives of those involved, most notably children, it no longer carries the social stigma it did for so many years. Reputations aren't sullied, and social position isn't affected (unless, of course, there's a salacious aspect to the divorce). The once-shameful "D" word is common, with two recent White House residents having been divorced and remarried (Betty Ford and Ronald Reagan) and, of course, that heir to the throne of Great Britain and Northern Ireland and future Defender of the Faith, Charles Philip Arthur George Windsor.

But little more than a generation ago, his mother, the queen, did not receive divorced people. She was forbidden by protocol to invite them as her guests. When that rule was amended in the mid-sixties so that the innocent parties of a marital rupture could receive the coveted gilt-edged invitations to royal events, it was considered a startling social development. Indeed, divorce had been the cause of the greatest scandal in the royal family for generations when, in 1936, the queen's uncle, King Edward VIII, abdicated his throne in order to marry the twice-divorced American Wallis Simpson.

That the king would put his personal happiness ahead of his duty to his country was anathema to his family. A year after the newly styled duke and duchess of Windsor were married, his mother, Queen Mary, wrote to him: "I do not think you have ever realized the shock which the attitude you took up caused your family and the whole nation. It seemed inconceivable to those who had made such sacrifices during the war that you, as their king, refused a lesser sacrifice.... All my life I have put my country before anything else, and I simply can not change now." A hard-line attitude then, but in 1947, ten years after the Windsors had been married, she had hardened further. She wrote to her second son, now George VI, denouncing the twice-divorced Wallis Windsor as "so pushing ... she leaves no stone unturned to remain a thorn in our sides and advertise herself whenever she can ... with two husbands still living ... so unnecessary and tactless."

Queen Mary was an imposing figure, and the dominant force in the life of her granddaughter, Elizabeth II. It was this unrelenting attitude toward divorce that led Elizabeth to make two very difficult personal decisions with regard to her immediate family and divorce. In the mid-1950s, just after she assumed the throne, the queen was faced with a potential scandal when her vivacious sister, Margaret, fell in love with Group Captain Peter Townsend, a former equerry to George VI, a dashing war hero, and, alas, a divorced man. Even though he was the innocent party in his divorce, Margaret was forced to choose between marrying Townsend or retaining her royal status. She could not have both, and the queen refused to support her sister and intervene on the couple's behalf.

A decade later, in the mid-1960s, Elizabeth's first cousin, the earl of Harewood, the son of her father's sister, Princess Mary, was involved in a divorce scandal when he fathered a child out of wedlock and set up house with his inamorata. His eighteen-year marriage came to a crashing halt; he was sued for divorce and later married the mother of this three-year-old son. On the advice of her ministers, the queen gave approval for the second marriage but exiled her childhood playmate from the royal family circle, going so far as to deny him an invitation to the 1973 funeral of their uncle, the duke of Windsor.

When President and Mrs. John F. Kennedy made a semi-official visit to London in June 1961 (ostensibly for JFK to attend the christening of his goddaughter Tina Radziwill, the visit also gave him a chance to brief Harold Macmillan about his recent conversations with Khrushchev and de Gaulle), the queen gave a dinner for them at Buckingham Palace. Lee and her then-husband, the exiled Polish nobleman Prince Stanislaus Radziwill, were included on the official guest list, but not without debate. Macmillan recorded in his diary that "after much hesitation the Queen waived her rule about divorce. Prince and Princess [Radziwill] were invited, although they had two or three partners apiece to date. She was very unwilling to do this, or to put their names in the court circular. . . . Had the Kennedys been staying at the American Embassy, I could have advised the Queen to omit the [Radziwills]. But since the President and Mrs. K. were actually staying with the Prince and Princess, it seemed impossible to do so."

Lest the queen seem intransigent, it must be noted that, upon her coronation, she became Defender of the Faith. In her role as the moral leader of her country, whose established religion did not recognize divorce, she was duty-bound to follow the conventions of the time. But this is the world that Diana was born into (almost literally—she was born within a month of the Kennedys' visit), and by the time her parents' marriage reached the crisis stage a few years later, attitudes toward divorce hadn't changed much at all. It was a shameful and regrettable business and one to be avoided.

For all the city's Jazz Age snappiness, divorce in New York in the 1930s was still a somber and scandalous rarity. Divorce might be fine in Hollywood, but movie people certainly weren't accepted into high society at that time. The state of New York made it difficult to obtain a divorce. Until 1967 the only acceptable grounds for divorce in New York was adultery. Alienation of affections, spousal battery, irreconcilable differences—none were acceptable reasons for dissolving a marriage in the courts of New York.

The Roman Catholic Church forbade divorce under any circumstances. This was the church that had split with England in the sixteenth century over the marital adventures of Henry VIII (who, paradoxically, created the very Church of England that also refused to recognize divorce). Very rarely did the Vatican's hierarchy grant an annulment, and in the 1930s it was almost unheard of. A Catholic woman seeking a divorce in New York in the 1930s found it hard going indeed. Even a Catholic woman with a social register husband, whose family belonged to Mrs. Astor's exclusive "Four Hundred" set, faced censure and disapproval on all fronts.

New York, 1940

Jackie's distrust of the press and all its attendant trappings can be dated to January 26, 1940. It was not the first time her name had appeared in the newspapers. Notwithstanding the conventional society dictum that a lady's name appears in the newspapers but thrice (at the occasions of her birth, her marriage, and her death), she had been a regular feature in the society pages dating back to her second birthday party, which was reported with gushing praise in the *East Hampton Star*. Her adventures at the county pet fairs and horse shows were all duly noted in the social papers.

But it was not the society column of the *New York Daily Mirror* that featured the Bouvier family that icy January morning. It was front-page news, SOCIETY BROKER SUED FOR DIVORCE, and featured photographs of the family and lascivious details of Jack Bouvier's extramarital love life. The scandal was enormous, and the shame

Jackie and Lee felt was escalated when the story was picked up by the Associated Press and other news services and printed throughout the country in both respected newspapers and tabloids alike.

In an odd way, the Bouviers' domestic drama was echoed in one of 1940's hit movies, the film adaptation of Clare Boothe Luce's play *The Women*. The plot of that fabled MGM extravaganza revolved around a society matron (Norma Shearer) with a precocious daughter who loved horseback riding (Virginia Weilder) whose marriage to a society broker is ruptured because of his affair with a conniving shop girl (Joan Crawford). The film is full of laughs, thanks to an all-star cast led by the riotously funny Rosalind Russell. It was Russell's first attempt at comedy, and on the first day, when she started to play a scene in a realistic manner, director George Cukor stopped her and said, "In this film [your character] is breaking up a family, and there's a child involved, and if you're a heavy, the audience will hate you. Don't play it as a heavy, just be ridiculous." Russell credits Cukor with establishing her reputation as a comedienne, but the director's perceptions were acute and spot-on correct. The emotional core of the movie is a scene when the young daughter, distraught at the impending divorce of her parents, breaks down into tears and asks an almost unanswerable question, "Please, Mother dear ... Daddy, Daddy darling ... why?"

It's not hard to imagine ten-year-old Jacqueline Bouvier asking the same question. Sadly, however, she knew the answer. For the previous four or five years, the tensions between her mother and father had escalated to the point where divorce seemed the only option. The Bouviers had had a trial separation in 1936, a six-month experiment that saw Jack moving out of 740 into a room at the Westbury Hotel (above his favorite stomping ground, the Polo Bar). They reconciled at the end of the six months, but it was only temporary. In the summer of 1938 Janet rented a summer house in Bellport, forty miles away from the East Hampton that the girls knew and loved. They spent that August with their father at the Bouvier family's estate, Lasata, but as much as they loved it, that summer was the first salvo in what would be an almost twenty-year-long bitterly contested game of tug-of-war between Jack and Janet for the affections of their two daughters.

As an adult Jackie would confide in her friend Peter Duchin that one of her earliest memories was of her father and mother coming into the nursery to kiss her good night before they went out to the Central Park Casino to hear her friend's father, bandleader Eddie Duchin, and his orchestra. Her memory was poignant in its details (the lushness of her mother's fur coat and the sweetness of her perfume) and bittersweet in her confession that it was one of the few times she remembered seeing her parents happy together.

Those happy times together were few and far between, and disappeared as the 1930s progressed. At the root of the problem, of course, were money and sex. When Jack and Janet first married, his net worth was $750,000 and he made millions during the course of their marriage (over $2 million on his liquor stocks alone when Prohibition was repealed). But his penchant for high living and risky bets had reduced his net worth to slightly more that $100,000 in 1936. His adulterous shenanigans would provide ample evidence for Janet to seek a divorce in New York. With the assistance of her father, she had hired both a lawyer and a private detective. The latter had assembled a dossier of names, dates, and places, as well as photographs, and it is this information that was leaked to the *Daily Mirror.*

But if Janet thought it was going to be easy, she was wrong, for Jack decided to fight back, and in a most ungentlemanly fashion. "Good taste" at the time decreed that in a situation like this, the man would withdraw from the marriage, often arranging to be caught in an adulterous situation with a paid companion. But Jack was having none of it. He had his lawyers take depositions from the couple's servants, who painted a uniformly unflattering portrait of Janet as a high-strung, shrewish harridan.

Bernice Anderson, the Bouviers' maid, recalled, "The children, with the atmosphere the way it was and their mother highly irritable and nervous, were not happy. . . . Jacqueline frequently spoke about running away.

"Jacqueline used to say on many occasions that she hated her mother. Jacqueline and her mother frequently had yelling spells, she would yell at Jacqueline. And Jacqueline would yell back at her mother. In fact they were both very high strung and Mrs. Bouvier seemed to be by far the worse of the two. The children were not very happy with their mother at Bellport or at Gracie Square. [After a second separation, James T. Lee had evicted Janet and the two girls from 740 Park Avenue, installing them in a smaller apartment in a building he owned at One Gracie Square.] They always seemed very happy when they were allowed by their mother to go see their father. In fact it was almost pathetic."

Jackie's nurse, Bertha Newey, testified that Janet was "always tired and upset so that when you [Jack] arrived home from the office she took it out on you." And furthermore, Janet's mother, "Mrs. Lee, losing her temper, as she usually did, attempted to slap Jacqueline in the face and I tried to shield her and received the blow myself. Which I very properly returned to Mrs. Lee."

Once, in 1937, Jackie rushed up to her nurse and said, "Look what they are doing to my daddy," and was so upset that she "was in tears."

Jack Bouvier fared much better than his embittered wife and was described as "the most careful of fathers, particularly regarding the children's routine, their going to bed, and their swimming exercises in the morning at the beach and Jacqueline's riding in the afternoon."

The depositions went on and on, each more damaging to Janet's reputation. In order to avoid any more embarrassing publicity, Janet decided to withdraw her divorce suit from the New York courts. She then reverted to the alternative choice that other affluent women of the time utilized; she decided to be, in the words of columnist Walter Winchell, "Reno-vated." Like the Norma Shearer character in *The Women*, Janet took up the minimum six-week residency in the then-rustic Nevada gaming city, as the state's divorce laws were much more liberal than New York's. In June 1940 the turbulent twelve-year-old union of Jack Bouvier and Janet Lee was dissolved.

For Jackie and Lee, their world would never be the same.

Divorce in their social circle was unusual, and the fact that they were Catholic added more shame to the stigma. It was rare enough for Catholics to be in the upper ranks of the Protestant-dominated society, but to be Catholic girls whose parents were divorced under the most unseemly circumstances heaped guilt on top of shame. Jackie, as she was older, was held out for ridicule by her peers. "All the kids knew," a cousin recalled, "and some made a point of needling Jackie." Even family holidays would become traumatic, as Thanksgiving and Christmas and Easter spent in the bosom of Grandpa Bouvier's large apartment at 765 Park Avenue would find Jackie and Lee the only children there without their mother. As Jack was a beloved brother and uncle, there were few kind words about Janet.

Jackie found a mechanism with which to deal with her emotional pain. They "shared the emotional difficulties of children with divorced parents," Lee would later recall. "Jackie was really fortunate to have, or acquire, the ability to tune out." She could choose to hear what she wanted and to ignore those things she didn't. She withdrew into herself, into her books and stories, developing a keen talent for poetry and storytelling.

Jack had weekend and holiday visitation rights with his daughters, and they eagerly looked forward to their time with him, which he was determined to fill with gaiety, laughter, and fun. He would pick them up in his navy blue convertible on Sunday mornings, announcing his arrival at Gracie Square with a secret signal of long and short toots on the car's horn. Since his new apartment on East Seventy-fourth Street was too small for him to house animals, he made arrangements with a neighborhood pet store to rent a dog just for the day, and off to the park the happy trio would go. There would be trips to F.A.O. Schwarz for toys and Saks Fifth Avenue and Bloomingdale's for clothes. Jack would end up borrowing more than pets for these outings, as his financial situation steadily worsened as his problems with alcohol increased. He would tap his family and associates for loans to help pay for the perennial good times that were his lifeblood with his daughters, especially Jackie.

Lee knew that there was a special bond between her sister and her father. When asked, as an adult, if he favored Jackie, she replied, "Of course he did. That was very clear to me." She didn't resent it, though, and was able to carve out some special father-daughter memories of her own, sharing his love of the sea. She attributes the favoritism to several factors: that "he had wanted a son more than anything . . . she was named after him, or at least as close you could get a girl's name to a boy's," that Jackie had had a four-year head start to bond with Jack, and that she very closely resembled Jack's dark good looks.

The girls loved their time with him and were reluctant to go home to their mother. Janet's difficult situation, as a divorced mother of two young girls, was exacerbated by her perception that she was the sole parent "telling them to brush their teeth and to sit up straight and mind their manners" while their father showered them with presents and indulged their every whim. It drove Janet to distraction that the girls preferred Jack to her. She had to find a new life for herself, a new marriage that would provide her with the security she needed and the social position she craved. That became her focal point in life, and balancing that with raising two young daughters created a great deal of inner turmoil in Janet, and she began to focus on Jack as not just an errant ex-husband but an enemy. For years, Jackie and Lee would hear nothing but vitriolic diatribes against Jack by Janet (and, in turn, against Janet by Jack). That Jack held a higher regard for his elder daughter was not lost on Janet. But she filed the hurt away, saving it like a trump card, to be used at a later date. In the view of her soon-to-be-stepson, Janet was "a very vindictive woman," and when she finally did pull out that card, it was to devastating effect and fundamentally changed her relationship with Jackie forever.

London, 1968

Diana Spencer shared with Jackie Bouvier parents whose age differences and mismatched temperaments led not only to the trauma of a childhood ruptured by divorce but to the more insidious distinction of a divorce gift-wrapped with disgraceful scandal. For when the Spencers' marriage reached its end, it brought to London society a scandal unseen since the nasty divorce a few years earlier of the duke and duchess of Argyle. In that infamous case, the duke was able to successfully introduce into evidence photographs showing his wife performing sexual acts on an unidentified man. The Spencers' divorce lacked details as salacious as those of the Argyles, but it did have dire consequences affecting the family dynamic.

When Frances Althorp, in love with Peter Shand Kydd, moved to London and filed for divorce, she had every expectation that she would be granted custody of her four children. The two elder girls were away at boarding school; she planned for both Diana and Charles to attend school in London. But a trio of unexpected events interrupted her plans. First, Johnnie decided to fight her for custody. Because he was the scion of one of the great aristocratic families in the land, the courts would look upon his plea with class prejudice and be prepared to favor the father rather than the mother. Second, two months before the divorce case went to trial, in the summer of 1968, Janet Shand Kydd named Frances as a correspondent in her divorce action against Peter. She was labeled a licentious lady. Third, and most devastating, Frances's mother, Ruth, Lady Fermoy, broke with her daughter and testified in favor of her titled son-in-law. That action destroyed the bond between mother and daughter. Since Lady Fermoy declined to speak publicly about her decision, it's difficult to know exactly why she did something so hurtful to her own daughter.

Was Lady Fermoy convinced that her grandchildren belonged with their father, that living with him was in their best interests? Or, as a member of the court (she was a lady-in-waiting to the Queen Mother at the time), did she side with the establishment, aligning her sights with Johnnie's glorious future, the splendor of Althorp House, the invitations to Royal Ascot, summer holidays at Balmoral? The man whom Frances loved was, in her view, little more than a tradesman, albeit a financially successful one. The history of the Shand Kydds' empire of wallpaper paled when compared with that of the Spencers. For Ruth it may have seemed a logical choice, but it was coldhearted and would have many painful ramifications in the years to come, most notably for Frances.

Diana would remember her mother as a very unhappy woman. Living without her children, who were relegated to weekend visits, was emotionally difficult for the thirty-two-year-old mother. "I remember Mummy crying an awful lot every Saturday when we went up for weekends; every Saturday night, standard procedure, she would start crying."

"What's the matter, Mummy?"

"Oh, I don't want you to leave tomorrow."

For nine-year-old Diana it was devastating. Diana would remember that her brother "hadn't realized how much the divorce had affected him until he got married and started having a life of his own."

People would later comment that Diana took the divorce of her parents in stride. Her father's cousin Robert Spencer would say that the divorce didn't affect Diana that much, because "after all, they were not particularly short of cash." It's interesting to note that of the four Spencer children, the two elder girls were away at boarding school when their parents split up and weren't home to witness the fights, see the tears, and try to block out the yelling. The two elder children, Sarah and Jane, have both enjoyed marriages that have lasted in excess of twenty years, while the two younger children, Diana and Charles, were both involved in painful marriages that ended in divorce.

However, the elder daughters suffered as well. Sarah suffered from a well-publicized case of anorexia nervosa. An eating disorder, as Diana would come to discover, is an attempt to bring ultimate control to one's life and is often triggered by a feeling of being out of control in the world immediately around you. Imagine an environment in which a child is "always seeing . . . mother crying," as Diana remembered, and a father who "never spoke to us about it." There was no place to turn other than inside oneself, and Diana always "felt different from everyone else, very detached." She never asked questions and found an emotional refuge in pets and animals. As an adult, Diana would speak of her menagerie of stuffed toys as "my family."

She remembered, "I adored animals, guinea pigs and all that. In my bed I'd have twenty stuffed bed animals and there would be a midget's space for me and they would have to be in my bed every night."

She needed the company, as nights were excruciating. She would hear her brother, Charles, crying out for his mother, his room too far away for her to conquer her fear of the dark to get out of bed and comfort him. She was obsessed with the dark, insisting on a night-light until she was almost a teenager. Those lonely nights, alone in the dark, listening to the plaintive wails of her baby brother, were to haunt her for the rest of her life.

Diana also suffered from feeling different from her schoolmates. "We had become horribly different at school [she and Charles], because we had divorced parents and nobody else did." If the tabloid papers didn't pick up the story of the Spencers' divorce, it was the talk of the aristocratic world to which both sides of her family were connected by blood and marriage. There was no escaping that Frances Althrop had been branded unfit to raise her children, not only by the courts but also by her own mother.

The pain and the humiliation and the loneliness that Diana suffered as a result of her parents' divorce would serve her well in later life. "The divorce helped me relate to anyone else who is upset in their family life, whether it be stepfather syndrome or mother or whatever, I understand it." She had experienced the same feelings herself.

Frances and Johnnie refrained from using their children as pawns, playing them off the other, in the torturous manner that Jackie's parents did. But they were unwittingly to cause their children, especially Diana, little traumas in the most mundane of circumstances. Diana remembered one episode that she called "the most agonizing decision I ever had to make." She was to be a bridesmaid for her cousin, and both parents had presented her with a pretty dress to wear at the rehearsal party. Choosing between the green dress from Frances and the white dress from Johnnie, being forced to show favoritism over the choice of a frock, was so upsetting to the young girl that she blocked out which dress she eventually chose.

Family occasions were difficult, but holidays were the worst. The custody agreement meant that each and every holiday was split. It was a series of grim journeys back and forth between the two households. It was traumatic, recalled Diana, "each individual parent trying to make it up in their area with material things rather than the actual tactile stuff, which is what we both craved for but neither of us ever got." With Sarah and Jane away at school, it was Diana and Charles who were placed on the train every weekend to travel back and forth, and it created a bond between the two youngest Spencer children. They looked forward to the day when they, too, could go away to boarding school. "We couldn't wait to be independent, Charles and I, in order to spread our wings and do our own thing."

There was one world in which Diana could spread her wings; interestingly enough, it was a world that also captivated the young Jacqueline Bouvier. Both found solace and comfort, not to mention light and beauty, in the world of the ballet.

There's a song in the Broadway musical *A Chorus Line,* called "At the Ballet," in which a trio of young dancers express the joy they find "up the steep and very narrow narrow stairway, to the voice like a metronome." In *A Class Act,* their musical biography of the show's lyricist, Edward Kleban, playwrights Linda Kline and Lonny Price re-create the collaborative process between Kleban and composer Marvin Hamlisch.

Ed:
I did my own interviews with each of the dancers—I don't wanna mention names—and what these kids had in common is they had lousy, miserable, terrible, awful childhoods. The only time they were happy was at the ballet. So there's your title: "At the Ballet."
Think philandering fathers . . .
Frustrated mothers . . .
Alcoholic frustrated mothers . . .

The song, with its plaintive refrain "I was pretty, I was happy, I would love to . . . at the ballet," perfectly encapsulates both the despair and longing of an unhappy childhood, with all the feelings of being unwanted, useless, and filled with shame, as well as the indescribable joy to be found in the dark, watching handsome princes and graceful swans, where "everything was beautiful."

Out of their painful childhoods came a lifelong passion for the ballet. Both at one time had hoped to be dancers. Jackie would later say, "I was a tomboy until I learned how to dance. Then I became feminine." As a young girl in New York, she attended a fashionable dance class but far preferred the ballet lessons she took. She was too tall to be a dancer and her feet grew too big, but she was passionate about ballet and collected books, and later art, relating to the dance. When she was a student at the Sorbonne in the late 1940s, she purchased a series of eighteenth-century ink-and-watercolor illustrations of the ballet, which she would place in her dressing room at the White House. She used her time in public life to promote the dance; the famed choreographer George Balanchine was one of her first guests at the White House, coming for tea the week after the inauguration. Ballet, both classical and modern, was performed at state dinners for the shah of Iran and the president of the Ivory Coast. When she left public life, the ballet was one of the few causes she threw her wholehearted support behind, being a patron of the American Ballet Theatre, chairing many of the troupe's gala benefits.

Diana, too, adored the ballet but, like Jackie, grew too tall to have any hope of being a professional dancer. She remembered her boarding-school years with great fondness, as "there was an enormous hall . . . I used to sneak down at night when it was all dark and put on my music and do my ballet there in this enormous hall for hours on end and no-one ever found me."

She attended the ballet at every possible opportunity and once charmed her dinner partner, Mikhail Baryshnikov, when she told him of standing outside Covent Garden in the rain to get his autograph.

When she became a royal princess, not only was she appointed patron of several ballet companies, but she used her position to commandeer the services of the English National Ballet's Wayne Sleep to create a pas de deux for the two of them. Dancing in a silvery slip dress to the Billy Joel song "Uptown Girl" was an evening of sheer bliss for the once-shy girl who dreamed of finding in the world of the ballet the tranquility and acceptance she could not find in her life.

Chapter Four

A Girl at an Impressionable Age

A Vassar girl with discrimination!
—Jackie, describing herself to Arthur Schlesinger, 1962

The academic department . . . you might as well forget about that!
—Diana, speaking about her school days, 1991

Some might argue that Jackie was a brain and Diana a dunce, but that is both inaccurate and unfair. Both were born with a natural intelligence and curiosity, and although Jackie's was cultivated along academic lines, Diana's grew under her instinctual tutelage.

Each woman received an education in accordance with the normal customs of their class. There was no P.S. 78 or CCNY for these two. Instead there were private schools close to home, followed by boarding schools in tranquil rural settings, a Seven Sisters college for one and study abroad for both. What is curious, though, is that each received an education better suited to the times in which the other lived.

Diana's education lacked the basic quality of Jackie's. Certainly prepared for the life of a country lady—a Laura Ashley life crammed with dogs and shooting parties, Wellington boots and cords—Diana received little in the way of preparation for assuming a major role on the world stage. But what she did learn from an after-school volunteer program would serve her well in public life.

Jackie's education gave her full confidence in her "social, administrative and intellectual abilities," as she had been "reared in the Puritan ethic of doing one's duty to the fullest." Her love of literature and art, nourished by exceptional teachers, gave her a strong foundation for the work she was to do in both the public and private spheres of her life. Her education did what educations are supposed to do, spark an interest and then fuel the passion for learning.

New York City, 1935

That passion for learning and an accompanying dollop of mischievousness first surfaced at the Chapin School, where she enrolled in 1935. Her intelligence and imagination were appreciated by her teachers, who were less fond of Jackie's willful stubbornness, which often led to pranks both silly (lobbing water balloons on the other girls) and malicious (dipping a classmate's braids into an inkwell). She was forever being sent to the headmistress, Miss Stringfellow, and sat in stony silence while she was being chastised. "Miss Stringfellow says a lot of things," young Jackie told her mother, "but I don't listen."

Jackie's classmates were in awe of her "spirit, boundless energy and humor," and it was at Chapin, in the fifth grade, that she first met Nancy Tuckerman, who would become her lifelong friend. They were roommates in the mid-1940s, when both attended Miss Porter's School in Farmington, Connecticut. Tuckerman, in a charming memoir of their friendship, wrote of being persuaded to overcome her fear of riding by taking Jackie's horse, Danseuse, for a brisk afternoon canter, which was strictly forbidden by school rules. Tuckerman injured her arm and, fearful of the repercussions, turned to Jackie, who blithely suggested she "tell the infirmary you fell out of a tree." That's just what she did, and not surprisingly, it worked.

Farmington, Connecticut, 1943

Family issues loomed large as fourteen-year-old Jackie prepared to enter Miss Porter's School, a prestigious academy just outside of Hartford, Connecticut. The summer before she entered the ninth grade, her mother remarried, placing Jackie and Lee in a new family. Janet had married Hugh D. Auchincloss II, a wealthy stockbroker who was a Standard Oil heir and owner of two large estates, Merrywood, just west of Washington, D.C., on the banks of the Potomac River in McLean, Virginia, and Hammersmith Farm, on Narragansett Bay in Newport, Rhode Island. Hugh Auchincloss was the opposite of Jack Bouvier: impassive, dependable, and quietly rich.

Jackie came to love her Uncle Hughdie, or "Unk," as she would call him. The marriage brought her a ready-made elder brother, Hughdie's teenage son, Hugh D. III, or Yusha. Yusha was two years her senior, handsome and charming. Jackie instantly considered him her brother, treating and thinking of him as such. Life at Merrywood and Hammersmith Farm returned Jackie to the luxurious milieu that she had known as a very young girl.

Black Jack was irked that this new family offered her the luxuries and pleasures that he could no longer afford, so he was pleased when his favorite daughter chose to attend boarding school so close to his base in New York. It removed her from the clutches of the Auchinclosses. (A nasty slogan, "Take a loss with Auchincloss," summarized Jack's feelings about his ex-wife and her new husband.)

Jackie's new family would grow, with the addition of Tommy and Nini, Hughdie's two children from his second marriage (to Gore Vidal's mother, Nina), and then "little" Janet and Jamie, children of the union between Janet and Hughie. Where once there had been four in her family, there were now nine.

Miss Porter's gave Jackie her first taste of freedom, her first escape from the domestic turmoil that had long been the most constant thing in her life. Her letters home were happy, full of the topics of adolescence: talk about friends, boys, plans for parties and weekend trips, and reports on her doings at school ("Tuck and I were out in the buggy with Donny [Danseuse] this afternoon. . . . We take the radio and cigarettes and have a heavenly time").

She was an outstanding student and yet kept from being known as a grind because of her sense of fun. In order to receive forbidden telephone calls from young gentlemen, she sent elaborate plans to Yusha to call the school office at a specific time and pretend to be his father, so they could talk and gossip. (Or rather, he could talk freely, she would have to restrict her comments to "Yes, Uncle," "No, Uncle." It was fun nonetheless.)

At Miss Porter's Jackie developed her interests in literature and drawing, studying the history of art with Sarah McLennen and English with Elizabeth Walker. Always a voracious reader, as a child she had read short stories by Chekhov. She also studied languages, getting A's in French and Spanish, both languages she would speak with ease. Given her fluency in French and her passionate interest in her father's cultural heritage, it was natural that she would want to study abroad. When the opportunity came in her sophomore year at Vassar, it was one that she couldn't ignore.

"She could draw just about anything," a friend would remember, "people, animals, objects of any sort, all in perfect scale." Her letters home were often enhanced by her illustrations; a letter to Yusha congratulating him on being so popular shows a bevy of young girls swooning over him with an irate Frank Sinatra, glowering and alone, off to the side. Her love of poetry grew, and she would become famous within her family and friends for the poems and stories she would write and then illustrate with her whimsical and sophisticated drawings.

In 1946, at the end of her junior year, fifteen-year-old Jacqueline Bouvier was awarded the Maria McKinney Memorial Award in Literature. The prize was a book of poetry and the poems within were so meaningful to her that she kept the volume in her bedroom on a bookshelf where she kept her "special treasures—books on art and ballet and poetry."

Poughkeepsie, New York, 1947

There would come a time when she would refer to the place as "that goddamn Vassar." But she didn't always harbor that sentiment about the "female college" founded by brewer Matthew Vassar in 1861. "It's so wonderful here," she wrote to a friend in the fall of her freshman year, "a whole different life and so much freedom. It really makes you be responsible. They don't look after you the way they did at Farmington." The combination of a keen intellect and a natural curiosity would give Jackie an advantage as she began her college studies.

Jackie and her freshman roommate, Edna Harrison, lived in Main 312. Vassar students then and now are justifiably proud of their Main Building. Designed by James Renwick, the architect of St. Patrick's Cathedral in New York and the first Corcoran Gallery in Washington, D.C., it was modeled after the palace of the Tuileries, which had been part of the Louvre in Paris until it was destroyed in 1871. The hallways are twelve feet wide (so that two young ladies wearing hoop skirts could walk side by side, or so legend goes), the rooms graced with high ceilings and tall windows. Jackie and Edna shared a large double room facing north, with a communal bathroom a few steps down the hall.

She studied Shakespeare, poetry, art, and religion and was to say that she was "fortunate to find superb teachers in these fields." Classes were small, about twelve to fifteen students, and the teachers, among them the Shakespearean scholar Helen Sandison, held each girl to high standards. Jackie's grades were quite good, although she was forever complaining that she never studied and even dashed off quick notes to friends during class ("I am writing this in Music 140, listening to early Christian wailing hymns and trying to concentrate over this awful din").

Jackie was popular among her Vassar sisters (she's remembered as being "great fun" and "a loyal friend"). But she was, by nature, something of a loner. When, after dinner and study hall, friends would gather in the high Victorian parlors on the second floor of Main, Jackie would rarely join them. Instead she would stay in her room, content in the solitary activities of reading, drawing, or keeping up with her voluminous correspondence. Just after the Christmas break in 1948, Jackie was distinguished further from her classmates when she was anointed Debutante of the Year by the columnist Igor Cassini, writing under the name Cholly Knickerbocker. The story, running on Tuesday, January 13, featured a flattering photograph of Jackie with long, wavy hair, wearing a sleeveless white evening gown with large ruffled flounces at the neckline and at the hem. Cassini wrote of her "classic features and daintiness of Dresden porcelain. She has poise, is soft-spoken and intelligent, everything the leading debutante should be. . . . Jacqueline is now studying at Vassar. You don't have to read a bunch of press clippings to be aware of her qualities."

The lure of New York City, just seventy miles down the Hudson, was often too strong to resist, and in her two years at Vassar Jackie spent few weekends on campus. Black Jack, in New York City, and Lee, at Miss Porter's, were her primary diversions. She wrote with great enthusiasm about spending the weekend with her father, driving his black Mercury to New Haven for the Yale–Coast Guard football game. He took her on a tour of his old haunts, including his fraternity tombs. At the game they ate hot dogs and waved banners while Jack gave Jackie his opinion of her various boyfriends, which made her laugh.

But the dreary train trips back up the Hudson to Vassar, chugging past Tarrytown and Dobbs Ferry, and Garrison and Cold Spring up to Poughkeepsie, coupled with the school's all-female and vaguely feminist atmosphere, began to wear on Jackie. She made plans to spend her junior year studying in France. As her sophomore year came to an end, she wrote that she felt "cooped up in this dungeon" and made summer plans ("All of June running around to weddings, part of July with Daddy, leaving August 23 for Paris").

She had come to Vassar by a traditional path, but Jackie's independence began to assert itself in her decision to go to the Sorbonne. Life in Paris, barely four years after the city's liberation from Nazi domination, was not going to be comfortable, let alone luxurious, and in some quarters was even considered dangerous (the dormitories of the Sorbonne, for example, were thought to be unsafe for single women). But Jackie's sense of adventure won out, and off she sailed for Paris.

Paris, 1949

She arrived there in October of 1949 after spending a month in Grenoble perfecting her French in an intensive language program. After the protected freedom of boarding school and college, she found life as an exchange student to be sublime. She lived with an impoverished aristocratic French family on the rue Mozart, where there were coldwater baths once a week and not a word of English was spoken. She loved her studies and used her free time to scour the flea markets for inexpensive art prints and books. Her family connections gave her entrée into the world of Parisian and diplomatic society.

And though she had little money (between both her parents, she had an allowance of sixty dollars a month), she was able to get student tickets for the multitude of cultural offerings—the theater, opera, and ballet—which she attended on an almost nightly basis. Less highbrow but equally enjoyable were the small cafés where she would listen to Edith Piaf and smoke Galoises through the night.

She used the base of Paris to travel extensively, touring France and visiting England and Switzerland, on a dazzling social whirl. On a more sobering note were trips to Germany (where she went to the concentration camp at Dachau and reported that "the Germans are still Nazis") and Austria—still under joint occupation—where she was detained for a short time by Russian soldiers for taking unauthorized photographs.

After she had finished her exams in June, Yusha arrived from Yale for a joint vacation that would take them to Scotland to visit his ancestral roots and to Ireland to visit hers. She was as interested in her Irish Lee ancestry as her French Bouvier. After more than a year abroad, she and Yusha returned on the French liner *Liberté*. Jackie came back to the United States far more sophisticated and worldly than her kilt-and-sweater-wearing Vassar classmates could ever hope to be, and she made a decision not to return to Poughkeepsie for her senior year. Instead, much to Jack Bouvier's indignation, she moved back to Merrywood and enrolled in George Washington University, where she received a degree in French literature in the spring of 1951.

Kent, England, 1973

Diana experienced more difficulty than Jackie did adjusting to school—and to her schoolmates. "My sister [Jane] was a prefect at West Heath, and I was pretty ghastly for the first term," Diana confessed in a later interview. "I was a bully because I thought it was wonderful to have my sister as a prefect. I felt very important." In fact, both her sisters had preceded her to the elite West Heath. Sarah passed through school with a reputation for being rebellious and was often sent to the headmistress, Ruth Rudge. Aggressive and athletic, she was on both the swimming and riding teams. Accomplished in the classroom as well, she passed half a dozen O-level (ordinary) exams. Jane was also an excellent student, earning both O-level and A-level (advanced) exams but was quiet and dutiful and a leader, serving as lacrosse team captain. So when Diana went there, in the fall of 1973, she had a hard act to follow.

West Heath is a typical English public school—similar to any of New England's many preparatory, or "prep," schools. Nestled in the rolling hills of the Kent countryside, it is close to Sevenoaks, a quintessential English village with it pubs and small cottages and winding roads. Knole House, the historic Tudor home of the Sackville family, is nearby, as are the fabled gardens of Sissinghurst, the country seat of Harold Nicolson and Vita Sackville-West.

The school has its own splendid gardens and thirty-two acres of woodlands. Founded in 1865, the school wasn't as valued for its academic programs as much as it was for its ambition to build "character" and boost "confidence." The student body, approximately 120 students, was made up of girls from aristocratic and wealthy families.

West Heath was a fairly exclusive school, partly because of its high tuition.

Diana was already at a disadvantage when she entered West Heath, as she started a term later than the other girls in her class. Friendships and cliques had already formed, and the other girls were familiar with the faculty and staff. Diana had to cope with the fact that the girls in her class had already started on their coursework. Her insecurity manifested itself in displays of girlish cruelty. Jane's presence wasn't much help to her, though, as the second term came. Many of the girls to whom she had been horrid ganged up on her and took revenge. By the third term she had calmed down. Her teachers could see that her temperament fell somewhere between that of the firebrand Sarah and the more docile Jane.

"Her mind, you often just felt, was elsewhere," recalled one of her teachers, Penny Walker. "Her sisters were fairly good academically. Sarah was a brilliant pianist. Jane wasn't far behind. She had to a lot to live up to." Diana enjoyed literature, reading Jane Austen and Thomas Hardy, and showed interest in the Tudor and Stuart dynasties in her history classes, but her teachers were aware that she had difficulty with her concentration. "I didn't shout out the answers in class," Diana remembered, "because I didn't think I knew them."

She adored sports and excelled at them, partly because of her height. As one of the tallest girls, she was on the tennis, netball, and field hockey teams and was almost as athletic as Sarah. She showed an independent streak similar to her sister's by sneaking into the assembly hall late at night, playing her music and dancing alone for hours.

She pulled her most outrageous prank one night when, on a dare, she agreed to slip out of the dormitory after lights out and sneak down the main drive, a half-mile walk, in the dark to rendezvous with another girl. The other girl, not as daring as Diana, never showed up. Diana, whistling in the dark, was amazed to see a series of police cars, sirens blazing, pull up the drive and stop in front of the school. When she got back to her dormitory, the headmistress, having discovered her absence, was furious. Both of her parents were called to the school, and though her mother was secretly amused—

"I didn't think you had it in you," she whispered to Diana—both parents admonished her. Miss Rudge was placated.

Like Jackie, Diana Spencer won prizes during her school years, though they were not scholarly ones. "I always won all the swimming and diving cups," she once recalled with a laugh. "I won all sorts of prizes for the best-kept guinea pig." Diana could be charmingly self-deprecating about her academic shortcomings, but the truth remains that she was as surprisingly undereducated for a young woman in the 1970s as Jackie was overeducated in the 1940s. But Diana would take one invaluable lesson from her days at West Heath, a lesson that would add dimension to her work as Princess of Wales.

The Sevenoaks Voluntary Service, a charitable organization, created a program with West Heath to sponsor volunteers to make regular visits to a hospital for the physically and mentally disabled. Diana willingly signed up, and this became her first experience of working with the people in circumstances less fortunate than hers. They would eventually become her core constituency.

The hospital was housed at Darenth Park, an imposing Victorian monstrosity hidden from the street by forbiddingly high walls. Muriel Stevens, who organized the twice-a-week visits, remembered that "Diana was never frightened. She was extremely relaxed in that setting, which for a young person of her age was incredible. It was intimidating to walk into that huge place and to see some of the severely handicapped people that we did have."

The patients were curious about the young volunteers and would grab at them and stroke their hair. Diana easily made friends with many of the patients, who enjoyed her boisterous laughter. "That joyous sound. You wouldn't know what it was she was laughing at, but at the sound alone you would find yourself smiling," Muriel remembered fondly. Part of the program included dancing, and dancing with people in wheelchairs is awkward at best. Thanks to her height and her dance training, Diana was able to dance backward by holding the arms of the wheelchair.

Her days at Darenth Park gave Diana several important lessons in dealing with vulnerable people and making them comfortable. Muriel Stevens was impressed that "we never had to remind Diana that touch was the main means of communication." Her ability to be tactile, to touch AIDS sufferers and land-mine victims with no sense of condescension, would be one of her main gifts to the world and was a lesson she learned as a schoolgirl, as valuable as anything an academic program could teach. But it would not save her skin academically: she failed her O-level exams again. She left West Heath before moving on to the sixth form. Diana, essentially, was a high-school dropout.

Gstaad, Switzerland, 1978

After she left West Heath, Diana's parents were at somewhat of a loss as to what to do with their daughter. She was just sixteen, too old to return home as a child and yet too young to go out on her own. She was sent to the Institute Alpin Videmanette, a finishing school near Gstaad in the Swiss Alps. Old-fashioned then, and now almost extinct, finishing schools were where young ladies went for "polishing"—a round of courses designed to create sophisticated hostesses who were well versed in running a large household, planning dinner parties, and having witty conversation. Miss Porter's once had a finishing program, but it was eliminated in favor of college-preparation studies in the early 1940s.

French was the official language at the institute; fewer than ten of the seventy-two students were English-speaking. Classes in cooking, dressmaking, and domestic science—the finishing-school equivalent of home ec—were all conducted in a language that Diana found difficult to master. She did not enjoy her time in Gstaad, except for the skiing. She and her friend Sophie Kimball skied all day long and, in violation of the school's practice, spoke English.

Almost from the moment of her arrival, Diana wrote emotional letters home, some twenty in all, begging to be allowed to return early. She finally convinced her parents that it was a waste of their money to keep her there. In April 1978, after just a few months, she returned to England and to her mother's apartment in Cadogan Square. She was ten weeks short of her seventeenth birthday and as ready as she would ever be to take on the world. She just needed to decide what she wanted to do with the rest of her life.

Jackie told *Ms.* magazine in 1979, "What has been sad for many women of my generation is that they weren't supposed to work if they had families. There they were, with the highest education, and what were they to do when the children were grown—watch raindrops come down the windowpane? Leave their fine minds unexercised?" Some women were exceptions to the rule, but they truly were exceptions. More often than not, they were professionals—a doctor or a lawyer. Women were given all the preparation, but the culture of the time kept them from making use of their skills.

Thirty years of progress in all areas, the women's movement in particular, hadn't really reached the landed gentry in 1970s Britain. They viewed the world through solidly old-fashioned rose-colored glasses. Higher education for women, at least aristocratic women, was a deviation from the norm. Schools existed in a very basic way to provide a little polish and style to the young ladies (in many cases, they were, literally, Lady So-and-So, daughters of dukes, marquesses, and earls). Though the doors had been opened for Diana Spencer and her sisters to pursue any career they chose, like most of the young women in their circle, they politely declined the invitation to walk through those doors. Marriage to a country squire, perhaps to a title or heir, seemed to be the highest aspiration. In that regard, Diana succeeded brilliantly.

Diana's future husband had held a place in her fantasy life even before she met him; she had decorated her room with a pin-up poster of Charles in one of his "Action Man" poses. The Prince of Wales enjoyed a daredevil image at the time, one tied to athletic ability and adventure. She may have enjoyed the fantasy, but in the fall of 1977, her sister Sarah was living the reality. She had been dating Charles for a few months and had invited him to a shooting party at her family home, Althorp.

Diana had just failed her four O-level exams and had gone home for a weekend to study for them again. She met Charles in a field.

Later he was to recall her as being "jolly" and "bouncy." She was over the moon with delight. She raced back to school after the weekend and went around crowing, "I've met him, I've met him." Perhaps it was that excitement that kept her from studying, as she failed her O-level exams again.

In the 1940s or 1950s, Diana's success could have made almost any aristocratic young American woman swoon with jealousy. After they graduated from college (if they did), these women—the women of Jackie's generation—could expect to put their finely educated minds on hold while they married and raised a family. Jackie's future sister-in-law Joan Kennedy once commented, "We all went to college in pursuit of a degree—our M.R.S." That did not hold true for Jackie. Though she acquired the ultimate M.R.S.—a man who would one day become President of the United States of America—in doing so, she was able to fully utilize her considerable abilities in the pursuit of excellence.

Chapter Five

Maidens

I loved being in a flat with the girls . . . it was great.
I loved being on my own.
> —Diana, describing her single life in London

I'll be glad to get out of this place and have a fascinating life.
I'm going to rent a South Sea island and live in luxury and sin.
> —Jackie, describing her future plans in 1947

Diana Spencer married less than a month after her twentieth birthday, young for her generation of women. Jacqueline Bouvier married six weeks after her twenty-fourth birthday, practically an old maid by the standards of the early 1950s. But what each shared was a short period of time, just two or three years, when they were young women about town. That taste of freedom, the excitement of holding your destiny in the palm of your hand, is exhilarating, as both Diana and Jackie were to discover during their brief time as single girls.

The years 1978 to 1981, after Diana had left school but before she married, were marked by two emotion-laden events: her father's remarriage and his near-fatal illness. The first introduced a rival for her father's affection—the "evil stepmother"—and the second rendered Johnnie Spencer totally dependent on his new wife. Earl Spencer's marriage to Raine Dartmouth did not bring about a happy collective family in the same way that Janet Lee and Hugh D. Auchincloss's union did. Diana's relationship with her father suffered from this emotional double assault; not only had he replaced her mother with another woman, but he came close to the ultimate in emotional abandonment—an early death. When he recovered, Diana found him a changed man. The comfortable father figure of her girlhood was gone forever.

Jackie graduated from college in 1951 and was married twenty-eight months later. Most of her contemporaries married early—the women at Vassar waited breathlessly at their class day lunch for the first of their classmates to run around the table, signifying that she had received an engagement ring. But Jackie wanted more out of life. "I've learned not to be ashamed of a real hunger for knowledge," she said at the time. Though she didn't have the freedom of her own apartment, living under her mother's supervision at Merrywood, she did take steps to find a career that would stimulate both her intellect and her creativity. Many years later, on the eve of her fiftieth birthday, Jackie looked back at that time of her life: "If I hadn't married, I might have had a life very much like Gloria Emerson's. She's a friend who started out in Paris writing about fashion—and then ended up as a correspondent in Vietnam. The two ends of her career couldn't seem farther apart, and that is the virtue of journalism. You never know where it's going to take you, but it can be a noble life."

Her innate sense of adventure would lead to flirtations with some interesting career choices and a brief but rewarding stint as a reporter and photographer for the *Washington Times-Herald* (where she would report on Queen Elizabeth's 1953 coronation). But Jacqueline Bouvier would follow the accustomed traditions of the time and "retire" once she became engaged in the summer of 1953, just as Diana Spencer would do eighteen years later.

London, 1978

Diana came home from Switzerland to a family situation fraught with tension. Not yet seventeen, disappointed at having failed at school, where her siblings had enjoyed notable success, with no plans for her future, she returned to find an unwanted rival. The birth of her brother, Charles, had erased Johnnie's disappointment at her gender. Diana had cherished the fantasy of being "Daddy's little girl." Now there was a big girl to take her place in Johnnie Spencer's heart.

Raine McCorquodale is a grandiose character in this story full of larger-than-life figures. The daughter of romance novelist Barbara Cartland, she found the blueprint for her life in her mother's books. With overstated manners and bandbox femininity, she acted and looked like a character from a road company version of a Noël Coward play: arch, exaggerated, and over-the-top. Underneath this heavily shellacked facade was an iron will and steely determination. Married since the late 1940s to the earl Dartmouth, in 1974 Raine began a romance with Johnnie Spencer that would culminate in a quick and quiet marriage in 1976 after she and Dartmouth divorced.

"Acid Raine" was the name bestowed upon her by her Spencer stepchildren. The four of them were united in their distaste for the woman who had bewitched their father. Shortly before Johnnie inherited his title and estates in 1975, he had become reacquainted with Raine when they met at a party. "It was a hot day and everyone was in the garden," Raine was fond of recalling. "When I went inside there was only one person there—John. He said, 'I haven't seen you in twenty years.' 'Things are so coincidental, aren't they?' I replied."

Raine was the countess of Dartmouth. It was a title older than that of Earl Spencer, but it came with little of the splendor and less of the riches. Five years after his divorce, Johnnie was ripe for a romance, and Raine pursued him with determination. At first their affair was conducted with discretion, using the move from Park House to Althorp (which became the family's home upon the death of Johnnie's father) as the reason for Raine's continuing presence. She was helping Johnnie redecorate and modernize the stately house. But Johnnie's children actively disliked this woman whom they viewed as taking their mother's place, and he soon enough found his discreet cover blown by his eldest daughter.

Having heard rumors of a romance, a reporter called Althorp and asked to speak to Johnnie. "Lord Spencer is in bed with Lady Dartmouth," Sarah responded with splenetic glee, "and I don't want to disturb them." A divorce for the earl and countess Dartmouth soon followed, with Johnnie being saved from the public humiliation that his Frances had suffered—Gerald Legge, Earl Dartmouth, declined to name him as a corresponent in his divorce suit. Raine and Johnnie married on July 14, 1976, in a registry office in London with only Raine's brother in attendance. None of the Spencer children attended, nor did any of Raine's four children: William Viscount Lewisham, the Honorable Rupert, the Honorable Henry, and Lady Charlotte Legge.

With Diana away at school, at West Heath and later in Switzerland, there were other matters to think about. Back in London, at age sixteen and at a loss as to what to do with herself, Diana couldn't help but focus on how her father's affections had been usurped.

She was loath to move to Althorp. It held no emotional pull; Raine was the mistress of the house. "I was itching to go to London because I thought the grass was greener on the other side," Diana said. But her parents wouldn't allow her to live in London until her eighteenth birthday. She took a job as an au pair, or mother's helper. The Whitaker family, friends of Diana's stepfather, Peter Shand Kydd, had a six-year-old daughter, Alexandra, and lived in Hampshire. She saw herself as "part of their team" but didn't show too much enthusiasm for the work ("It was all right") and soon, in the summer of 1978, launched a successful campaign to be allowed to live in London. Her parents relented, and so she went to live in her mother's apartment in Cadogan Square and was enrolled in a cooking school.

She had just started at the cooking school when her father suffered a stroke and nearly died. Diana had a haunting premonition of his attack before it happened, telling friends at a house party in Norfolk, "I've got this strange feeling he's going to drop down, and if he dies, he'll die immediately; otherwise, he'll survive." When the telephone rang the next morning, she told those at breakfast "that will be about Daddy." Indeed, the call came from the hospital where Earl Spencer was lying gravely ill.

Johnnie had suffered a massive cerebral hemorrhage in September 1978. Raine's behavior in the ensuing months saved her husband's life but irreparably damaged her relationship with her stepchildren. Like Jill Castle, the obsessed heroine in Sidney Sheldon's *A Stranger in the Mirror,* Raine devoted her considerable energy, talents, and will to her husband's recovery. She went behind the backs of his doctors to obtain experimental medicine and utilized such unconventional methods as bringing a record player into his hospital room to play Puccini and having the ghost of Johnnie's father exorcised from the house at Althorp.

She also restricted the children's access to their father, at times literally standing at the hospital door and blocking their entrance. She told one friend that she "did not need teenagers throwing tantrums" at his bedside. Jane was the only one of the Spencer children who was even civil to Raine, barely managing to say hello. The others were outright rude to her and shouted at her over Johnnie's comatose body. His recovery took months, and Raine maintained a daily vigil at his side. She virtually dragged him back to life, and although she told a close member of her family, "I simply adore him," some of her critics (and there have been many) pointed out that if Johnnie had died, Raine's position would have been tenuous; she would have been forced from Althorp with insufficient financial provision made for her future.

Johnnie did recover, but Diana noticed a pronounced change in his nature, telling one friend, "He was one person before and he was certainly a different person after . . . basically a changed character."

By the summer of 1979, Diana had reached her eighteenth birthday and came into funds from her American great-grandmother. She purchased an apartment in Earls Court and had finally gotten a diploma—in the cooking course she had taken in Wimbledon. ("I quite liked it but . . . I got terribly fat. I loved sauces; my fingers were always in the saucepans.")

Diana loved the freedom her new life offered her. She shared her apartment with three friends and kept her social life quiet ("I wasn't interested in having a full diary"). She was kept busy, finding jobs as a cleaning lady and baby-sitting for friends of her sisters. She devised a code word for the Sloane Ranger types for whom she worked, calling them the "velvet hairbands" and finding them "pretty grim employers."

By the start of 1979, Diana had balanced her work week between two jobs, teaching three days a week at the Young England Kindergarten and working as a nanny for a young American boy for the other two. The kindergarten, near Victoria Station, was run by two friends of Jane Spencer who were impressed with Diana's rapport with their young charges. They hired her to teach drawing and dancing. "Miss Diana" was immediately popular with the dozen or so young children she taught.

She was also popular with Mary Robertson, the American woman who hired her to care for her toddler son, Patrick. Mary found Diana to be sensible and grounded, recalling that "I really had no concerns about her being flighty or irresponsible." Mrs. Robertson, with her Harvard M.B.A., was an astute businesswoman who had brought her young son to London and was very careful about whom she hired to care for her little boy. She had been impressed with the way that Diana focused her attention on Patrick during their first interview, mussing his hair and playing with his toys. Diana was hired, and Mary Robertson became Diana's first adult friend from outside her aristocratic circle.

Diana was a young single woman in London. As was customary, she would spend a few years enjoying life in the big city and then marry. She dated ("I had crushes, serious crushes on all sorts of people") but an instinct deep inside her told her not to go too far with any one relationship. One former boyfriend commented, "The relationship was not a platonic one as far as *I* was concerned, but it remained that way. She was sexually attractive but always a little aloof." As a child, Diana had always felt that she was going somewhere different in her life, telling her father when she was thirteen, "I know I'm going to marry someone in the public eye." An inner voice told her to remain chaste, a virgin, a maiden. She was careful to maintain her sexual innocence. When Charles came back into her life in the summer of 1980, she was the ideal candidate for the job of Princess of Wales. She was so perfect, in fact, that her name was literally at the top of a list of eligible young women prepared by Buckingham Palace and vetted for Charles by, among others, Camilla Parker Bowles. A virgin, an English girl, an aristocrat with a beautiful and seemingly docile personality, Diana was the ideal royal wife.

Washington, D.C., 1951

"I have always known that I wanted to 'do something' with my life but I could never visualize just how to go about it." Jackie expressed those thoughts just as she was about to graduate from George Washington University in the spring of 1951. Well educated and well traveled, she had followed her mother's dictum to return to Washington to establish a home base at Merrywood. Janet was eager for her to settle down in one place "in the home," as Janet put it and postwar Washington was an intriguing place for an intelligent young woman—a small city that was a hub of world power.

Jackie's first job after college was with the CIA. The Central Intelligence Agency, formed in 1947 by President Harry Truman's National Security Act, evolved from World War II's Office of Strategic Services (OSS). In its charter it was charged with "coordinating the nation's intelligence activities and correlating, evaluating and disseminating intelligence which affects national security." Long a bastion of the WASP establishment (during the war it was said that OSS stood for "oh so social"), the agency recruited from the Ivy League and Seven Sisters colleges and was a highly sought-after job for young college graduates, both male and female. It was the ideal place for people who wanted to "do something" with their lives, and Jackie had pestered CIA director Allen Dulles, a friend of Hughdie's, for a job there. The position she was hired for required security clearance. She described it as a "special job on a certain project" that would take place from October 1951 through January 1952.

Nothing has ever been written about her tenure there, and, intriguingly, there is no record of any of Jackie's activities from October 1951 to January 1952. She and Lee traveled in Europe during the summer, a trip that was a graduation present for Lee, who had just finished Miss Porter's and was about to go to Sarah Lawrence. The Bouvier sisters created a delightful scrapbook of their trip, which they later published in the 1970s under the title *One Special Summer*. They returned from Europe on September 15, and Jackie's job as the Inquiring Photographer for the *Washington Times-Herald* started in January 1952, but there's no record in any of the multitude of biographies that have been written about Jacqueline Kennedy Onassis that cover her activities in the late fall and early winter of 1951.

She had a command of the French language that certainly qualified her to work for the Agency as a translator in the French mission. As of May, she hadn't learned how to type, so it was unlikely she held a secretarial position. At the start of the Cold War, international activity demanded translators who were fluent in French: there were communiqués from the French sector in Berlin, the Fourth Republic in France, and Indochina and Algeria. An expert translator, one who had lived in France and understood the nuances of the language and its street slang, would be a prized employee.

It's no surprise that Jackie impressed the Central Intelligence Agency; she had impressed her teachers for years. Dr. McClanahan, her English professor at George Washington University, commented: "Miss Bouvier is excellent and writes much better than do most students and her critical sense is perceptive. She has done better than 'B' work this year."

Jackie had also impressed her would-be employers at *Vogue* magazine. While she was in Europe in the summer of 1950, Janet Auchincloss had seen an advertisement in the magazine announcing their Prix de Paris contest. When Jackie returned she hastily submitted her application, late. ("I cannot type myself. I am taking a secretarial course this year but as yet it still takes me ten minutes to peck my way though a sentence.") The girl who promised to type Jackie's essays got caught up in homecoming activities, so on Halloween 1950 Jackie wrote to *Vogue,* asking for an extension.

The thirty-odd pages that constitute Jacqueline Bouvier's entry for the Prix de Paris are the most extensive autobiographical material available to scholars. Two authorized biographies, Molly Thayer's *Jacqueline Bouvier Kennedy* and *Jacqueline Kennedy: The White House Years*, are close seconds. They were shaped by Jackie's editing and strict control. But the eight essays for *Vogue* are remarkably candid, witty, and insightful. The self-portrait is charming ("I am afraid I will never be very successful over a hot stove"), the makeup tips a delightful time capsule of mid-twentieth-century beauty products

(Dorothy Gray's Special Dry Skin Mixture and ammoniated tooth-paste are two of her recommendations). For smokers there's a suggestion of a weekly peroxide rinse, as "nothing will be counted against you faster than a dingy smile."

Jackie chose "nostalgia" as a theme for an issue of *Vogue* and wrote about Venetian doges, Directoire dandies, Babe Paley wearing Charles James, and Madame Pandit Nehru in Mainbocher. She wrote of an obscure F. Scott Fitzgerald story, "Please Show Mr. and Mrs. F. to Room No. . . . ," and made a list of current events that she predicted would be nostalgic memories in twenty years' time. Among the episodes that caught her fancy that year were Margaret Truman's singing, the Ingrid Bergman/Roberto Rossellini "uproar," and Gloria Swanson's comeback in *Sunset Boulevard*.

There's a poignant short story, "The Violets," about a young woman at the wake of her beloved grandfather. With its references to relatives bickering over who gets what piece of furniture and what flowers aren't elaborate enough to display, it's easy to see the story as a fictionalization of the death of her paternal grandfather, "Grampy Jack" Bouvier, who died in January 1948.

The last essay, a critique of a *Vogue* article on perfume, is constructive in its criticism and offers an alternative layout, including quotes from Shakespeare, Oscar Wilde, and Milton's poetic drama *Samson Agonistes*—"Coveted by all the winds that hold them play / an amber scent of odorous perfume, her harbinger."

Jackie closes her self-portrait by confessing that her most annoying fault is "getting very enthusiastic over something at the beginning and then tiring of it halfway through." But her enthusiasm for the *Vogue* contest was thorough enough for the judges to comment on her writing style, bright mind, and fashion flair. She won first prize but turned it down, in part, because of her commitment to the CIA. She did try to negotiate a January start date and went so far as to fill out an application form on May 21, 1951. Jackie affirmed that she was not a communist or affiliated with any group that advocated "the overthrow of our Government by any force or by any illegal or unconstitutional methods."

In January 1952 Jackie became the Inquiring Photographer for the *Washington Times-Herald*. It's ironic that the woman who would come to resent the intrusion of the press in her private life would take a job in which she was required to interview and photograph private citizens. But her job, obtained again through her stepfather's circle of friends, was one suited to a young woman with strong social connections. The *Times-Herald*'s former owner, Cissy Patterson, used to round out her staff with such women, among them Jack Kennedy's effervescent sister Kathleen and his first love, Inga Arvard.

A man had been writing the "Inquiring Photographer" column, but Frank Waldrop, the editor, had wanted to see it written from a female perspective. The job was simple: take photographs of passersby and ask them questions about topical and human-interest subjects. With a creative mind behind it, the column could provide insight into how people felt about the world around them. Jackie's questions were always witty and probing—"Noël Coward says all women should be struck regularly, like gongs. Do you agree?" "If you had a date with Marilyn Monroe, what would you talk about?" "The Irish author Sean O'Faolain says the Irish are deficient in the art of love. Do you agree?"—and she was well regarded by her boss.

"She was a business-like little girl," Waldrop told Jackie's official biographer, Molly Van Rensselaer Thayer, "nice, quiet, concentrated, obviously very, very earnest in wanting to be a professional. She was self-sufficient, good at listening and she handled her job efficiently."

One day early in 1953 Waldrop sent Miss Bouvier up to Capitol Hill, where he had arranged for her to question the Republican vice president, Richard Nixon, and, from the Democratic side, the newly sworn-in junior senator from Massachusetts, John F. Kennedy. Jackie asked her future husband and his future political rival what it was like to observe the Senate pages—the college students who assisted senators—up close. Nixon's reply was straightforward and dull; Jack Kennedy's flashed with his typical wit: "I've often thought that the country might be better off if we Senators and the pages traded jobs."

As Jackie was heading out of the *Times-Herald* newsroom to interview JFK, Waldrop grabbed her and warned, "You behave yourself. Don't get your hopes up. He's too old for you—besides, he doesn't want to get married." She smiled enigmatically at him, grabbed her bulky Graflex camera, and headed up toward Capitol Hill.

Chapter Six

The Men They Married

His greatness weigh'd, his will is not his own,
For he himself is subject to his birth;
He may not, as unvalu'd persons do,
Carve for himself, for on his choice depends
The safety and the health of the whole state;
And therefore must his choice be circumscrib'd
Unto the voice and yielding of that body
Whereof he is the head.

—William Shakespeare, *Hamlet*, 1.3

So spoke Laertes to Ophelia when she asked her brother about the Danish prince. In hindsight, and from a distant vantage point, one wishes that he had advised young Diana Spencer and Jacqueline Bouvier as they contemplated their marriage choices. Charles Windsor and John F. Kennedy were very far removed from Hamlet, but Laertes's knowing analysis of the dynastic needs of princely men could easily apply to them.

They were different in the most basic ways. First, Charles was born to greatness, whereas JFK achieved it after having the quest for greatness thrust upon him by a father with Shakespearean ambition. Apart from being the heir to his mother's throne, Charles was a firstborn child. Jack Kennedy was a second child, a second son, the "spare" who would come in handy in the event of the death of his elder brother. Second, the Windsor family dynamic was completely the opposite of the Kennedys'. Charles grew up in a family in which his mother was the power figure, with a father who played a secondary and far less significant role ("I'm a bloody amoebae" was the discreetly edited complaint of Prince Philip). JFK grew up in a family modeled on paternal domination and maternal submission. It wasn't so much "Father knows best" in Joe Kennedy's domain, it was "Father knows everything and don't you be a donkey and think otherwise." Third, their personalities were completely different: Charles was sensitive and self-pitying, JFK was detached and pragmatic.

Charles and Jack shared an experience that shaped both their character and their personalities. Both grew up starved for maternal love. Their subconscious personae were shaped by this deprivation. Each shared a deep-seated fear of abandonment and anger because of this fundamental betrayal of the mother-son bond, and this fear manifested itself in a long-standing reluctance to commit to marriage and a constitutional inability to honor his marriage vows.

It would be harsh to classify Queen Elizabeth and Rose Fitzgerald Kennedy as bad mothers. Certainly both had but the best of intentions, eager to bring their babies into a world filled with love and security. If the circumstances of their lives, often beyond their immediate control, created a scenario in which their actions did not match their maternal intentions, it's difficult to blame them. But neither Charles nor JFK grew up with a strong emotional bond to his mother, and each transferred this internalized feeling of deprivation to the relationship he formed with his wife.

The right choice of marital partner was crucial to their professional success. To paraphrase a comment Prince Charles made to a group of news reporters, the decision of whom to marry was not one in which the heart should rule over the head. Each man needed a consort who would be equal to the job that, in Charles's case, fate had thrust upon him, and in JFK's, his domineering father had.

Both Charles and JFK had dated on extensive number of women, some suitable, others conspicuously not, and both remained unmarried until their thirties. By then, both were set in their bachelor ways and, on a very real level, regarded matrimony as an essential element for a well-rounded CV, rather than as a joyful and natural part of life. For Charles the need for a wife of suitable stature was more visibly pressing, as whoever he married would one day be queen of England and the mother of the future king. Perhaps the most telling and perceptive words that Charles was ever to speak about his personal life was his offhand answer to a question posed during the joint interview he and Diana gave just after their engagement. "And in love?" asked the BBC. Diana quickly blushed, looked down, and giggled out her answer, "Of course." Charles looked slightly bemused at the question and answered, "Whatever 'in love' means." He might just as well have quoted Tina Turner: "What's love got to do with it?" For love, which would be a nice side benefit if it were to develop, was hardly a necessary ingredient.

Jack Kennedy was also vague about love, late in his life telling a friend that he wasn't the "heavy lover type." Although he had been, in his own words, "interested once or twice," he had never been in love. A ladies' man in every sense of the word, Jack could charm just about any woman alive—and, if he had the opportunity, did. He was thirty-six years old before he married. He was successfully elected to the U.S. Congress three times and unseated the illustrious Senator Henry Cabot Lodge Jr. in 1952 by specifically courting the women's vote. His plurality in that election, 70,000-odd votes, was roughly equal to the number of ladies invited to "Kennedy Teas," political rallies masquerading as demure social teas, hosted by Rose Kennedy or one of Jack's sisters. More than a few women attending harbored a secret desire to land the handsome millionaire political scion.

When JFK finally settled down (after being pressured by his father, who scornfully told him that "any man reaching forty and still not married runs the risk of being considered queer"), he told his fiancée that he had decided a year earlier that she was the one but that he hadn't been ready at the time. Now he was. "How *big* of you" was the twenty-three-year-old Jacqueline Bouvier's reply. Her decision to accept his proposal was a momentous event, changing more than just their lives; it affected the course of American history for two generations.

The intertwined stories of Diana and Jackie are distinguished, in an odd way, by some of the most splendid architecture in the Western Hemisphere. From the official residences at Buckingham Palace and the White House, rich with historic association and replete with priceless collections of art and furnishings, to splendid private homes like Kensington Palace, Althorp, and Hammersmith Farm, symbols of a vanishing era of great private wealth, and luxurious apartments at 1040 Fifth and 740 Park Avenues, modern-day mansions in the sky, the stage settings for these two stories are as opulent as imagination, taste, and a great deal of money can create.

Eighty-three Beals Street can make no claim to extravagance, luxury, or architectural distinction. Yet from its wood-framed clapboard humbleness emerged John Fitzgerald Kennedy. He was born in the house on May 29, 1917, in a bedroom on the second floor. Furnished with a twin bed each for husband and wife, the room was the largest of three bedrooms, which shared the floor with a small boudoir and the house's sole bathroom. Young Jack Kennedy was to live at 83 Beals Street for only four years, for his father's success in business and his mother's success in enlarging the family brought about both the means and the need to move to a large house around the corner, on Naples Road.

The Kennedy family is an American success story. Jack was the second child of a family of nine, four sons and five daughters. Joseph Patrick Kennedy, the patriarch, was a self-made man, the son of a saloon owner and the grandson of Irish immigrants who were among the great wave of young men and women making the harsh ocean voyage across the Atlantic in the 1840s. Ireland was a country wracked by poverty and famine. In some ways the life they faced in America was even harsher than the one they had left behind, for this New World was not filled with milk and honey, but with prejudice, disease, and suspicion. It was a hard life wherever they landed in the United States, and Joe Kennedy's grandparents had settled in Boston, the Puritan city on the banks of the Charles River, a city where "the Lowells spoke only to the Cabots, and the Cabots spoke only to God." In many of the city's famous purple windows (tinted by an imperfection in the sand used in the glassmaking process) were signs and plaques adorned with four dreaded letters, N.I.N.A. The initials stood for "No Irish need apply" and were as hurtful and divisive to the nineteenth-century Irish Americans as the placards segregating "whites" and "coloreds" were to African Americans a hundred years later.

Joe Kennedy fought this prejudice his whole life. He began his successful rise by attending the city's most prestigious schools, Boston Latin High School and Harvard College, and was further elevated by his marriage to Rose Fitzgerald in 1914. Rose Elizabeth Fitzgerald was the prize catch in Irish Catholic society. She was one of the most celebrated young women in the city, thanks in part to her charm, intelligence, and attractiveness, but also because her father was the illustrious mayor, John "Honey Fitz" Fitzgerald. In making Rose his wife, Joe Kennedy was definitely marrying up. He would create a great fortune by shrewdness and conniving, and use that fortune to fuel his aspirations of familial glory.

For twenty-nine years the focus of that glory was his eldest son, Joseph P. Kennedy Jr. He was the star of the family, the one whom the rest of the children looked up to and idolized. He was healthy, athletic, and vibrant, with an abundance of charm and inherent leadership qualities. It was Joe Jr. who was destined for great things and Joe Jr. who was his mother and father's favorite.

What was Jack's role? And what effect did being "second best" in the eyes of both his parents mean for him? A sickly child, confined to beds and hospitals for long stretches of his childhood, he grew up under the shadow of his elder brother's mystique. Rose Kennedy writes of his being frail and thin and missing family outings and holidays because of illness. Rose would have the cook give him an extra portion of food or the last spoonfuls of rich gravies that accompanied the roasts. He would combat his physical fragility with a robust intellectual curiosity and a vivid, original wit that could sting.

April 3, 1923

Jack said, "Gee *you're* a great mother to go away and leave your children all alone."

In her memoir, *Times to Remember,* Rose Kennedy uses this quote to illustrate what she called his "elfin quality," but in fact she goes on to allude to feeling "distressed" and "hard hearted" by her five-year-old son's caustic retort. Rose was about to take a six-week vacation, not with her husband and children, but alone with her sister Agnes, to visit the American West. Driven by her "insatiable curiosity about the world," Rose would leave her five children, ages two to eight, in the care of their nursemaid and the wife of one of Joe's business associates and travel to California. While she was touring Hollywood studios, there was an outbreak of measles in the family, but Joe withheld the information from her so that she wouldn't worry or cut short her vacation.

The trip to California wasn't an anomaly for Rose. Long vacations away from her family were a regular feature of her life. First the trips were throughout the country, and then later there were twice-a-year trips to Europe. As Joe's fortune grew, Rose enjoyed the means with which to escape from home again and again. By the early 1930s, when her family had grown to nine children, she was a devotee of Paris couture and was entirely comfortable leaving her children in the care of her friend Mary Moore, a good doctor, and "good household help" while she stayed in France, arranging fittings and visiting museums. "Every time Mrs. Kennedy had a baby, she hired another nurse and took another trip abroad" was the memory of one of Jack's grade-school teachers.

It was unusual maternal behavior, and though they may have been necessary for Rose's emotional survival, the frequent absences from her children had direct consequences on their sense of security. Jack quickly adapted and learned how to get whatever bits of emotional warmth Rose was able to give him. He confessed to a friend that when his mother would leave on one of her frequent trips, he used to cry all the time until it dawned on him that his outbursts irritated her. "Better to take it in stride," he realized, if he wanted to get any maternal affection at all.

Young Jack retreated into a world of books during his frequent convalescences. He read Robert Louis Stevenson, Rudyard Kipling,

Harriet Beecher Stowe, *Arabian Nights, Pilgrim's Progress,* and *King Arthur and the Round Table.* As he grew older, he read Marlborough, Fox, and Burke. His tastes were far more secular than those of his family. "When we were reading *Lives of the Saints,* he was reading Carlyle," his sister Eunice recalled. Jack used the escape found in sweeping historical epics to combat feelings of loneliness and isolation. And from these long afternoons, curled up alone with a favorite story, came a strong sense of emotional detachment that would, in his adulthood, manifest itself in his inability to fully trust any intimate relationship, a strong aversion to being physically touched, and a keen ability to compartmentalize his life, each disjointed fragment kept apart from the others.

It wasn't until Choate that Jack began to pull away from the orbit of his elder brother. He had followed Joe from one school to the next, from the Dexter School in Brookline, to Noble and Greenough, then off to Choate and Harvard. At Choate he had met his lifelong boon companion, Kirk LeMoyne Billings, known affectionately as Lem. A second son himself, Lem was able to crack through the facade that Jack had built for himself in a way no one else in his life was capable of doing. He could cajole him out of his moods, and make him laugh and relax. Having a friend like Lem—a friend who understood him completely and, more important, accepted him completely—gave Jack the ability to come out from under the shell of being "Joe Kennedy's kid brother."

At Harvard, Jack distanced himself from Joe. Since his father was the ambassador to Great Britain, Jack had unique access to diplomatic sources and material. His senior thesis, an examination of England's lack of preparation for the war against Hitler's Germany, first won honors and was soon after published under the title *Why England Slept.* The book caused a buzz, appearing on both the *New York Times* and *Washington Times-Herald* bestseller lists and giving Jack a leg up in the never-ending fraternal competition.

The advent of World War II and America's entry into the war provided the Kennedy boys with a worldwide stage on which to compete. Both young men enlisted in the navy, with Joe training to be a pilot and Jack a PT boat skipper. Joe was stationed in England and Jack in the South Pacific, where, on August 2, 1943, his PT boat was sliced in half by a Japanese destroyer. Thrown into the ocean with several badly injured shipmates, Kennedy led an impressive and ultimately successful survival campaign, and was awarded the Silver Star.

When Jack was roundly and very publicly cheered as a bona-fide war hero, his elder brother felt a little angst. Jack had bested him, and equaling the score became the compelling goal of the 375 days Joe had left to live. He drove himself harder and harder, and his squadron mates witnessed him kneeling in prayer and driving an angry fist into his bunk again and again. He knew that he had a chance to earn the navy's highest honor, the Navy Cross, if he completed a series of successful bombing raids. By May 1944 he had completed the thirty-five required missions. Then, to the consternation of his parents, he volunteered to stay on, writing to Joe and Rose that "I . . . was due to start back in about two weeks but volunteered to stay another month." On August 12 he volunteered to fly a particularly tricky mission, where he would pilot a plane over the English Channel, set it on an automatic course, and then parachute to safety. But the plane, loaded with almost twelve tons of explosives, never reached its target. It exploded, illuminating the night sky. Joseph P. Kennedy Jr. was dead.

The death of his brother Joe was a pivotal event in Jack Kennedy's life. In the midst of mourning his eldest son, Joe Kennedy transferred his ambitions for Joe onto Jack; within two years, Jack would embark on one of the most successful political careers in U.S. history.

He was elected to Congress in 1946, 1948, and again in 1950. By then the Kennedy political machine was gearing up for national office. After debating a run for governor of Massachusetts, they set their sights on the Senate seat occupied by Henry Cabot Lodge Jr. To unseat Lodge would be a victory on many levels, not the least of which was the triumph of the Irish Catholic over the Boston Brahmin. It became a family cause; Joe financed the campaign (the suitcases filled with cash are a Massachusetts political legend), Rose and her daughters graced the famous "Kennedy teas," and Bobby managed the effort. Kennedy won a solid victory, even more impressive as it bucked the nationwide Republican trend that swept Dwight and Mamie Eisenhower into the White House.

For Kennedy to reach the next level of success in his career, it was imperative that he marry. But he was in no great hurry to do so. He wrote to one friend that his political success had been "based up to now almost completely on the old sex appeal" and that he was too old and set in his ways to be married. But he knew he had to, and set about the task.

Jack Kennedy had a voracious sex drive and had had dozens of girlfriends, starting at Choate. Several of them had been well-born Catholic girls, like Frances Cannon, Charlotte McDonnell, and Olive Cawley. He got along well enough with them, but the first real serious romance of his life was with a woman named Inga Arvad, a Danish journalist he met during the war and with whom he enjoyed a passionate affair. There were two major counts against "Inga Binga," as Jack called her. First, she was married to a Hungarian film director named Paul Fejos and had been divorced before that. Second, as a journalist based in Berlin, Arvad had interviewed many members of the Nazi hierarchy, including Adolf Hitler himself, meeting him during the 1936 Olympic Games in Berlin. A few years later Arvad was in Washington, working at the *Times-Herald* with Jack's sister Kathleen, a lively and vivacious young woman who had been the toast of London during her father's ambassadorship. Arvad's past had aroused the suspicion of the FBI, and with America's entry into World War II in 1941, she had been tagged as a possible spy; she was followed and her home was bugged. She was twenty-eight when she met Jack Kennedy, four years her junior. Her warm and passionate personality appealed to the young man, long starved of maternal warmth. Their relationship was a first for Jack, deeply complex and emotionally intimate. It floundered from the dual pressures of naval and fatherly disapproval. The FBI alerted the navy regarding the identity and background of Jack's paramour. Joe Kennedy knew that a relationship with a divorced blond security risk would do Jack more harm than good, and he insisted they break up.

In the first six years of his public life, Jack dated often, even sharing his bachelor existence with his sister Eunice in a small house on Thirty-first Street in Georgetown. When, at thirty-five, he began to think seriously about getting married, he had his choice of ardent young women, all eager to marry one of the most eligible bachelors in the country. What they didn't know was that he was a playboy very set in his ways, addicted to sexual adventure—the result of a childhood deprived of warmth and understanding. His devil-may-care attitude of ironic detachment was an artfully constructed mask. Underneath it was a little boy lost. Finding the perfect match for him would be no easy task for the most determined cupid.

London, 1948

The birth announcement that hung on the fence outside his grand-parents' home did not announce the birth of a son; instead it announced with great pride the birth of a *prince*. The pride came from the fact that this prince was the first child born in the direct line of ascension to the throne in the twentieth century. Second only to the marriage of the baby's parents a year before, this joyous news lifted the spirits of the country in the stark years after the great victory of World War II.

Charles Philip Arthur George Windsor was born in Buckingham Palace in November 1948. His mother was Princess Elizabeth, heiress presumptive to her father, King George VI. Charles's father was the former Prince Philip of Greece and Denmark. Philip had renounced his foreign title when he became a British citizen and on his wedding day was created His Royal Highness, the Duke of Edinburgh. In one of the very few examples of Elizabeth leading a "normal" life, she took the royal equivalent of a married name and was called Princess Elizabeth, Duchess of Edinburgh, for the first four years and three months of her marriage.

A word about British titles, which can be incomprehensible to the uninitiated. The rules regarding royal and aristocratic titles are, by their very nature, arcane. The rules of royal nomenclature have been reworked twice in the last century. The first came during World War I, when George V changed his family name to Windsor (prompting the German kaiser to mischievously announce that he was looking forward to a production of *The Merry Wives of Saxe-Coburg und Gotha*). George V used the opportunity of anglicizing his family name to winnow out the ranks of princes and princesses, narrowing those able to be called "royal" to those in direct line to inherit the throne, their wives, and children of sons but not daughters. That's why Prince Andrew's daughters are princesses but Princess Anne's two children have no royal title.

Normally the eldest sons of dukes take their father's second title as a courtesy, while younger sons are given the courtesy title Lord and daughters the courtesy title Lady. But the rules of precedence dictated that instead of being called earl of Merioneth, the children of the duke and duchess of Edinburgh would be styled Royal Highness and be called Prince and Princess. So Charles became Prince Charles, and when his sister was born in 1950, she was Princess Anne, not Lady Anne Mountbatten-Windsor. The second change in the rules came in the 1990s, after three of the queen's four children divorced. It limits the use of "HRH" and the titles Prince and Princess. When Prince Edward married Sophie Rhys-Jones, it was the first time in a hundred years that the married son of a sovereign did not become a duke. Edward and Sophie are called the earl and countess of Wessex, with the understanding that he will inherit the Edinburgh dukedom upon the death of his father.

With all the talk about royal titles, it's easy to forget that there was a time when Prince Charles was widely known as "Action Man," a title given him by the popular press in the 1970s when he seemed to be the embodiment of the dashing adventure seeker, a James Bond with larger ears and better pedigree. Far removed from the docile little boy in the pale blue coat and the gawky teenager who was stiff and uncomfortable in public, Charles the Action Man was seen everywhere, doing everything. He would be photographed parachuting and paragliding, he would play polo and ski, he would date aristocratic young women as well as glamorous movie stars.

It was in his Action Man persona that he first came into the romantic consciousness of the teenage Lady Diana Spencer. Throughout the 1970s he was acknowledged as the most eligible bachelor in the world, and Diana was certainly not the only young girl dreaming of a fairy-tale wedding and becoming the Princess of Wales. But the Action Man image was just that, an image. Charles the man was very different from Charles the prince and Charles the image. Of all the characters in this story, he had the most carefully regimented life. He was born with his future mapped out, and on his head lay the hopes for the future of the monarchy. The pressure on him was enormous, and his inability to make even the simplest choices himself (where to live, what to do, when to wake up in the morning) was extraordinarily frustrating. His life was not his own.

Charles was born just as the British empire began its decline. India, the "jewel in the crown," had recently been granted independence. His maternal grandparents lost their titles of emperor and empress of India. Britain had won World War II, having led the way during the darkest hours of the battle, in the early days before the United States had entered the fight. But with the victory came little glory. Harsh restrictions on food and fuel continued even after the war, and a sense of social unrest was heavy in the air. Winston Churchill's Conservative Party was voted out of power and the post-war Labour government fought through legislation to continue to deconstruct the inequities of the class system.

For the aristocratic and upper classes, the postwar era was a time of great change, and that change, coupled with Britain's slow but steady decline as a world power, gave them very little to celebrate. The marriage, in 1947, between Elizabeth, the lovely young princess whom the populace had watched grow up before their eyes, and Philip, the "Viking from across the sea," was the first major royal event since the end of the war. In their union were generations of tradition, a celebration of a glorious past, and dreams of an illustrious future.

Elizabeth had been born third in line to inherit the throne, after her uncle David, then Prince of Wales and later King Edward VIII and duke of Windsor, and her father, then duke of York. At the time of her birth there was no reason to think that she would ever be queen. The Prince of Wales was expected to marry and have children. Even if he didn't, there was every chance that her own parents would have another baby, a boy, who would supersede her in the order of succession. It wasn't until "Lilibet," as she was called, turned ten and her uncle David abdicated in favor of his younger brother that she became the heiress presumptive.

Who Elizabeth would marry was a question discreetly asked from the time she became heir to her father's throne. The range of royal choices had been limited by the two World Wars, and there were simply not that many princes of appropriate birth, nationality, and religion who qualified. Though the royal family had relaxed its rules about marrying into the aristocratic classes, the heiress to the throne must marry a royal prince.

Luck and the determination of Lord Louis Mountbatten came into play. Mountbatten, a prince who lost his royal status in the aftermath of World War I (his German surname, Battenberg, was literally anglicized to Mountbatten), was a maternal uncle of the young Prince Philip. He had engineered a meeting between the two young people in the summer of 1938, during a royal visit to the naval college at Dartmouth. Elizabeth was immediately smitten with the handsome blond youth. It was a true love match for Elizabeth. If it seemed like an arranged match, it was an example of how well arranged matches could work out, for Philip brought to his job an understanding of the role he'd be required to play, an admirable discretion that proved quite useful over time, and a grudging respect for the rules of the game.

The primary rule of the game, of course, was to continue the line, and so children were necessary. Charles and his sister, Anne, were born in the early years of the Edinburghs' marriage. Their lives, and those of their parents, were to go through a cataclysmic change in 1952 when George VI died an early and unexpected death. Elizabeth became queen a full decade or two before she had expected to. This not only put a temporary stop to enlarging their family (there is a ten-year gap between Anne and Andrew, born in 1960, with Edward to follow in 1964) but also put unforeseen burdens on the young couple.

Elizabeth had been raised in a manner typical of aristocratic households, whereby the prevailing wisdom was that children were meant to be seen but not heard. She had been brought up in a loving household, certainly in more relaxed circumstances than the rigid formality of her father's childhood. Nevertheless, the day-to-day duties of raising Lilibet and her younger sister, Margaret, were left to nursery maids and governesses. Children were bathed and dressed and sent in to visit their parents at teatime for an hour or so. It was the way she had been raised, and the way her children would be raised.

But she was queen and the inherent obligations created a deeper divide between mother and son than mere social circumstances would have dictated. All through his childhood, Charles and his mother were separated for months on end. When the Edinburghs were first married, Philip retained his commission in the Royal Navy and was stationed in Malta. Elizabeth would join him there, leaving Charles in London in the care of his nanny and his grandparents and his paternal great-grandmother, Queen Mary, widow of George V. Royal tours would follow, meaning weeks and months of separation. There is one famous incident in which the queen, returning home from a trip to Australia, was greeted by her five-year-old son with an officious handshake, as if he had little clear memory of who she was and even less of an emotional connection to her as his mother.

Charles grew up a timid and sensitive boy. He rarely saw his mother and, he told his official biographer, felt as if he continually failed to meet his father's high expectations. The more tender side of Charles's nature, his sensitivity and soul-searching spirituality, were an abomination to Philip. A blustery man, Philip bridled within the confines of the royal establishment and tried to bully his son as a means of toughening him up for the rigors that life had in store for him.

Part of the toughening-up process came in the choices of schools to which Charles was sent. There was Gordonstoun in Scotland, where boys took ice-cold showers every morning and slept through the winter nights with the windows open three inches from the top. Charles was miserable there, often tearfully complaining to his grandmother, with whom he made a strong emotional bond. Trinity

College in Cambridge followed Gordonstoun, with a semester spent in Australia, where Charles was able to meet people from very different backgrounds.

He followed his education with a long stint in the navy. About the time he entered the navy, he met a woman with whom he would form his strongest emotional relationship, Camilla Shand. At the time they were both single, and Charles fell in love for the first time in his life. But duty intervened, and he went off on an eight-month tour in the Caribbean. While there, he learned that Camilla had accepted a proposal of marriage from Andrew Parker Bowles, who had been her on-again, off-again boyfriend for six years. Charles, left with a "feeling of emptiness," forged on and quickly became a royal playboy, seriously dating more than a dozen women, all of whom provided fodder for an ever eager press. He dated many girls from aristocratic circles, including Lady Jane Wellesley, daughter of the duke of Wellington; Lady Sarah Spencer, Diana's eldest sister; Amanda Knatchbull, the granddaughter of Lord Mountbatten; Davina Sheffield; and Anna Wallace, nicknamed "Whiplash Wallace" for her ferocious temper. Charles and Anna had been dating in 1980; when they broke up, he was both despondent and eager to pick up the pieces of his love life.

"It's awfully difficult, because you've got to remember that when you marry, in my position, you are going to marry someone who perhaps is one day going to become Queen. You've got to choose someone really carefully. . . . People expect quite a lot from somebody like that . . . and it has got to be somebody pretty special."

That was Charles's sentiment at the age of twenty. Twelve years later, at thirty-two, and fresh from his breakup with Anna Wallace, he was ready to fall in love again.

Chapter Seven

Courtship and Engagement

He'd found the virgin, the sacrificial lamb,
and in a way he was obsessed with me.

—Diana, in 1991, describing her then-fiancé

They'll kill me before I ever get to marry him. I swear they will.

—Jackie, in 1953, describing her sisters-in-law-to-be

Both Diana's and Jackie's courtships by their husbands lacked conventional romance. Granted, the Prince of Wales and the dashing young congressman with a multimillionaire father were considered prime catches in the marital sweepstakes. With women making themselves available to them at every turn, neither Charles Windsor nor Jack Kennedy had any need to pursue a woman with the traditional box of candy and handful of flowers. But the detachment with which they went about finding a wife, their life partner, was out of sync with both the postwar 1950s and the romantic revival years of the early 1980s. While it would be inaccurate to say that either relationship was devoid of true affection, both women were clearly shortchanged in the romance department.

Jackie brought to her courtship a healthy skepticism; she was, after all, the daughter of a first-class rake. He had taught her what was attractive to a man, and she was an apt pupil. Acquiring a ready-made elder brother as a teenager introduced her to a world of prep-school boys and Yalies. A year in Paris had exposed her to the most romantic of men in the most romantic of cities. She knew men and knew what to expect from them. Not long after her return to Washington, she became engaged.

Diana knew men, too. But the men she knew were the fictional heroes in her stepgrandmother Barbara Cartland's romance novels. Diana's dating experience was limited, and once she set her sights on Prince Charles, she understood the need to keep herself chaste. Charles had to marry a virgin. Even in the 1980s it was unacceptable for any woman to come to the throne with a sullied past or a history of former lovers. Diana was an innocent. She thought she knew what she wanted but was unaware of the forces around her who had a hand in shaping her destiny. She was pleased with the results of her courtship with Charles, but the process left her unsatisfied—as in the old Peggy Lee song, she asked herself, "Is that all there is?"

Both women were essentially cast in the role of fiancée, Jackie by her future father-in-law, Joe Kennedy, and Diana by a consortium that included her grandmother, the Queen Mother, and two of Charles's lovers. That is not to say that there was no love involved; of course there was, by all four partners. But the love there came in many varieties. For each aspect of genuine love, there was love tempered by past experience, love masquerading as storybook romance, love turned cynical by hurt and disappointment.

And in the midst of all this came the glare of publicity. Jackie was so enthralled—at least at first—by the idea of her being newsworthy that she created a scrapbook, carefully pasting the engagement notices and photographs that appeared in newspapers across the country. She annotated each entry in her spidery handwriting, from the *New York Times* to the *St. Louis Post-Dispatch*. As reporters would call her at Hammersmith Farm, she would answer their questions and apologize charmingly for not being well versed in the skill of being interviewed. She had been on the asking end until recently, leaving her job at the *Times-Herald* shortly before her engagement was announced. The newspaper stories could have come from Hollywood screenwriters, for they all followed the script laid out by the Kennedys. The society girl from an old family, well bred and well educated, marrying the most eligible bachelor in the country. The tone of the reportage was respectful and in line with the wholesome and upwardly mobile optimism of the times.

For Diana the press attention fell on her like a ton of bricks. From the moment she was identified as Charles's new love interest in the fall of 1980, and for the rest of her life, Diana was, as her brother would say so memorably at her funeral, "the most hunted person in the modern age." At first the press was charmed by her, and she by them. She formed easygoing, flirtatious relationships with reporter James Whitaker and photographer Ken Lennox, among others. They would find ways to protect her, at least in the early days, when Whitaker would warn her that there were some things she just should never divulge to him. She played the press game perfectly, perhaps taking Jackie's advice to offer "minimum information with maximum politeness." She appeared to be perfect, and the press played up that aspect. Perhaps the only flaw they saw in her was that she might be too tall for Charles.

Both Diana and Jackie endured unsettling revelations during their engagement, and Diana was humiliated enough to entertain serious doubts about going forward with her wedding. Neither one of their fiancés consulted Emily Post to guide his behavior during his engagement. Some of the indignities were minor; neither couple shared in the excitement or romance of choosing an engagement ring. Joe Kennedy picked out Jackie's, and Queen Elizabeth had an array of sapphires delivered to Buckingham Palace. ("Her eyes popped out when I chose the largest one," Diana confided to a servant.) Both husbands-to-be showed a lack of consideration: both Charles and Jack took off on extended trips during their engagements, Charles for duty and Jack for pleasure. But some of the indignities were staggering; both men continued to sleep with other women almost literally up till their wedding day.

Why did Jackie, and later Diana, put up with this behavior? Were they so close to grasping their brass rings that a little tarnish didn't matter? Were they intrigued by the challenge of taming two such robust bachelors? Or were their hearts filled with hope, what Emily Dickinson called "the thing with feathers—that perches in the soul— and sings the tune without the words—and never stops—at all"?

London, 1981

She didn't know it, but her name was on a list: a list of young women of the appropriate age, social background, and of sterling character. The list contained only a dozen or so names, and Diana's was at the top. Like scouts for a sports team, or Hollywood talent agents, the men who ran the monarchy had a vested interest in its future, and the need to recruit new blood into the family became a priority as Charles entered his thirties. The habit of the British royal family marrying other royals had largely ended; Prince Philip and Princess Marina, who married the duke of Kent in 1934, were the last two. So while the press speculated about Princess Caroline of Monaco or Princess Marie-Astrid of Luxembourg, the establishment was looking at English girls, daughters of the nobility or landed gentry. As one of the queen's friends would later say of Diana, "On paper, it seemed like the ideal match."

Looking at the externals, Diana did appear to be perfect. The Spencers were as grand a family as the Windsors and were even related to them, descended, through an adulterous liaison, from Charles II. If her father had dynastic ambitions for his daughter, his service as courtier had taught him how to get the job done without seeming to push. Diana was beautiful, appearing modest and shy. She was young, but her youth was an asset in terms of her lack of experience with men. Most important, she seemed to possess a docile personality, one that could be molded and shaped to fit the Windsors' needs.

Diana's first invitation after making the list came in November 1978, when she was asked to Prince Charles's thirtieth-birthday party. It was odd not only in that she was just seventeen but also that he was still seeing her sister Sarah. Sarah was more than a little put out, griping, "Why is Diana coming as well?" But both Spencer girls ended up going to the dance. Diana thoroughly enjoyed herself, despite being one of the youngest people there. She found Buckingham Palace "amazing" and later bragged that she wasn't at all intimidated by her surroundings.

Diana apparently made a good impression, for at Christmastime she received a second royal invitation, to attend a weekend shooting party at Sandringham, where the royals took a ten-week winter break. Her sister Jane's marriage to the queen's assistant private secretary gave her access to the royal orbit, but it wasn't until a year later that Charles took significant notice of her.

It was during a weekend in the country in the summer of 1980 that the relationship reached a new level. Diana joined the party at the invitation of Philip de Pass, whose parents were hosting the Prince of Wales for a polo match. "Would you like to come and stay for a couple of nights?" she remembered being asked. "You're a young blood, you might amuse him." But it wasn't Diana's bonhomie that attracted Charles as they sat on a bale of hay eating barbecue. With one perceptive comment, she tapped into a deep-rooted emotional longing, and he began to see her in a different light.

Being royal means you are continually surrounded by people who make a great effort to please you. In that world of aristocrats and courtiers, flattery and obsequiousness have been raised to an art form. If people aren't actively trying to curry favor, they make a concerted effort to stay away from controversy, especially regarding any emotional issues.

"You looked so sad when you walked up the aisle at Lord Mountbatten's funeral," Diana told him, bringing up the most emotionally devastating moment of Charles's life. "It was the most tragic thing I've ever seen. My heart bled for you when I watched it. I thought, It's wrong, you're lonely, you should be with someone to look after you." Those words cut through the complex emotions that Charles wrapped around himself like a protective shield, and grabbed hold of his heart.

It was a bold stroke, simultaneously compassionate and canny. No one spoke to Charles that way, certainly not those closest to him. His parents compartmentalized their emotions, becoming adept at suppressing them as an unproductive use of energy. At the time of Mountbatten's funeral, Prince Philip nagged and picked on Charles until the younger man was driven into a fury. Philip's intention was to keep Charles from crying during the service: shedding tears over the violent death of a much-loved uncle was foreign to Philip's code of behavior.

Charles was more sensitive than his father was, and Diana, in speaking to him with such honesty and insight, made a profound impression on him. Here was someone who understood him and sympathized with his position. In an interesting parallel, the conversation recalled one between the last Prince of Wales, Charles's great-uncle David, and Wallis Simpson. When they met in the early 1930s, also on a weekend in the country, Wallis found herself seated next to the prince at dinner. Making small talk, the prince asked her if, as an American living in Britain, she missed central heating. Wallis's response—"Sir, you disappoint me. Every American woman is asked that in Britain. I had expected more from the Prince of Wales"— captivated David as much as Diana had captivated Charles. People didn't speak to royalty in that manner. In his memoirs, the duke of Windsor remembered that conversation as the first time any woman had shown a real interest in him. The relationship that began at that dinner brought the monarchy its gravest constitutional crisis in modern times.

The runner-up in the constitutional-crisis derby started at a dinner as well. Diana, like Wallis before her, was not having a conversation with a *prince,* she was talking to a man. Charles, being addressed as a man, was both moved and aroused. Diana recalled, "The next minute he practically leapt on me, and I thought this was very strange." Charles asked her to leave the party the next day and return with him to Buckingham Palace. She refused, feeling that it would be awkward for her hosts. Charles, unused to any woman refusing him, was intrigued and added Diana to the guest list for the traditional sailing event at Cowles, where she would spend a week on the royal yacht *Britannia.*

The week at Cowles was Diana's first exposure to Charles's friends en masse. They were an older crowd, and their curiosity about Diana made her feel that "they were all over me like a bad rash." Another invitation soon followed, to attend a concert at the Royal Albert Hall, with a late supper afterward at Buckingham Palace. Diana's grandmother Lady Fermoy was invited as well, and it was as her grand-daughter that Diana's presence was explained. Charles intensified his interest and asked Diana to go up to Balmoral for the annual Brae-mar Games in the early part of September. By then he had started telling his close friends that he had found the girl he wanted to marry.

The press discovered Diana as well. The hunt was on, and Diana displayed remarkable poise for a young woman from a privileged background. The attention was round-the-clock and tested her in-genuity. She would load her car with suitcases filled with sheets, leave it running and dash back into her apartment, then sneak out a back window to make an effective getaway. She was never rude to any of the reporters, answering their questions while walking down the street with her head lowered and eyes firmly planted on the ground. She was called "Shy Di," and the adept way with which she handled the pressure impressed the establishment.

The press and, through them, the public fell in love with Diana and decided that she was the one for "the job." Charles's parents were also impressed, and as the Christmas season and New Year approached, pressure grew on Charles to make up his mind and propose. There was intense pressure on the whole royal family, ul-timately forcing a rare emotional outburst from the queen. "I wish you would all go away!" she shouted at a pack of reporters and photographers who had assembled at Sandringham, anticipating an engagement announcement timed with the New Year's celebration.

It did not come, and the pressure increased throughout January. Prince Philip, typically, could not bring himself to speak with Charles about it. He wrote to his son, advising him that if he did not propose to Diana, he was duty-bound to break off with her as quickly as possible; otherwise, her honor would be tarnished. The Queen Mother weighed in, telling her favorite grandchild, "Diana Spencer, that's the girl you should marry. . . . If you do [love her], grab her because if you don't, there are plenty of others who will." Elizabeth did not approach her son directly but told a friend that she and Philip were concerned about Charles's indecisiveness and worried about the negative repercussions that might fall on Diana.

Charles was in a self-confessed "confused and anxious state of mind." He told a friend that he wanted to do the right thing for his country and his family but was, in his words, "terrified of . . . making a promise and then . . . living to regret it." Seeking some relief, he left Sandringham early and went on a skiing holiday to Switzerland with close friends who were supporters of Diana. Not all his friends supported her, but because of his position, few offered him frank advice. The protocol was always to follow his lead, so Charles, faced with the most important decision of his life, was left largely to his own counsel. He decided to propose. Just before his return to England, he called Diana and said, "I've got something to ask you." He then invited her to meet him at Windsor Castle the next afternoon, and on February 6 he asked her to be his wife.

"He was deadly serious," Diana remembered. "He said, 'You do realize that one day you will be Queen.' Yes, I said, I love you so much, I love you so much, and he said, 'Whatever love means.' And then he ran upstairs and rang his mother."

It would be three weeks before the announcement was made public; plans were made for Diana to take an extended vacation at her stepfather's sheep ranch in Australia. Ostensibly, this was to give her time to think over the enormous step she was about to take, but her answer had been a swift yes, so she and her mother started making lists of things they had to do. She was hurt and disappointed that Charles did not call her once during the three weeks she was away.

When she returned, the engagement was announced and they posed for photographs (with Charles standing on a step above Diana to appear taller) and sat for an interview with the BBC. On that day her life changed completely. She acquired a protection officer and, for security reasons, moved out of her apartment. After she spent a few days at Clarence House as a guest of the Queen Mother, a suite of rooms at Buckingham Palace became her base of operations.

Unfortunately, there was little for her to do. The Lord Chamberlain's office handled almost all of the planning for the wedding, from setting the date to choosing the menu for the wedding breakfast. After carefully checking the various diaries of the senior members of the family, July 29 was selected as the most convenient date.

Charles insisted on St. Paul's Cathedral over the more traditional Westminster Abbey so more people could be invited. Diana was allotted one hundred of the 2,600 invitations. One of the queen's ladies-in-waiting, Susan Hussey, would talk with Diana about royal protocol, but by and large her days were free. She felt isolated and lonely in the drafty hallways and oversize rooms of Buckingham Palace. She practiced tap dancing in the elegant Music Room and wandered into the kitchens to talk with the servants (until she was told to stop, as future princesses did not befriend the help). Charles went off on a long-planned trip to Australia and New Zealand, leaving Diana alone and increasingly uneasy.

The major source of her unease was the growing realization of the importance of Camilla Parker Bowles in Charles's life. Diana knew that Camilla and her husband, Andrew, were part of the Prince of Wales's circle; she had stayed at their country home before her engagement. She knew that Charles and Camilla had dated ten years earlier. Camilla, now married and a mother of two, didn't seem to be a rival for Charles's affections, but there was something about the relationship that Diana found unsettling. When Diana came to Clarence House on the day the engagement was announced, she found a letter from Camilla propped on her bed, suggesting they have lunch. They met while Charles was in Australia, and the older woman set about establishing her turf.

"You're not going to hunt when you go and live at Highgrove, are you?" she questioned. Diana answered no, that after a bad fall and a broken arm, she had given up horses. Camilla relaxed, having carved out a place for herself, and the lunch continued along chatty lines. Diana later came to realize that she had been too immature to understand the real agenda behind the seemingly innocent questions.

Still, Diana's suspicions grew. The previous November there had been a small scandal when the newspapers reported that a blond woman, presumed to be Lady Diana, had slipped onto the royal train to spend the night with Prince Charles. Buckingham Palace issued a flat-out denial, as did Diana. She knew she hadn't been on the train, but she had a pretty good idea who was. She began to pay more attention to Mrs. Parker Bowles, and was disturbed with what she learned. Camilla knew the details of Charles's private diary and what the couple's plans were. She kept whispering instructions to the young woman: "Don't push him into doing this" and "Don't do that." Charles, who deplored confrontation, would evade Diana's questions about the woman he identified as his "very good friend."

Diana had other things to worry about as well. Now that she was hidden behind the gates of Buckingham Palace, the press turned to her family for news. Her mother kept a discreet silence, but her father and stepmother posed for pictures outside of the palace and gave many interviews. Barbara Cartland talked to so many reporters, touting Diana's qualities, that Diana struck her name off the guest list. Even closer to home, Diana's uncle Lord Fermoy announced to the press that his niece was indeed a virgin.

To the observing public, oddball relatives aside, everything seemed perfect. Diana was a bright spot in a spring and summer racked by economic turmoil and deadly riots throughout Britain. Every public appearance found Diana relaxing into the role she would soon occupy. She might not have been born royal, but she approached the job with poise and grace. The eyes of the world would be focused on London the last week in July, and the prestige of Great Britain rested on her shoulders. All the American television channels were planning to broadcast their morning news shows from the lawns across from Buckingham Palace. The wedding would bring an economic boom, with hundreds of thousands of tourists expected. Souvenirs of all sorts were being readied, and there was an interest and enthusiasm in the monarchy that hadn't been seen in years.

Diana's enthusiasm was wavering. Her means of dealing with a life that was slipping from her control was to take complete control of the one aspect of her life that was still hers to command—her body. Her anxiety manifested itself in bulimia. She internalized her rage at the situation and began to throw up her meals on a regular basis. She lost enough weight during her five-month engagement that her waist shrank from twenty-nine inches to twenty-three. Charles had been the trigger for the self-destructive behavior; during their engagement photo session he put his arm around her waist and said, "Oh, a bit chubby here, aren't we?" It was an incident that she remembered vividly, and it drove her to take action. At first she was secretly thrilled with her ability to disgorge her food. She thought it was an effective means of relieving tension.

The tension reached a climax a few days before the wedding, when Diana discovered that Charles was giving Camilla a heavy gold-link bracelet that he had had custom-made for her. It had a blue enameled disk engraved with the intertwined initials *F* and *G*, for Fred and Gladys, Charles's pet names for himself and Camilla. Diana learned of this through a member of Charles's staff; when she confronted him, she exploded in a rage. He cut her off and took the bracelet with him to an intimate farewell rendezvous with Camilla just two days before his wedding.

Diana was devastated. This was not the way she had imagined things would turn out. She went up to her suite in Buckingham Palace and sat with her two sisters. She confessed her fears to them, adding, "I can't marry him. I can't do this; this is absolutely unbelievable." Her sisters tried to cajole her, but their response pointed out just how little control she had over her life.

"Bad luck, Duch, your face is on the tea towels, so you're too late to chicken out."

Washington, Hyannis, and Newport, 1952–53

The language of their romance has become so well known that it almost seems like movie dialogue: "He leaned across the asparagus and asked me for a date"; "He'd call me from some oyster bar on the Cape with a great clinking of coins, to ask me out to the movies the following Wednesday." In a way it was scripted dialogue, for they were carefully crafted answers to reporters' questions. Jacqueline Kennedy, as she was by then, knew the story she wanted to tell, and the intimacies she was willing to share with the public. There is an exotic quality in the way she presented their courtship, down to the vegetables—asparagus was far removed from the lives of meat-and-potatoes Democrats in the 1950s.

The dinner with the asparagus was at the home of Charles and

Martha Bartlett, who Jackie would later say had been shameless matchmakers the night they invited Jack Kennedy and Jacqueline Bouvier to their small house on Q Street in Georgetown. Bartlett was a journalist, covering Washington for the *Chattanooga Times*, and was independently a friend of both of them. He had dated Jackie during her Vassar years, admiring her "marvelous sense of humor" and finding her totally unaffected despite her high-society background. He and Jack had been friends since the end of the war, when Jack had briefly flirted with a career in journalism. Bartlett had an instinct that Jackie's blend of gamine and sophisticate would appeal to Jack Kennedy. "I thought she was a girl with extraordinary promise," he recalled, "and it seemed to me she would be a marvelous wife" for his friend, who needed, he felt, to settle down. Jack was intrigued enough to ask Jackie out for an after-dinner drink. As they approached her car, Jackie was bemused to find a sometime boyfriend sitting in the red leather seats of her black Mercury convertible. The car, which had been a present from Black Jack on her seventeenth birthday, was parked with the top down, and the man, recognizing it, just hopped in to wait for her. Jack, slightly embarrassed, mumbled something about taking a rain check and slinked off into the night.

That night may not have been the first time they met. Dinah Bridge, an English friend of the Kennedys', was staying with Bobby and Ethel just after the birth of their daughter Kathleen, in 1951. She remembers sitting at the breakfast table one morning with the new parents, Jack, and his sister Jean. "Around the corner of the front door came this beautiful girl in riding clothes to pick up Jean to go riding. And I believe I am right that that was the first time he'd ever really taken note of her."

But even that might not have been their first meeting. In 1948, during her sophomore year at Vassar, Jackie wrote to a friend that she had met on the train between Washington and New York "a young red haired Congressman whose father had been an ambassador." They had flirted for most of the four-hour trip, and when the train arrived in New York she had to dash across town to Grand Central to make a connection to Poughkeepsie. In the letter she enigmatically declined to name the man, but there's no doubt as to his identity.

It was four years later, in the spring of 1952, that they started what Jackie would later describe as a "spasmodic courtship." Thanks to his Senate race, Jack was spending most of his time in Massachusetts. Hence, the long-distance phone calls and the "great clinking of coins." They would date sporadically over the summer as the Kennedy political machine went into overdrive. Somewhere in the smoke-filled back rooms of Massachusetts politics, the machine was making noise about the thirty-five-year-old candidate's marital status. Coupling a war hero's record with the glamorous image of a dashing bachelor was a means of winning an election. Once the election was over, though, bachelorhood became a liability. If Kennedy entertained any notion of creating a national image or harbored a desire for higher office, he would have to be married and have a family.

Jackie had marriage on her mind as well in the spring of 1952. She was engaged in January and planned on being a June bride. Her intended, John Husted, was a Wall Street broker whom she had met the previous winter. After a monthlong courtship, he proposed in the Polo Bar at the Westbury Hotel, Black Jack's old stomping ground. Jack Bouvier liked Husted—they had Yale and Wall Street in common—and was thrilled at the idea of Jackie's living in New York, far from the clutches of the Auchinclosses. Janet Auchincloss was not thrilled at all. She was as close to apoplectic as her disciplined gentility would allow. Husted was *not* what she had in mind for Jackie; Janet anticipated marriage to a Rockefeller, a Mellon, or a Vanderbilt. She did not keep her lack of enthusiasm from Jackie; just the opposite. While going through the mechanics of social custom—a formal announcement in the *Times-Herald* (which failed to mention Jack Bouvier's name), an engagement party at Merrywood (remembered as "a chilly affair" by one of the guests)—she nagged Jackie day and night to break off the engagement. Janet's harping didn't work, but the reappearance of Jack Kennedy in her life did. In the second week of March, Jackie returned Husted's sapphire engagement ring. Janet, triumphant, sent a retraction to the newspaper.

In May, a few weeks after the breakup, the Bartletts had another dinner party: Martha suggested to Jackie that she bring Jack Kennedy as her date. Dinner at the Bartletts' mixed good food with lively conversation and often ended with a spirited round of word games. "Lots of games were played," one guest recalled, "and [Jackie] was sort of put through her paces. . . . She stood up extremely well."

Jackie recognized the evening as the turning point, the moment when their feelings toward each other rose to a higher level. She knew instinctively, she told a biographer in 1960, that "he would have a profound, perhaps a disturbing influence on her life." An inner voice told her that this was a man who did not want to marry, that he would bring her heartbreak, but she "swiftly determined that the heartbreak would be worth the pain."

It would be a year from that night before Jack proposed; in the interim, two of the people closest to Jackie and Jack nudged them closer toward the altar by taking the marital plunge themselves. In April 1953 Lee Bouvier married Michael Canfield, a publishing heir who was rumored to be the illegitimate son of the duke of Kent, the uncle of Elizabeth II. That Jackie had been bested in the wedding sweepstakes by her younger sister was underscored when Lee deliberately tossed her bouquet to Jackie during the reception at Merrywood.

Jack Kennedy was closer to his sister Eunice than he was to any of his other siblings. "They were so alike that they were almost one human being," Dinah Brand remembered. "Eunie's" wedding to Sargent Shriver, in May 1953, came after a seven-year courtship. It was designed as an extravaganza to showcase the family's wealth and position: St. Patrick's Cathedral with Cardinal Spellman officiating, a bridal gown designed by Christian Dior, and a wedding reception at the Waldorf-Astoria Hotel.

Jackie was not among the seventeen hundred guests sipping pink champagne and dancing to "April in Portugal" at the Waldorf. She had been invited but, after a year during which Jack still refused to commit, remembered her father's long-ago advice. She made herself scarce, traveling to London to report on Queen Elizabeth's coronation for the *Times-Herald*. Janet, who knew something about capturing the heart of a wealthy man herself, encouraged her to go: "I should think he would be much more likely to find out how he felt about you if you were seeing exciting people and doing exciting things instead of sitting here waiting for the telephone to ring."

Janet and Hughdie financed the trip, and Jackie sailed on the *Queen Mary* with her friend Aileen Bowdoin. The trip brought Jackie to the periphery of the royal circle. The duke and duchess of Windsor were on the same crossing. They were returning to Paris, as they had not been invited to watch his niece crowned queen. In London Jackie and Aileen stayed in an apartment that belonged to Lady May Abel-Smith, one of the queen's ladies-in-waiting, whose duties required her to move into Buckingham Palace during Coronation Week. Jackie's sketches of everything from the Windsors' dogs to Lauren Bacall dancing a fox-trot with Prince Philip's cousin at Perle Mesta's ball, together with her colorful stories, appeared on the front page of the newspaper several times during the week. Jack Kennedy took notice of them. Apparently absence *did* make the heart grow fonder, and Jackie returned to her borrowed flat one evening to find a telegraphed proposal of marriage.

Janet suspected that something was in the air when Jack called her from Cape Cod, asking for Jackie's return travel plans. "I know that plane," he told Janet. "That plane stops in Boston, and I'm going to meet her there." Jackie had flown with over a hundred dollars' worth of excess-luggage charges, a heavy suitcase filled with books on history for her fiancé. Wanting to look her best after the long transatlantic voyage, Jackie was annoyed that the plane's bathroom had been coopted by the actress Zsa Zsa Gabor, who spent the last hour of the flight primping and fixing her hair and makeup. Jackie had peppered the glamorous actress with questions about her beauty secrets. Zsa Zsa, rather bitchily, remembered a young woman with bad skin and kinky hair who shyly said that she hoped her beau would be at the plane to meet her in Boston.

As they disembarked, Gabor recognized the lean and handsome Jack Kennedy and raced to his open arms. "Jack, Jack, my darling Jack," she cooed as he gave her a warm embrace. He then turned to

Jackie and said to the actress, "Have you met Miss Bouvier?" Zsa Zsa looked at the woman who had pestered her for hours on the plane, turned back to Jack, and purred, "Don't you dare corrupt her, Jack."

"Oh," Jackie purred right back, linking her arm through Jack's, "but he already has."

Jack neglected to introduce Jackie as his fiancée to the glamorous actress, yet another example that their romance was different from most. He also made her postpone the announcement of their engagement until after the *Saturday Evening Post* had run its cover story on him. "Jack Kennedy, the Senate's Gay Young Bachelor"—Jack disliked the title of the article, fearing it made him appear lightweight (this was before the word *gay* took on its current meaning)—was set to appear in mid-June. A cover story in one of the country's most popular magazines was a publicity coup for the brand-new senator, and it would be unwise to let anything interfere with the magazine's plans.

The engagement was finally announced on June 24, and Jackie spent the following weekend in Hyannis Port, where the Kennedys had a party to celebrate the happy news. Jackie wrote to Rose Kennedy upon her return to Newport, thanking her for the weekend but adding, "I never realized how wonderful it is to love your husband's family. I thought if you liked your in-laws—that was fine—and if you didn't it didn't matter, because your life was with your husband." As Jackie would soon learn, marriage to Jack Kennedy was marriage to the Kennedy clan. She met the whole family that weekend and "liked them all so much."

That feeling was not, at first, universally mutual. Rose Kennedy, in her memoirs, writes: "There may have been doubts about her among one or another of Jack's brothers or sisters or cousins at first." It's an extraordinary admission, given that the book is rife with half-truths and evasions. Rose attributes the doubts to the fact that Jackie was soft-spoken and shy—"at least in comparison with most of our brood"—but the truth seems to lie a little deeper.

Jackie had understood the dynamics at play as she walked into the big house on Scudder Avenue and prepared to meet the clan en masse: "Obviously, if you really liked the elder brother and you were rather shy you might have been a little nervous." Any woman entering that scene would have had to run the gauntlet. Jackie, with her interests in art and literature, her love of solitary sporting activities like horseback riding and swimming, was in for an especially hard time. The Kennedy girls were reluctant to include her in their sisterly embrace. Jack's three sisters and Bobby's wife, Ethel, treated Jackie's Hyannis Port weekend as a rough-and-tumble sorority hazing. They nicknamed her "the Deb" and mocked her "babykins" voice. When she told Ethel that she had once dreamed of being a ballet dancer, Ethel looked down at Jackie's size-ten feet and said, "With those clodhoppers? You'd be better off playing soccer, kid." Jackie, in turn, called them the "rah-rah girls" and told her sister, Lee, that they ran all over one another like a pack of gorillas.

Reporters and photographers were called in that weekend to record the engagement, but one important element was missing: there was no engagement ring. "I haven't one yet," Jackie told the reporters. "Jack and I have looked at dozens of them. Some I didn't like and others weren't the right type." Ultimately, it was Joe Kennedy who supplied the engagement ring. He turned to his friend Louis Arpels, owner of the fashionable jewelry store that bore his name, and together the two men chose an elegant design that matched a 2.84-carat square-cut emerald with a 2.88-carat square-cut diamond, joined together on a platinum band set with small diamonds.

That it hadn't actually come from Jack perhaps made it easier for Jackie to redesign the ring during her second year in the White House. She had Van Cleef & Arpels remake the ring, adding twenty round and marquise-shaped diamonds, hiding the original shape of the ring completely. The jewelers were slightly perturbed by her wishes, for the additional diamonds took what was once an elegant ring, its simplicity set off by the handsome pairing of emerald and diamond, and turned it into what was essentially a cocktail ring, lovely, yes, but hardly special. When Jackie asked for her secretary's opinion of the redesign, she did not like what she heard. "I told her, 'To me it looks much too bulky and takes away from the whole beauty of the ring.' 'Oh,' Jackie fumed, 'you're just like Jack.' "

Jackie had hoped for a quiet wedding, telling a reporter for the *Boston Traveler*, "It will have to be small. If it were large, it would have to be very large. And we wouldn't want it that way." As she would soon find out, she would be denied not only the size of wedding she wanted but also even her choice of guests and the dress she would wear. Joe Kennedy knew what this wedding represented; he was introducing to the country a future President and his bride. With his Hollywood experience, he knew how to make the wedding a spectacular event. Janet Auchincloss, with her acquired social graces and mores, was no match for him. A big wedding was what Joe Kennedy wanted, and a big wedding was what Joe Kennedy got.

The last straw in Jackie's unconventional courtship came when Jack set off for a three-week vacation in the South of France the month before his wedding. "She said Jack was going to [Hôtel du Cap] Eden Roc in Cap d'Antibes for his vacation, and he wasn't taking her," said Betty Beale, a society columnist. Given his history of extramarital affairs, the trip could hardly be classified as "one last bachelor fling." Going on the trip demonstrated a certain level of selfishness on Jack's part and was a clear indication of his ambivalent attitude toward marriage.

He was even more ambivalent in a letter he sent that summer to his navy friend Paul "Red" Fay. "Dear Old Pal, After a breakup with the bad and the beautiful Aline Olmstead—one fine girl. I gave everything a good deal of thought—and am getting married this fall . . . I am both too young and too old for all of this [and I] will need several long talks on how to conduct yourself during the 1st 6 months." He never even mentions Jackie by name but goes on to say that "the bride's mother . . . had a tendency when excited to think I am not good enough for her daughter and to talk just a bit too much."

That was Jack Kennedy's mind-set a few weeks before his marriage. Jackie's premonition that he would bring her heartbreak was right on the mark.

Chapter Eight

Wedded Wives

*I just had tremendous hope in me, which was slashed by day two.
They thought I could adapt to being Princess of Wales overnight.*
— Diana, on her "grim" honeymoon

*Since Jack is such a violently independent person, and I, too, am so
independent, this relationship will take a lot of working out.*
— Jackie, in the early days of her marriage

Their wedding days had been stolen from them by circumstances
beyond their control: Joe Kennedy's extravagant plans, Queen Elizabeth's lofty position, Black Jack Bouvier's drinking, and Camilla
Parker Bowles's presence in Prince Charles's heart. The early years
of their marriages were a blend of discovery, happiness, betrayal, and
disharmony. The pressure of creating a marriage under the glare of
public scrutiny was harsher for Diana, but Jackie suffered from the
expectations of being the wife of a public figure, too.

Diana Spencer and Jacqueline Bouvier, like millions of other
young women, had dreamed about their wedding days since girlhood. Unlike most young women, neither of them was able to make
her dreams come true. Jackie wanted a small wedding and a gown
of simple, modern design. Diana wanted her three roommates to be
her bridesmaids and all her friends to come to her wedding reception. They weren't allowed to make any decisions about the size and
style of their weddings. In a twist of tradition, and an indication of

what was to come, it was the groom's family who made those decisions and paid for the festivities.

Both Diana and Jackie behaved like the Thoroughbreds they were on their wedding days. They masked the bitter disappointment they were feeling and played their roles to perfection. No one who saw them would have guessed that anything was amiss. Their poise was admirable and necessary—admirable because they displayed grace under pressure, necessary because they would face far worse disappointments as they adjusted to their new roles. As brides of eldest sons, their marriages turned them into the rising stars of their new families. They immediately eclipsed the others who had married into the family, and both eventually overshadowed the family themselves.

Both Diana and Jackie had difficult transitions to make. The Windsors and the Kennedys were two tough clans to marry into. Inbred, fiercely loyal, and self-reliant, both families subjugated the individual in pursuit of the common goal. Though both young women appeared to acquiesce, each possessed a will of iron. The more the families tried to control them, the more futile the task proved.

Diana and Jackie faced tasks that were equally futile. Each married a man who was firmly entrenched in his bachelor existence. Each man was twelve years older, and each was settled in his ways. Each was unfamiliar with the compromises necessary to make a marriage work. Fidelity would become the thorniest issue each couple would have to face, but it was certainly not the only one. Each couple struggled to work out the issues of differing temperaments, emotional isolation, and conflicting wills.

The actress Katharine Hepburn once summed up the subtextual appeal of her fellow RKO stars Fred Astaire and Ginger Rogers—he gave her class, and she gave him sex appeal. That aphorism can be applied to Jackie and Diana as well: Jackie gave the Kennedys class, and Diana gave the Windsors sex appeal.

Jackie polished Jack, developing his interests in art, music, and poetry. She guided his transformation from politician into statesman. Rose Kennedy recognized this in her daughter-in-law, commending Jackie for bringing "so many things that helped round out and fulfill

his character. . . . It would be hard to imagine a better wife for him."
It was not always easy, but Jackie knew that it wouldn't be. Over
time, the Kennedys' complex relationship evolved into a bond of deep
affection and respect.

Diana relaxed Charles, introducing pullover sweaters and slip-on
loafers to his wardrobe. Her presence in the royal family rejuvenated
the monarchy. The fairy-tale appeal of her story captured the imagination of the public and made the monarchy more relevant to a
younger generation. Diana's job was harder, because she and Charles
had very little in common. There was great disparity in their interests, outlooks, and temperaments. Diana and Charles had a mutual
infatuation that was not based on any intellectual or emotional in-
timacy. Their marriage lasted fifteen years, half again as long as Jack
and Jackie's ten, but was doomed to fail from the start.

London, July 1981

It was a grand ceremony, which the British do better than anyone
else in the world, and it had gone off splendidly. The weather was
warm and bright. Tens of thousands of people lined the streets, their
mood boisterous and celebratory. The ceremony was perfect, save for
two small mistakes: Diana transposed the order of Charles's names,
taking Philip Charles Arthur George as her husband, while Charles
stumbled over his pledge of fidelity, promising to give her *her* troth,
not his. In hindsight the two mistakes are telling and Freudian:
apparently she did not want to marry him, and he was unable to
commit himself to her.

No one cared and few even noticed. As Charles and Diana
emerged from St. Paul's, the waiting crowd roared its approval.
Though there was hope in her heart, the reality of her new life closed
in on her as soon as they returned to Buckingham Palace. There the
queen hosted a wedding breakfast for 122 people. There were just
twelve members of the Spencer family invited, including Diana. She
was joined by her parents, her stepparents, her two sisters and their
husbands, her brother, her maternal grandmother, and a paternal

great-aunt who was a duchess. Her aunts, uncles, and cousins weren't invited, nor were her three roommates or any of her other friends. There were more staff members and clergy invited to the wedding breakfast than family and friends of the bride. Still, Diana was given 10 percent of the 122 invitations. For the ceremony, she had been allotted less than 5 percent.

The guests at the breakfast included the entire royal family, a large contingent of foreign royalty, Prince Philip's sisters and their German families (who had been pointedly excluded from his wedding, held so soon after World War II), and the entire Mountbatten family. They sat down to a menu of chicken breast stuffed with minced lamb, creamed corn, green beans, and new potatoes. The Welsh Guards orchestra played selections from Broadway shows and the theme from *Love Story,* but there was no dancing. Diana didn't record any thoughts about her wedding reception, but another royal bride did. They offer a poignant insight into the festivities from the perspective of the leading lady.

In her memoirs Sarah, duchess of York, writes of her wedding breakfast: "It was lavish and proper and dull, that lunch. At one point we raised a glass, yet no one made a toast, for that was not traditional! I felt suddenly washed by regret. All the pomp had been fine, but I wanted to be a regular bride—I wanted Andrew's best man to get up and make a funny speech, and for someone else to say what a jolly good person I was, or how badly I'd ridden my ponies. I had somehow missed out on the little, vital things." It's sad to imagine, but probably true, that Andrew and Fergie's wedding lunch was more relaxed and fun than Charles and Diana's.

Sarah had one last memory of her wedding day, and Diana undoubtedly shared a similar moment: "As I went upstairs to change into my honeymoon clothes, a nest of ladies-in-waiting hovered about me, jostling for position. They all wanted to be on the right side of the Queen's new daughter-in-law, and I fell for it, took them as sincere. But where was my mum and the people who loved me?"

The honeymoon could have been a romantic idyll, a sixteen-day cruise around the Mediterranean. Charles had ideas other than romance on his mind; he brought with him a collection of books by

Sir Laurens van der Post, a South African philosopher. Every night he would read a book, and every day at lunch he would try to discuss it with Diana. She, naturally, was reluctant to turn her honeymoon into a sun-drenched tutorial. Van der Post arrived in person when the honeymoon continued at Balmoral. Charles invited him to talk with Diana, who was nervous and agitated upon her return, showing classic signs of "buyer's regret." She had bought into the idea of being Princess of Wales, but the reality was turning out to be something different.

"They each ought to have married someone like the Queen Mother," was the astute observation of Lady Angela Oswald, a lady-in-waiting to Queen Elizabeth. "They each needed someone warm, who would have really looked after them. They each needed it and neither of them was capable of giving it to the other."

Part of the problem was that Charles was a fussy bachelor, used to getting his own way and definitely not used to sharing—sharing the attention of the crowds, sharing his time, sharing his staff. The staff was the first casualty of the marriage; several veterans either quit or were fired. Among them were the prince's private secretary and his long-serving valet (who went out and wrote a pair of gossipy tell-all books). The press hinted that Diana was on a binge, sweeping away as many elements of Charles's bachelor life as she could. She was to learn that she could not control him, no matter how hard she tried.

So much was going on that first year that it's no surprise she thought she could gain control of her life through her bulimia. She had turned twenty, married, and become pregnant within a ten-week span. That she married not only a man but also an archaic institution, and did so before a million preening eyes, added untold pressure. She understood the rules of protocol; her marriage to Charles made her the third-highest-ranked woman in the country. In all public ceremony she came after the queen and the Queen Mother. But she learned to her dismay that this extended to her private life as well. She would soon come to suspect that she ranked even lower than third when it came to Charles's affections. Her bulimia became appalling. Sometimes she vomited four or five times a day. Charles was the worst possible partner for her in this regard. Not understanding the illness, he treated Diana with contempt, mocking her at mealtimes ("Is that going to reappear later?").

The birth of her first son brought Diana a reprieve from the depression and anxiety. She adored being a mother. Breaking royal tradition, she insisted that William accompany Charles and her during their first international tour to Australia and New Zealand.

Charles had been left behind during all of Elizabeth and Philip's overseas tours. Elizabeth herself, as a two-year-old princess, had been left with her grandparents for six months when her parents were away. Bringing their child with them was both perfectly natural and precedent-shattering. It was startling for the royal family to behave like "normal" people, and Diana was credited with rejuvenating the staid attitudes that had separated the monarchy from the people for many years.

Her second son, Harry, was born in 1984, and by then Diana was the most popular member of the royal family. The queen discovered as much firsthand one evening at a royal command performance when photographers clamored around Diana and largely ignored her. Elizabeth had never experienced that before, and once the novelty wore off, she was not amused. Frivolous stories about Diana's clothes and hairstyles took the limelight away from not only her official duties but also those of the rest of the Windsors. Resentments, some petty but others justified, grew and were gossiped about in the press. A feud with Princess Anne was reported, based on the fact that she hadn't been asked to be Prince Harry's godmother. Though Diana and Anne would never be best girlfriends ("I don't rattle her cage, and she's never rattled mine"), there was no feud. Yet they were trotted out and put through the charade of laughing and chatting for the photographers.

Diana started to find her equilibrium after Harry's birth. On the exterior she was buffed and styled to a *Dynasty* gloss. Inside she began to rebel against the strictures that the establishment imposed upon her. She couldn't find love inside her marriage—she found it outside. She couldn't establish a working partnership with her husband—she launched a solo career. She couldn't survive by playing by Windsor rules—so she made up her own.

Newport, 1953

Jackie's wedding was a perfect introduction to the life she would live as a politician's wife. If politics is the art of compromise, her wedding was the social equivalent of a winning campaign. She married a man who stimulated her in every way possible. That was the endgame, and she had won. There was a price to her victory. Black Jack's exclusion from her side on this special day was a painful disappointment, but Jackie took the other compromises in stride.

"Oh, Mummy, you don't have a chance," Jackie remembered thinking the day Joe Kennedy arrived in Newport earlier that summer to lay out his plans for her wedding. Janet opposed almost everything Joe suggested, so he flew up to Hammersmith Farm to lay down the law, Kennedy-style. It would be a large wedding, celebrated by a dozen priests and officiated at by Archbishop Cushing. There would be hundreds of people invited to the church and hundreds more to the reception. Photographers and newsreel cameramen would record every moment. Jackie adored Joe and watched in amusement as he steamrolled her mother.

Jack requested that she wear an old-fashioned wedding gown. Jackie turned to her mother's dressmaker, Anne Lowe, to create a lavish dress. As part of the Prix de Paris, Jackie reflected on the significance of a wedding gown: "There will be one or two moments in your life when you will want the prettiest dress in the world, something that will be as important as the occasion you wear it for. It should be a dress that years later, laid away in folds of tissue paper, will be your own very special piece of nostalgia."

Thirty years after her wedding, she would tell designer Carolina Herrera that her wedding gown "was the dress that my mother wanted me to wear and I hated it." But for the Prix de Paris, she wrote of a wedding dress that was "enormously full skirted," and it's hard to imagine that she didn't have some say in the design of the elaborate dress.

The wedding itself was a baptism by fire. Less than an hour after learning that her father would be forbidden to walk her down the aisle because he was drunk, Jackie drove to the church with her mother and stepfather. The Auchincloss brood, Yusha, Lee, Nini, Tommy, Jamie, and little Janet, followed in a second car. What they saw as they turned onto narrow Spring Street astounded them.

"What a mess" was Yusha's first thought when he stepped out of the limousine. Joe Kennedy's publicity machine had succeeded. A crowd of three thousand people waited outside the church, jostling for position and climbing up the walls of the church to peek in the windows. Police had to link arms and form a human chain so Jackie could get from the car to the church. "She didn't want to have her picture taken by all these hordes of photographers," Yusha recalled. "They were pushing their cameras at her. I was almost hit in the face by one."

Joe Kennedy told reporters outside the church that Jack Bouvier had taken ill, but back at Hammersmith Farm the gossip spread that he had been too drunk to perform his duties. Yusha regretted that "privacy had become public [and that] possible conciliation had turned confrontational." Jackie hid her fury at Janet, whom she blamed for Black Jack's disgrace, and prepared to greet the twelve hundred guests.

As one of Jackie's closest friends, Yusha understood the particular tension she was under that day. He remembers thinking, "As an usher, brother, brother-in-law and friend, I was glad to see them leave for Acapulco."

They spent their wedding night in New York, at the Waldorf-Astoria Hotel. In Mexico the honeymooners stayed in a villa lent them by the Mexican president. From there, three days after the wedding, JFK cabled his parents. "At last I know true meaning of rapture. Jackie is enshrined forever in my heart. Thanks mom and dad for making me worthy of her."

They fished and swam, and enjoyed each other. While there, Jackie wrote to her father, telling him that she understood the pressures on him that day and that she felt she had walked down the aisle on his arm. A man who read the letter characterized its author as "a rare and noble spirit." After two weeks they flew to California, staying at Santa Barbara's San Ysidro Ranch. From there they went to San Francisco, where they stayed with JFK's navy pal Red Fay and his wife, Anita. Fay noted a tension between them. He realized that "the kind of honeymoon any young bride anticipates" did not include a stay with an old shipmate and his wife.

The Kennedys were back in Washington by November, and for the next three years lived either with their in-laws or in a series of rented houses. Their wedding gifts stayed in boxes (except for the ones Jackie didn't want and subsequently sold), and their lives were rootless. It wasn't until 1956 that they bought Hickory Hill, a six-acre estate three miles from Merrywood. But the stillborn birth of a baby girl in August 1956 made the house unbearable for Jackie, and they sold it to Bobby and Ethel. It wasn't until 1957, when Jack bought a three-story brick house in Georgetown, that the Kennedys finally had a home.

By then Jack and Jackie were battle-scarred from four tumultuous years of marriage. In October 1954, just over a year after their wedding, Jack had undergone the first of two operations to correct a chronic and painful condition in his lower back. An infection nearly killed him and required a second operation that offered low odds of survival. Jackie nurtured him through his convalescence, during which he created the Pulitzer Prize–winning biography *Profiles in Courage*.

Jack dedicated the book to Jackie, and her behavior during his illness impressed his family and friends. Any thoughts that she was a lightweight disappeared as she dressed his oozing back wound and kept up his spirits by encouraging him to paint and write. "My wife is a shy, quiet girl," he once said, "but when things get rough, she can handle herself pretty well."

The summer of 1956 was the nadir in their relationship. Pregnant for a second time (she had had a miscarriage in 1954), Jackie went to Chicago for the Democratic National Convention, where Jack's name was put in contention for vice president. Though he failed to get on the ticket, it was a huge victory for him. His graceful concession played well on television—giving Joe Kennedy the inspiration to market Jack "like cornflakes" in order to take advantage of the new medium. Both exhausted from the effort and exhilarated by its outcome, the Kennedys went back East. Jack dropped Jackie off in Newport with the Auchinclosses and then left for a recuperative vacation on the French Riviera. Though Jackie longed for him to stay with her, he refused. The baby wasn't due for another month, and he wanted to get away.

On August 23 Jackie began to hemorrhage and gave premature birth to a daughter she had planned to name Arabella, but the baby girl was born dead. Her husband wasn't there to comfort her; he was thousands of miles away on a forty-foot yacht in the middle of the Mediterranean. It was Bobby Kennedy whom Jackie saw as she regained consciousness; it was Bobby who gave her the sad news about her baby, and it was Bobby who arranged for her burial in Newport's St. Columba's Cemetery. Jackie established a strong emotional bond with her brother-in-law: "You knew that if you were in trouble, he'd always be there for you."

At first Jack didn't see why he should return to Jackie's side. There was, he said, nothing to be done. The news had taken three days to reach him, and the story had made the front page of the *Washington Post* (SENATOR KENNEDY, ON SAILING TRIP, UNAWARE OF WIFE'S MISCARRIAGE). His father forced him to return, warning him that "if you want any woman to ever vote for you again, haul your ass back home."

He returned to face an emotional quagmire. "Jack and Jackie's differences in outlook, interests and manner became more obtrusive. They were both bitter, disillusioned, withdrawn, silent as if afraid that conversation would deepen the wound" was Lem Billings's observation. As JFK's closest friend, he had unique insight into Jack's character. The couple separated for a while, and rumors spread that they would divorce.

It was during this difficult period that Gore Vidal has suggested that Jackie had affairs, with actor William Holden, among others. There is scant evidence to back up his claims, and Vidal is known for a malicious wit. But it would be understandable if Jackie decided to spread her wings at this juncture in her life. Though she understood the bonds of matrimony, she had seen in her father's behavior just how tenuous they were.

It's not surprising that Jack Bouvier and Jack Kennedy got along with each other. They met over dinner in February 1953, and any doubts in the elder man's mind about the son of a bitch Joe Kennedy's son were soon dispelled. "They were very much alike" was Jackie's understated assessment. "They talked about sports, politics and women—what all red-blooded men like to talk about." Part of JFK's appeal, according to Yusha Auchincloss, was that "she could see Black Jack in JFK . . . they had the same sense of charm, they were both lovable rogues." Jack Kennedy had a respectful relationship with his father-in-law, gently teasing him in their correspondence about the Harvard-Yale football rivalry.

The fact that she adored Black Jack made it easier for Jackie to see past JFK's womanizing. ("All Kennedy men are like that, it doesn't mean anything," she later told her sister-in-law Joan.) Perhaps it was the fabled million dollars that Joe Kennedy allegedly offered her to stay in the marriage ("Why one million, why not ten?" was her supposed response). Perhaps it was a fear of following in her mother's footsteps, casting off one philandering husband and embracing a staid, conventional life with a second. For whatever reasons, Jackie stayed with JFK and in November 1957 she gave birth to their first child, a daughter. She was named Caroline Bouvier Kennedy, honoring Jackie's deep affection for her sister and father.

Jackie survived these trials of marriage. Now she embarked upon the most rewarding role in her life: motherhood.

Chapter Nine

The Mothers-in-Law: Elizabeth Windsor and Rose Kennedy

> *Hammersmith Farm, Newport Rhode Island,*
> *Monday [June 29, 1953]*
>
> *Dear Mrs. Kennedy,*
> *... I do mean to thank you for the weekend too. It was such a*
> *perfect one—and I would have made a terrible mess if you hadn't*
> *told me how to hold my arms for photographers—and how to pick*
> *out engagement rings....*
> *Much love,*
> *Jackie*

> *After all I've done for that fucking family.*
>
> —Diana, on the Squidgy tape

Rose Kennedy first met the then-Princess Elizabeth at Windsor Castle on Palm Sunday in 1938. During the two and a half years Joe Kennedy was ambassador, Rose frequently socialized with the royal family and enjoyed a cordial relationship with Elizabeth's parents, George VI and Queen Elizabeth, as well as the king's mother, Queen

Mary, and his brother the duke of Kent. But it is with Elizabeth that Rose, unknowingly, shared a special bond.

They were mothers, and mothers-in-law, to some of the most intriguing personalities in contemporary history. Their mothering skills, tempered by their unique life circumstances, shaped the characters of the men who would marry Diana and Jackie. Their iron-willed characters, forged with a devotion to duty, shaped the tumultuous relationships they had with their famous daughters-in-law.

Rose Elizabeth Fitzgerald and Elizabeth Alexandra Mary Windsor were both born into one life and forced, by circumstances beyond their control, into another life altogether. Whatever disappointments or disillusionments they suffered were internalized, buried deep within their psyches. There were never any cracks in their public facades, but their private turmoil deeply affected their mother-child relationships. The iron will and staunch control they exercised over their lives created women with a need to control and to ignore unpleasant realities and hindered their ability to create loving and constructive relationships with their daughters-in-law.

London, December 1936

She was called "Lilibet" because her younger sister, Margaret, couldn't quite pronounce "Elizabeth." At ten she was a lively and vivacious child, but her comfortable world was about to change forever. Her parents were then the duke and duchess of York, the title traditionally reserved for the second son of the monarch. Her mother, the former Lady Elizabeth Bowes Lyon, was the daughter of a Scottish earl and the first nonroyal woman to marry into the British royal family for generations. The family lived across Green Park from Buckingham Palace, at 145 Piccadilly. The five-story house is gone now, destroyed by German bombs in 1943. Walking through the neighborhood today, with its Hard Rock Cafe and Hilton Hotel, it's hard to see what it was like sixty-five years ago, a genteel district of aristocratic families, coal-fueled fires (which helped create the fog for which London was once famous), and uniformed governesses taking their young charges out for a brisk stroll.

Though Elizabeth was born third in line to the throne, there was never any expectation that she would become queen of England. Queen of a foreign country, perhaps, as in the recent past her family had provided consorts for the thrones of Germany, Spain, and Norway. But, in the aftermath of World War I, marriage to a British nobleman was more likely. There were dukes who had riches and estates that surpassed those of the crown, and Princess Elizabeth might one day find herself the chatelaine of one of the famous stately houses of Britain—Chatsworth or Blenheim Palace or Woburn Abbey. A life in the country, a grand life surrounded by horses and dogs and grandchildren, was the expected future for Elizabeth of York.

That is until fate, in the person of Wallis Simpson, intervened. The American-born Simpson, from an old yet impoverished Baltimore family, had moved to London in the early 1930s with her second husband. There, through her American connections, she first met and later besotted the dashing Prince of Wales. Their romance was conducted in the open within the upper reaches of London society but kept secret from the general population by the press. It was a cause of great concern for George V and Queen Mary, who were eager for their eldest son to marry and provide an heir. Their four other surviving children were all married, and by 1936 there were five grandchildren, but David, as he was known in the family, displayed no interest in finding a suitable royal princess to make his consort.

When George V died in January 1936, David became King Edward VIII and for ten months ruled over a country unaware that a grave constitutional crisis was developing over his love affair with a woman who had divorced one husband and married a second. A crisis would be averted as long as Wallis stayed married to Ernest Simpson and remained the king's mistress (London society joked about *The Un-Importance of Being Ernest*). Wallis did divorce Simpson in October 1936, and a few weeks later the crisis came to a head. In early December Edward VIII prepared to abdicate in favor of his younger brother the duke of York.

"I'm afraid there are going to be great changes in our lives, Craw-fie," the duchess of York tearfully confessed to Marion Crawford, Elizabeth and Margaret's governess. Crawfie, who had been with the family for five years, broke the momentous news to the two girls. She told them what had happened and that they would be moving into Buckingham Palace.

"What!" Elizabeth exclaimed. "You mean forever?"

"Does this mean you're going to become Queen?" Margaret asked her older sister. "Poor you."

Poor Elizabeth, indeed. When Uncle David signed the Instrument of Abdication on December 10, 1936, her life was stolen from her, and the effect on the ten-year-old girl was devastating. Her parents were justified in their anger at David and Mrs. Simpson for bringing this monumental change to their lives, and especially to the life of their eldest daughter. Although it may have been the best result for the country (George VI and his queen were ideal figureheads to lead Britain through World War II, and their daughter has been a sta-bilizing presence on the throne for half a century), it was a terrible burden to place on an unsuspecting child.

Elizabeth's success as queen has, sadly, not been matched by her success as mother. Her devotion to duty cost her dearly in her re-lationship with her four children. Three have been divorced, one has remarried, and there's no way of knowing the effect on her six grandchildren. The belief in sacrificing personal happiness to adher-ence to duty was bred into Elizabeth from an early age. What's more, it was made clear that any deviation from that stance would bring dire consequences. The duke and duchess of Windsor (as David and Wallis became) were exiled from the royal family for the rest of their lives. The duke was officially welcomed back to England just three times in the last thirty-six years of his life, for the funerals of his brother and mother and for the unveiling of a memorial to his mother in 1967. The duchess was officially welcomed back just twice, for the latter event (a fifteen-minute ceremony in which she stood, finally acknowledged as a member of her husband's family) and for the funeral of her husband in 1972. So when problems arose in the marriage of Charles and Diana, Elizabeth was capable of responding only as a sovereign and not as a loving parent.

Having been born into the royal family, the queen simply did not know how to assist any outsider in adapting to life within it. She could no more understand Diana's difficulties in adjusting to her new role as a royal princess than she could teach her the Pythagorean theorem. Elizabeth was incapable of showing love and sensitivity.

At a dinner at Balmoral during the Waleses' honeymoon, the queen took a friend aside and said of Diana, "Look at her, sitting at the table glowering at us! I don't know what we can do. The only time she bucks up is when Charles speaks to her."

The friend tactfully offered some advice: "Perhaps if you look around the table . . . ," indicating that the other guests were much older than Diana, sharing little in common with a twenty-year-old bride. It was a gentle hint that the queen could expand her guest list to make her new daughter-in-law more comfortable. But it was sharply rebuked.

"I don't care," the queen responded. "She'll just have to buck up."

It was a remark worthy of the imperious queen from *Alice in Wonderland*, a remark that showed little, if any, compassion or understanding for the situation and displayed an attitude that would eventually undermine the very monarchy that Elizabeth had devoted most of her life to serving. It was, in the long term, best for the monarchy to welcome Diana into the fold, to prepare her for the role she had taken on, and to adapt itself to make the best use of what she had to offer. Instead, Diana was lost inside a viper's nest of indifference, strict adherence to antiquated traditions, gossip, and political rivalries cloaked in exquisite manners. There was a huge disconnect between the world of the "establishment" and modern Britain, and when Diana tried to build a bridge between the two worlds, she was continually thwarted, often in petty and demeaning ways.

It wasn't only Diana who received this shabby treatment. Princess Michael of Kent, the wife of Queen Elizabeth's first cousin, had been a member of the "firm," as the family calls itself, for just over a year in 1979 when Earl Mountbatten of Burma was assassinated. As the family prepared for the first state funeral since that of Winston Churchill in the mid-1960s, Princess Michael asked the queen what the proper attire was for such an event. She received a note with a one-word reply—"Black"—and after the funeral was sent a rebuke—"When I say black, I mean black. Not a black handbag with gold clasps."

It wasn't, as one biographer has suggested, that Elizabeth was unkind; she was just unimaginative. It was impossible for her to comprehend how intimidating Buckingham Palace, with all its formalities and fiefdoms, could be to an outsider. When Diana was first engaged to Charles, she was given a suite of rooms at the palace and basically left to her own devices. Charles disappeared, off on a long trip to Australia, and there was no one to tutor Diana in the endless details of being "royal." There was no 'Enry 'Iggens for this Eliza Doolittle, no Pygmalion for this contemporary Galatea. Elizabeth, who had limited experience dealing with young women, soon came to see that they had little in common and left Diana to her own counsel. Was it any surprise that Diana befriended the Buckingham Palace servants, who were nearer her own age and shared many of her tastes and interests? But the palace establishment isolated her further, restricting her access to the servants and tactfully chastising her for her inappropriate choice of companions.

The situation went from bad to worse. As the Waleses' marriage started to implode, Elizabeth wisely took no sides and, though concerned, kept her distance. At one point she suggested to Diana that bulimia was the cause of the couple's marital troubles. She couldn't, or perhaps she refused to, see that the eating disorder was a symptom of a more deeply rooted problem. That attitude led Diana to isolate herself from her mother-in-law and to seek counsel from others. When in time the warfare between Charles and Diana started to explode, Elizabeth quickly and decisively closed ranks with her blood family and effectively exiled Diana with nearly the same force as her uncle David had been exiled so many years before.

One aspect of the relationship between Diana and Elizabeth that is rarely touched upon is jealousy. Diana was perceptive enough to understand that in joining the royal family, she became a rival of the queen's—not in a real sense, as Elizabeth was a reigning queen and Diana would only be a queen consort, but Diana was an irritating daily reminder that a newer, younger, more beautiful royal superstar had arrived. Diana told one biographer, "The relationship [between her and the queen] certainly changed when we got engaged because I was a threat, wasn't I?" Elizabeth may not have felt threatened, but she was well aware of Diana's popularity. She was heard to complain, "My mother's a star, my daughter-in-law's a star, where does that leave *me*?"

By the time Diana first appeared in the public eye, in the winter of 1980–81, Elizabeth had been queen for nearly forty years and had long held the top spot as the most important member of the royal family. The Queen Mother was much loved but played a secondary role to her daughter. Princess Margaret was the royal everyone loved to hate, rising and falling in public favor with great regularity. The other females in the royal family were loved (Princess Marina, the duchess of Kent), hated (Princess Anne, for most of her young adult life), or ignored (the shy duchess of Gloucester), but all were minor characters when compared with the queen.

All that changed as the press and public quickly came to adore "Shy Di," she of the blushes, bangs, and modestly turned-down eyes. She quickly became the nation's favorite cover girl—she was the impetus behind the launching of two magazines devoted solely to covering the Windsors: *Royalty Monthly* and *Majesty*. At first the family was amused; it was unusual to see someone else at the center of press interest. But when the attention grew, their bemused acceptance turned sour. Prince Charles was the first to express his annoyance. He had limited experience in playing second fiddle and became so envious of the situation that, long before their personal relationship turned acrimonious, his office began to create separate schedules for the couple.

But Charles wasn't the only one touched by the green-eyed monster. Buckingham Palace would claim that the queen was above such silly things as petty jealousy. A well-known story told about the former prime minister Margaret Thatcher has her, early in her tenure, calling the palace to ask what color the queen would be wearing to an official function, only to be coldly rebuffed: "The Queen *never* notices what anyone else is wearing." But in November 1984 Elizabeth did take notice of Diana's new hairstyle, and in the words of her great-great-grandmother Victoria, she was not amused.

The opening of Parliament is one of the most important events on the queen's calendar. It is a formal occasion in which the queen reads a speech prepared for her by the prime minister's office, which outlines the government's agenda for the coming year. Since Parliament sits in the name of the sovereign, the queen proclaims that "my government" shall do this and that. Often attended by senior members of the royal family, it takes place in the morning, and the required dress is formal, with the queen wearing her crown and the other ladies in tiaras.

Diana wore the elaborate Cambridge Lover's Knot tiara that had been a wedding gift from the queen, who had inherited it from her grandmother Queen Mary. Made by the jeweler Garrard in 1914, the tiara replicated a design of Queen Mary's grandmother, a German princess who had married the first duke of Cambridge in 1818. Its intricate pattern of lover's knots made of diamonds supporting pendants of irregularly shaped natural pearls required a formal hairstyle, so, appropriately, Diana chose to put her hair up in a chignon. The resulting hairstyle was considered major news; it was the first time she had worn an upswept style. She headlined all the newspapers, knocking the queen's speech off the front page. The royal family was furious with her, considering her actions a deliberate attempt to upstage the queen. Prince Philip was designated to express the queen's displeasure, and he vented his fury on Diana. She was, in turn, hurt, baffled, and angry. She had done nothing more than what any woman with long hair would do under the same circumstances. Indeed, Princess Anne often wore her hair in a similar style. But the intensity of the family's anger over such a trivial matter clearly indicates that the hairstyle flap was a manifestation of a more fundamental issue: the family had come to see Diana as a usurper. She had become the focal point of the royal family from the day she married into it. She was the future, and they were the past.

Palm Beach, Florida, December 1961

"Well, you might remind her that we're having some important guests for lunch. It would be nice if she would join us." With those words, Rose Kennedy indicated what she expected from her daughter-in-law.

There were ten weeks between the election of John F. Kennedy in November 1960 and his inauguration in January 1961, and while it was a momentous time for everyone in the family, perhaps no one was more affected than the First Lady–elect, Jacqueline Kennedy. For in addition to making all the adjustments to her life and plans for her future, she had given birth, prematurely and not without difficulty, to her second child, John F. Kennedy Jr., on November 25. What she needed, what was medically required for her recuperation, was complete rest—and that was not to be found in the Palm Beach home of her in-laws.

When Jackie's secretary relayed Rose's message about lunch, Jackie repeated the request, mocking Rose's singsong voice. Jackie stayed in her bedroom, ignoring the lunch, and the secretary, Mary Gallagher, noticed from then on a distinct chill in the relationship between the two women. Though they had never been close, Jackie had always practiced a well-mannered cordiality that became more forced during the White House years and their immediate aftermath. It wasn't until her marriage to Aristotle Onassis that Jackie and Rose became close; it's as if her hard-earned life lessons enabled Jackie to appreciate Rose in a way she had not been able to before.

Rose Fitzgerald Kennedy shared with Queen Elizabeth II not only an iron will and a devotion to duty but also an ability to turn a blind eye to any reality that did not please her. Elizabeth may have been born in splendor in London's Mayfair neighborhood, and Rose born in a coldwater apartment in Boston's North End, but both women learned to subjugate their own wishes to follow a destiny made for them by their fathers.

Elizabeth's destiny was, of course, part of her birthright. Rose's was part of the American immigrant experience. Her father was John "Honey Fitz" Fitzgerald, one of the most successful Irish Americans in Boston's history. Best known as the five-time mayor of the city, Honey Fitz was also the first Democratic congressman from Massachusetts. He ran for the Senate in 1916 but lost to his WASP archrival, Henry Cabot Lodge. His wife, Rose's mother, was as retiring as he was gregarious, so it was Rose who stood next to the mayor, becoming the most well-known young lady in the city.

It was precisely that position, as Boston's "princess," that was to lead to the first of the many crushing disappointments that would be a leitmotiv of her life. Rose was intelligent, possessing a fine and curious mind, and had received an excellent education for a young woman in the early part of the twentieth century. She graduated from Dorchester's Latin School and had been accepted at Wellesley, one of the Seven Sister colleges dedicated to the education of women. Wellesley, like Vassar, Radcliffe, Bryn Mawr, Smith, Barnard, and Mount Holyoke, was a secular college and a stronghold of the Protestant establishment. Few Catholics were among the students at these schools. In an early case of political correctness, Honey Fitz, at the urging of Archbishop O'Connell, refused to give Rose permission to attend Wellesley. Mindful of the sentiments of his constituency, Honey Fitz ordered a convent education for Rose, first in Holland and then at the Manhattanville College of the Sacred Heart in New York. Rose was bitterly disappointed and long felt that she had been cheated out of the education she had longed for. The religious base at the core of convent schooling precluded an enormous amount of intellectual debate, and the decision to force Rose to go there did limit the scope of her education.

Falling in love with Joe Kennedy helped Rose get over her disappointment. The pair courted for seven years, as Honey Fitz felt that the brash young Kennedy was not good enough for his daughter. But Joe's success in the business world could not be ignored, and the couple wed in October 1914. Part of the reason she married Joe was to escape her father's unyielding influence. But, like Ibsen's Nora Helmer, Rose found herself going from being her father's daughter to her husband's wife.

Rose had nine children in a span of seventeen years. Early on in her marriage, she experienced another bitter disappointment when she discovered that her husband didn't apply the same energy to his marital vows as he did to his business dealings. Rose was often left alone at home, first in Brookline and later in New York, as Joe's business took him all around the country. She was soon to learn that marriage to Joe Kennedy did not bring the partnership that the teachings of the Catholic Church had promised her. He was not a faithful husband, he did not seek her opinions on major family decisions, and he was rarely at home. In 1920, after five and a half years of marriage, Rose left Joe; walked out on her three children— Joe, Jack, and Rosemary—and returned to her parents' home. It was the desperate move of a very unhappy woman who was pregnant with her fourth child. Honey Fitz laid down the law. She had no alternative but to go back to her husband and family. That was her duty as a Catholic wife and her responsibility as a mother. Daughter Kathleen, nicknamed Kick, was born shortly after Rose returned home, and was followed, over the next dozen years, by Eunice, Patricia, Robert, Jean, and Ted. Rose became an efficient mother, masking her hurt and disappointment behind an index-card filing system that kept track of each child's doctor's appointments, illnesses, and growth. What she simply was not was a warm and tactile mother. There's no doubt that Rose loved her children; she was just incapable of breaking through her wall of resentment and reserve to express her love in a way that satisfied the emotional needs of her brood of nine.

Rose created a life for herself in which she managed to find fulfillment in the trappings of wealth and luxury; regular trips to Europe, expensive jewelry and custom-made clothes, a staff of servants to run her home, and nannies, nurses, and governesses to oversee the day-to-day upbringing of her children.

Joe used his success in the business world, specifically the fortune he had accumulated, to enter the political arena. Large contributions to the presidential campaigns of Franklin Roosevelt resulted in appointments to several federal agencies, including the U.S. Maritime Commission and the Securities and Exchange Commission. In 1938 FDR appointed the brash Irish Catholic Joe Kennedy to the most prestigious post in the diplomatic community, London. As the first Irish Catholic American ambassador to the Court of St. James, Joe could thumb his nose at every Boston Brahmin who had ever snubbed him.

Being the wife of the ambassador brought Rose the social acceptance and happiness that she had long craved. Joe's years in London were uneven at best, and disastrous at worst. He did not have the diplomatic self-control that such a position requires, and it was not long before Roosevelt began to circumvent his ambassador, sidelining Joe. His isolationist views, which he was not shy about expressing, made him very unpopular in London; his defeatist attitude turned unpopularity into loathing. The stint in London was the end of Joe's career in public service, a career that he had once hoped would take him all the way to the White House.

Rose was bitter about Joe's behavior, accusing him of throwing away so much of what they had worked for. "We had everything, everything," she wrote of their time in London. "Afterward I was very angry at him. . . . I was made to suffer for it. I lost my friendships. We lost our prestige. . . . I wonder if he ever knew how much I lost because of him." Her brief resurgence into the limelight over, she retreated to the family's two homes—summers in Hyannis and winters in Palm Beach.

Rose suffered three shocking losses during the 1940s—the deaths of Joe Jr. and Kick, and Rosemary's exile from the family. Joe's death was traumatizing but not completely unexpected; he was a casualty of war. Kick's death, in a 1948 plane crash, was the cause of both great sorrow and great shame for Rose. So deep was her shame that, twenty-five years after Kick's death, she lied about the circumstances in her autobiography, *Times to Remember*. Kick, who had once married outside of the Catholic Church, had threatened to do so again, and was killed with her married lover, the Earl Fitzwilliam, when their chartered plane crashed in France. Rose glossed over the situation surrounding their death and deliberately misreported the circumstances, saying that that Kick was flying with "a group of friends" when tragedy struck.

Guilt and shame played a large part in the story of Rosemary Kennedy. Pretty, emotional, and somewhat slower than her exuberant siblings, Rosemary was mildly retarded. Though the Kennedys had found a way to make her feel a part of the family without taxing her limited resources, in the years following the family's return from England, Joe began to worry about her future and sought out a radical procedure as a potential solution. Rosemary received one of the first prefrontal lobotomies performed in the United States, and her operation was tragically botched. She was rendered incompetent and moved from the family home to a convent in Wisconsin, where she still lives. What is truly shocking about the Rosemary story is that Joe arranged for both the operation and the convent without Rose's knowledge or consent. When she returned from one of her periodic trips, Joe presented her with a fait accompli. The Kennedy family did not acknowledge Rosemary publicly for the next twenty years. At Joe's behest, they simply excised her from their lives.

Rose hid her despair and focused her internalized anger on maintaining an external perfection. She swam and golfed and kept her figure trim, spending most of the spring in Paris buying clothes and most of the summer on the Riviera being entertained by café society. In the 1950s her children began to marry, and the ranks of the Kennedy family swelled to include Ethel Skakel, Sargent Shriver, Peter Lawford, Steve Smith, Joan Bennett, and, in 1953, Jacqueline Bouvier.

Rose warned her daughters-in-law about the hazards of being married to a politician, at least a politician from the Joe Kennedy mold. "They might be hearing and reading all sorts of scandalous gossip and accusations . . . and they should understand this and be prepared from the beginning."

From the beginning, Jackie maintained a correct relationship with Rose, penning exquisite notes on her pale blue stationery from Merrywood and Hammersmith Farm. "It seems to me that very few people have been able to create what you have," she wrote shortly after her engagement was announced, "a family built on love and loyalty and gaiety." She invited Rose to criticize her if necessary. "If you ever see me going wrong I hope you will tell me—because I know you will never find fault unless fault was there." Rose took Jackie at her word; the notes and letters came regularly for the next few years. Yet the two women had different outlooks on life, and their differences and emotional temperaments kept them apart.

As with Diana, Jackie's marriage made her a rival for her mother-in-law's position. But unlike with Diana, the 1960 election actually elevated Jackie to the role of First Lady of the land, a title that Jackie detested, preferring to be called Mrs. Kennedy. It was only in the second year in the White House, when a telephone operator said to her, "I have Mrs. Joseph Kennedy on the line . . . ," that Jackie turned to J. Bernard West, the chief usher, and said, "I guess I am *the* Mrs. Kennedy, I am the First Lady." From then on, she accepted the title.

With the election of her son to the presidency, Rose anticipated a return to the social whirlwind that had brought her such fulfillment during her years in London. She saw herself assuming a role similar to that of Queen Elizabeth, the Queen Mother, almost a second First Lady. She was a continued presence in the White House, forcing the protocol department to revise their official rankings; as the wife of a former ambassador, there was a specific rank for Rose Kennedy. But she wanted a special place, and one was created for her. Rose Kennedy, and subsequent presidential mothers, ranked below the President and First Lady, below the vice president and his wife, below the justices of the Supreme Court and their wives, below the Speaker of the House and his wife, but above all the members of the Senate and House, the cabinet, the military establishment, and the diplomatic corps. Rose even managed to insinuate herself into the Kennedys' triumphant visit to Paris in May 1961.

When social secretary Letitia Baldrige placed Joe's and Rose's names on a suggested guest list for the dinner honoring the governor of Puerto Rico (the famed dinner at which Pablo Casals came out of his self-imposed exile and gave a concert in the East Room), Jackie struck a line through their names, noting in the margins that "He won't come—she will and [as Jackie's sister] Lee will be staying here—too much confusion." Jackie resigned herself to the situation, though, adding with a sigh, "She'll probably say she's coming anyway." She did. Photographs of the evening show Rose sitting in the front row of the concert and rising to congratulate Casals after his performance. In his tactful memoir, *Upstairs at the White House,* Chief Usher West states that Rose most often came to the White House when Jackie was away.

Rose lived vicariously through Jackie's triumphs in the White House, substituting for her as hostess on a number of occasions, including a state dinner for the emperor of Ethiopia in October 1963. A few weeks after that evening, Rose Kennedy returned to the White House again, this time to share with Jacqueline Kennedy the horror of the President's funeral. She arrived on Sunday evening, the night before the funeral, and left on Monday afternoon, returning to Hyannis Port to be with Joe, who, felled by a stroke, was unable to attend.

The relationship between Jackie and Rose reached its nadir a week after the assassination, when, tired and distraught, Jackie lashed out at her mother-in-law during a long conversation with the reporter and historian Theodore White. Painting a romantic picture of her husband as a frail and sickly boy, left alone with his books about King Arthur and the Knights of the Round Table, Jackie claimed, "His mother really didn't love him. . . . She likes to go around talking about being the daughter of the Mayor of Boston or how she was the Ambassador's wife. . . . She didn't love him. . . ."

White was sensitive to his surroundings, to Jackie's emotional state and the reasons why he had been granted an interview with the recently widowed First Lady (she wanted to make a statement to the American public through *Life* magazine). Exercising great tact, he made no mention of her emotional outburst in any of his accounts, and it was only after his death, and the death of Jacqueline Kennedy, that his notes were opened to scholars.

Grief-stricken and in shock, Jackie remembered some whispered confession from Jack that revealed the extent of his feelings of childhood abandonment and used them to frame her husband as a romantic hero for the ages. Ten years later her attitude toward Rose had softened, and during the 1970s the two women grew closer.

Jackie contributed many reminiscences to Rose's autobiography, saying, "When I married Ari, she of all people was the one who encouraged me. . . . She's been extraordinarily generous. Here I was, I was married to her son, and I have his children, but she was the one who was saying, if this is what you think is best, go ahead."

A short time after Joe Kennedy died in 1969, Rose was sailing on the *Christina* with Ari and Jackie, and as the women were talking, something caused Rose to tear up. She stopped the conversation, took Jackie's hand, and said, "Nobody's ever going to have to feel sorry for me," and held her chin up high. Jackie looked at the woman she had once mocked, and saw that through the tragedies and the triumphs was a remarkable person. "I thought, 'God, what a Thoroughbred.'"

Chapter Ten

The Windsors and the Kennedys

Windsor Castle
May 22, 1940

Dear Mr. Kennedy,

Thank you very much indeed for the lovely pictures from "Pinocchio." They are so cleverly done. I think I like the one of Pinocchio's head best, or perhaps the one of them on the raft.

We saw the film the day before my birthday and we all liked it very much. I think I prefer it to "Snow White."

I am so sorry for the delay in thanking you but in the muddle of leaving a Royal Lodge to come down here, the pictures were not given to me till yesterday.

I hope you, Mrs. Kennedy and the children are well.

Yours very sincerely,

Elizabeth

The House of Windsor was born royal, the Kennedy clan made royal by popular appointment. Both families have made substantial contributions to their respective countries, and both have faced public acclaim as well as public disapproval. Their stories have occasionally intersected over the past sixty years. During Joe's tenure as ambassador, he and Rose enjoyed a cordial relationship with King George VI and Queen Elizabeth, based partly on personal regard and partly on strategic imperatives. The relationship between the two families reached a new height in the next generation, when their children, Jack and Lilibet, both heads of state, met as equals.

Beyond the prominent positions the families held in their countries, they also shared a family dynamic. Both the Windsors and the Kennedys were ruled by a dominant figure—the queen and Joe Kennedy, respectively. Their spouses were not regarded as equal partners but as subordinates—Philip by the rules of protocol, and Rose by her husband's chauvinism. Both families were insular, neither one welcoming newcomers with open arms. Perhaps if you were cut from the same cloth—Ethel Kennedy and Sarah Ferguson, for example—you were more accepted (at least in the beginning in Fergie's case), but those perceived as vulnerable or soft—Joan Kennedy, Princess Margaret's husband, Lord Snowden—were in for some pretty rough going.

For two generations the Kennedys have been regarded as America's "royal family," heirs to a great political and social dynasty. Rose Kennedy enjoyed the royal comparison; her close-up look at the Windsors had deeply impressed her. She modeled her behavior on theirs and, from the time of Jack's presidency, saw herself as an American Queen Mother. But it was two women who married into these families, Diana Spencer and Jacqueline Bouvier, who did the most to forever alter both the style and substance of each.

London, 1938

The connection between the Kennedys and the Windsors began when Franklin Roosevelt, in a delicious blend of political payoff and social mischief making, appointed Joe Kennedy ambassador to the Court of St. James. An Irish Catholic maverick, denied membership at WASPy country clubs, now held the most prestigious post in the diplomatic world. The Kennedy family arrived in London in waves, first Joe in February 1938 with Kathleen, then Rose with the younger children, and finally Joe Jr. and Jack (who were both at Harvard), Eunice, and Rosemary. The Kennedys took London by storm; the exploits of the ambassador's nine children were regular features in the popular newspapers. Joe's tenure as ambassador began with a stroke of luck. He hit a hole in one while playing golf, and his quip "I am much happier being the father of nine children and making a hole-in-one than I would be as the father of one child making a hole-in-nine" endeared him to the British public.

Shortly after their arrival, the ambassador and Mrs. Kennedy received an invitation from the king and queen to spend a weekend at Windsor Castle. Given the rising threat from Nazi Germany, a warm alliance with the United States was imperative. Both George VI and Elizabeth made a special effort to charm them. The Kennedys sat in the place of honor at meals (to the right of the hosts) and were given a lavish two-bedroom suite with a personal maid and valet. A special Roman Catholic Mass was arranged for them on Palm Sunday morning, at which Joe was invited to give one of the readings. The Kennedys spent an informal afternoon in the garden with the royal family. Joe found the twelve-year-old Princess Elizabeth "very smart, well mannered and intelligent and industrious." Thoroughly charmed by the royal family, Joe suggested they visit the United States, sensing that his countrymen would warm to the couple as he had, which would help popularize their cause. Both families felt that the weekend was a great success. Joe's blunt but accurate comment to his wife sums up his feelings nicely: "This is a helluva long way from East Boston, Rose."

From such a good beginning, however, came a very bad end. Joe's tenure as ambassador lasted a short two and a half years and was not successful. To be fair, it came at a time when an experienced diplomat would have been more helpful than a political appointee in such a sensitive post. As Europe drew closer and closer to war in the closing days of the 1930s, Britain's position became more precarious. Joe came to be known in England as an isolationist and a defeatist. His stubborn independence and thirst for personal publicity irritated President Roosevelt. The President began communicating with the British directly, circumventing his ambassador.

Despite all this, the dictates of protocol brought the increasingly unpopular ambassador into regular contact with the king and queen. Perhaps because they saw so many of the same figures from the aristocracy at function after function, they seemed amused by the brash Mr. Kennedy. He had his three eldest daughters—Rosemary, Kathleen, and Eunice—presented at court (while excluding other American debutantes). At a formal dinner in the summer of 1939, Joe sat next to the queen. They joked, with Elizabeth laughingly referring to the huge crinoline skirts on her evening gowns, "I have a hard time fitting into these chairs with these new dresses, but tonight I don't seem to overflow." They talked of a recent fracas involving Rose Kennedy's refusal to dine with the duchess of Windsor in Paris. "I know of no job I might occupy," Joe told her, "that might force my wife to dine with a tart." Elizabeth laughed, saying it served the duchess right.

The ambassador and his wife did not charm everyone in England. Henry Channon, the Chicago-born interwar politician and diarist known as Chips, found Kathleen "entrancing" and Jack "amusing" but did not warm to Rose. "She is an uninteresting little body, though pleasant and extraordinarily young looking to be the mother of nine. She has an unpleasant voice and says little of interest. She too keeps a diary and I always like people who keep diaries; they are not as others, at least not quite." As for Joe, Chips's attitude mirrors what most of England was thinking by November 1939: "I trust that Joe Kennedy is wrong, for he prophesies the end of everything, and goes about saying that England is committing suicide."

One Kennedy was an unqualified triumph—Kick. "She was a star," her sister-in-law Lady Anne Tree remembered. "So full of gaiety and light. Not at all bitchy like so many of the other girls." Kick charmed everyone, but she had a wicked tongue when in the safe confines of the clan. "They are very sweet," she wrote about the royal princesses to her family after the war, "but Princess Elizabeth is very royal and very hard to talk to. She has a sweet face but dresses so badly. Her evening clothes make her look much fatter than she really is."

Joe quit his post at the end of 1940, effectively ending his career in public life. By then all the Kennedys were safely back in the United States. After America entered World War II a year later, Kick would return to London, for she had fallen in love with an Englishman.

London, 1944

They had met six years previously at a garden party at Buckingham Palace. She was the effervescent daughter of the American ambassador; he was heir to one of the noblest titles in Britain. He was so highborn that he was mentioned as a possible husband for Princess Elizabeth. His name was William John Robert Cavendish, marquess of Hartington, and he was the eldest son of the duke of Devonshire, owner of Chatsworth. Billy's mother, called Moucher, was Mistress of the Robes to the queen, Elizabeth's senior lady-in-waiting.

Kick and Billy's story is perhaps the one true fairy-tale romance in this entire saga. It has all the elements: a charming heroine, a dashing hero, true love, and powerful forces trying to keep them apart. The powerful forces at work were the couple's two religions, Roman Catholicism and Anglicanism. What should have been a social coup for Rose was turning into a battle: both sides had much to lose, and each clung to its position with equal stubbornness. Finally Kathleen gave in. She married Billy in a civil ceremony in May 1944, with her elder brother Joe the only member of her family present.

France, 1948

When tragedy struck the Kennedy family on May 13, Chips Channon made a diary entry that neatly encapsulates Kathleen's story: "The newspapers blaze with more sad news: Kik [sic] Hartington has been killed in an air-smash; also Peter Fitzwilliam. They were a glamorous couple—gay, dashing, attractive, carefree, colossally rich—and very much in love. Or at least he was. He has been wanting to marry her for some time but she objected, as a lapsed Roman Catholic, to his getting a divorce from Olive, who is his official widow. . . . Kik [sic] Hartington had an ill starred life. She began by being a vivacious simple American girl when Joe Kennedy, her father, was made Ambassador here. She was gay enough, susceptible enough, to become be-glamoured by English life (and it was very grand then), and when Billy fell in love with her, and wanted to marry her, she couldn't resist and courageously defied the Roman Catholic Kennedys and married him: her gay, debonair brother Joseph was best man at their war-time wedding. Both he and Hartington were killed shortly afterwards. She seemed heartbroken and then, in time, recovered her spirits. . . . Then the fabulous Lord Fitzwilliam appeared. . . . Now they have died together."

The Kennedys were devastated by her death. Joe, who had been in Paris hoping to make some sort of arrangement that would enable Kick to marry a soon-to-be-divorced Protestant, was awakened in the middle of the night and told of the plane crash. From his suite in the Hôtel George V, he wrote: "No one who ever knew her didn't feel that life was much better that minute. And we know so little about the next world that we must think that they wanted just such a wonderful girl for themselves. We must not feel sorry for her but for ourselves." Joe accompanied his daughter's body back to England. Kick was buried at Chatsworth, and the duchess of Devonshire selected her epitaph: "Joy she gave / Joy she has found." Joe was later to express his disappointment that the queen didn't send a message of condolence to Rose.

London, 1948

A few weeks after Kathleen's death, Jackie attended a garden party at Buckingham Palace. She was on her first trip to Europe and had wangled the invitation through the undersecretary of the treasury, Edward Foley, who was a friend of Hughdie and Janet's. She was presented to the king and queen and shook hands with Winston Churchill. At nineteen, it was Jackie's first glimpse of royalty.

Jackie would return to London throughout the 1950s, first as a reporter covering the coronation in 1953 and then regularly after Lee moved there in the mid-1950s. Lee's first husband, Michael Canfield, took a leave of absence from his publishing career to serve as a special assistant to the American ambassador, Winthrop Aldrich. The young couple led a glamorous life, and during the troubled years of her marriage, Jackie often sought refuge with them. In the late fifties Lee divorced Canfield and married Stanislaus Radziwill, an exiled Polish nobleman who used his defunct title, prince. Lee now called herself Princess Radziwill and moved in the glittering social circle of the British aristocracy.

London, June 1961

John Kennedy made a triumphant return to the city he had known as a college student. He came back as President of the United States and the leader of the free world. He acknowledged his ties to Britain in a short speech he made upon arriving from Vienna: "I come not to Great Britain as a stranger. I spent many months here in the days before the Second War. Two of my sisters had the good judgment to marry citizens of Great Britain and tomorrow I am about to assume my most sober responsibility, which is to become the godfather of a new English citizen. So I am glad to be here."

The Kennedys' stay in London was brief. JFK would not be there two full days, and Jackie only slightly longer. There was the christening of Lee and Stas's daughter, Tina, with a reception following at the Radziwills', a luncheon given by Prime Minister Harold Macmillan, and a formal dinner at Buckingham Palace.

"The Queen was pretty heavy going," Jackie confessed to Gore Vidal. "I think [she] resented me. Philip was nice but nervous. One felt absolutely no relationship between them. She was human only once." Perhaps resentful of the protocol issue raised by the Radziwills' past divorces, Elizabeth hadn't included any of the royals whom the Kennedys had asked to see, Princess Margaret and the duchess of Kent among them. "Anyway," Jackie told Gore, "the Queen got her revenge. No Margaret, no Marina, no one except every Commonwealth minister of agriculture they could find." Jack flew back to Washington right after the dinner, still dressed in his evening clothes.

Jackie was outspoken about the evening at Buckingham Palace at a small dinner at which Cecil Beaton was one of the guests. "About dinner with the Queen last night," he recorded in his diary, "she said they were all tremendously kind and nice, but she was not impressed by the flowers or the furnishings ... or by the Queen's dark blue tulle dress and shoulder straps, or that flat hairstyle."

A year later, in March 1962, Jackie returned to London on her way home from a trip to India and Pakistan. Elizabeth invited her for a private lunch, just the two of them, at Buckingham Palace. Jackie's public remarks displayed the courteous and tactful side of her character: "I thought the Queen's clothes were lovely and she was most gracious."

Elizabeth was pregnant with her fourth child when John Kennedy was assassinated. She telegraphed her condolences to Jackie: "I am so deeply distressed to learn of the tragic death of President Kennedy. My husband joins me in sending our heartfelt and sincere sympathy to you and your family. Elizabeth."

The reaction to JFK's assassination in Great Britain was extraordinary. David Bruce, the American ambassador in London, sent a confidential report to Secretary of State Dean Rusk, stating that "Great Britain has never before mourned a foreigner as it has President Kennedy. The tributes to his memory have been multitudinous, untinged by distinctions of race, religion, or class. . . . Many demonstrations of effectionate [sic] respect spring from the hearts of those who believe he might have become the creator of a new world order. Like other symbols, this one is not subject to analysis, and is mystically interpreted."

Bruce went on to pay tribute to Jackie: "The beauty, grace, elegance, gallantry, dignity, and attractiveness of Mrs. Kennedy added luster to the Presidency. . . . She was, in herself, a national asset."

Prince Philip led the British contingent to the funeral, which included Andrew and Deborah Devonshire, Kick's brother- and sister-in-law. In the White House after the funeral, Jackie received Philip in her private salon. As they sat sipping Bloody Marys, she asked his advice about greeting the dignitaries gathered in the staterooms below. Philip's reply was swift: "I'd advise you, you know, to have the [receiving] line. It's really quick and it gets it done." Jackie followed his advice and received the guests in her favorite room, the

Empire-style Red Room. Saying good-bye to Philip, she curtsied as he left the room. Two years earlier, en route to London, she had asked Angier Biddle Duke, the chief of protocol, if she should curtsy to the queen and Philip. No, he told her firmly, the wife of a chief of state never curtsies to anyone. That afternoon, hours after burying her husband, she turned to Duke and smiled sadly, saying, "Angie, I'm no longer the wife of a chief of state."

Runnymede, England, May 1965

After her husband's death, Jackie wondered whether her life would become an endless round of driving "down a Kennedy Parkway to a Kennedy airport to visit a Kennedy school." But the trip to England came at the invitation of Queen Elizabeth and was therefore special. The queen was going to dedicate an extraordinary memorial to JFK—an acre of land at Runnymede, where the Magna Carta had been signed in 1215. The idea had been Elizabeth's, and her speech paid warm tribute to the man she had first met when she was twelve years old. The queen acknowledged the special regard the British had for JFK, "whom in death my people still mourn and whom in life they loved." Wearing white, which is a color of royal mourning, Jackie responded in kind, saying that it was "the deepest comfort to me to know that you share with me thoughts that lie too deeply for tears."

Jackie's official party included several members of the Kennedy administration, who gave her a vermeil box to commemorate the event. "It meant so much—your coming to England with me," Jackie wrote to Dave Powers. "I don't think any of us will forget Runnymede."

The trip to England was also emotional in that Maud Shaw was leaving the Kennedy household. The nanny had taken care of Caroline and John for eight years and was planning to accompany them to London for the Runnymede ceremony. "Mrs. K. has just told me she will not need me to return to the states," she wrote to President Kennedy's secretary, Evelyn Lincoln, on March 22, 1965. "I must say it was a bit of a shock. What I am sorry [about] in a way is the loss of my wages & social security credits until I can retire on pension in September." She was fired four months before her retirement but decided to put on a brave face. "Lots [are] worse off than I am," she wrote to Lincoln. To spare the children's feelings, she and Jackie decided not to say anything other than that Miss Shaw was going to stay behind in England to visit her family for a while.

In preparation for their presentation to the queen, Miss Shaw taught Caroline how to curtsy and John how to bow. Standing in for the queen, the nanny instructed them to say, "Good afternoon, Your Majesty." Caroline did it perfectly, and then it was John's turn.

"Good afternoon, My Majesty," said four-year-old John.

"No, John," Shaw told him. "That's not quite right. We have to call the queen 'Your Majesty.' Try it again."

Again and again he bowed and said, "Good afternoon, My Majesty." Caroline collapsed in a fit of giggles as John indignantly shouted, "You said she was *my* Majesty. That's what I said." Jackie watched with amusement as he practiced until he got it right.

There was an enormous bond of affection and trust between Jackie and Maud Shaw. Miss Shaw had been a part of their lives since Caroline was eleven days old. When they first met, a month or so before Caroline was born, Jackie told her that she had had an English nanny as a child and that she and JFK admired the way the English brought up their children. Jackie entrusted Shaw with the excruciating task of telling Caroline that her father had died; she completed that dreaded task with skill and compassion. So highly did Jackie regard Miss Shaw that during the reception at Windsor Castle following the Runnymede ceremony, she took care to make a formal presentation to the queen: "Your Majesty, I would like to introduce Miss Shaw, who looks after my children." The nanny was overwhelmed and touched by Jackie's thoughtfulness.

The separation from her nanny was painful for Caroline and eventually distressing to Jackie, who was shocked when Miss Shaw published her memoirs of the Kennedy years. "Since the news of my [*Ladies' Home Journal*] writings I haven't heard again from Mrs. Kennedy," Maud Shaw wrote to Evelyn Lincoln in February 1966.

"I have felt a little troubled from time to time—but on the other hand I felt I had done nothing out of place by just pattering about the president and his children. At Xmas & from Switzerland I had a letter and a p.c. from both the children . . . so I hope she will continue to let the children write to me."

Caroline, too young to hold a grudge, wrote to Miss Shaw for years. That Jackie allowed her daughter to do so despite her own feelings for her ex-employee points out another element of Jackie's good mothering. Maud Shaw's most treasured possession was a gilt-edged scrapbook of their years together that Jackie had lovingly created and inscribed, "You brought such happiness to all our lives and especially to President Kennedy, because you made his children what they are."

Upperville, Virginia, November 1985

The two most famous women of the twentieth century met just once, over lunch at Bunny Mellon's farm in Virginia. Diana and Charles had come to Washington to open *The Treasure Houses of Britain,* a huge show celebrating the five-hundred-year history of private patronage and art collecting by the British aristocracy. Their four-day trip to Washington spurred an exhaustive social competition for invitations to the three formal events planned for the weekend—the gala opening at the National Gallery, a dinner dance hosted by President and Mrs. Reagan at the White House, and a reception at the British embassy. But the most exclusive invitation of all was for a quiet Sunday lunch at the Mellons' farm, Oak Spring, set in a little village of rolling hills near Middleburg, the heart of Virginia's hunt country.

The Mellons had planned an informal lunch with two goals in mind: to give the royal couple a respite from the rounds of official entertaining, and to introduce Diana to some people closer to her own age. Most of the socialites and officials she met in Washington were of her parents' generation or even older (President Reagan was fifty years her senior). To that end, Bunny Mellon had invited John and Caroline Kennedy. Jackie was invited, too, and she looked forward to meeting the young woman whose life bore so many similarities to her own.

"Jackie admired Diana at first," her half brother, Jamie Auchincloss, said. "She saw something of her younger self in the princess." Yusha Auchincloss agreed. "They were very much alike, they had the same sense of mischievousness. There were many parallels between their two lives. Both of them were very young when they were thrust onto the world's stage, and despite some difficulties they both grew into their roles."

Jackie told one of her Doubleday colleagues that she respected Diana for "rising to the occasion after her marriage" and that she found Diana "beautiful, elegant, charming and very stylish." They joked about Diana's writing an autobiography and enjoyed Bunny's simple but luxurious hospitality.

As Diana's marriage began to unravel in the late 1980s, Jackie's admiration for Diana turned to sympathy. "Jackie felt very simpatico with Diana," Yusha recalled. "Jack was very circumspect in his extracurricular activities. Even when Jackie was away [from the White House], I never saw Jack flirt with another girl." The sympathy that Jackie felt for Diana turned to disapproval when it became clear that Diana was using the press to fight her battles with Charles. "Diana and Jackie shared the problem of having to cope with powerful, philandering husbands," one of Jackie's friends said. "In their approach to this they differed greatly. Jackie was made of sterner stuff."

The two never met again, but Diana was moved by Jackie's death. She told a friend that she had wept at the death of a woman she barely knew but considered a role model. On her cream-colored stationery engraved with a large red D and a coronet, she wrote to both Caroline and John, expressing her deepest sympathy. She wrote how much she admired Jackie and looked to her as a role model for bringing up children in the public eye. She was later to tell friends how impressed she was with the way John Kennedy handled his fame. She hoped William would follow his example.

Chapter Eleven

Mothers

A child's stability arises mainly from the affections received from his parents, and there is no substitution for affection.

—Diana, 1986

I was reading Carlyle and he said one should do the duty that lies nearest you. And the thing that lies nearest me is the children.

—Jackie, 1962

One of the shared triumphs of Diana's and Jackie's lives is that they excelled in the most traditional of female roles, that of mother. They were exceptional mothers, as even their most ardent detractors would admit. Few mothers are prepared to raise children as the objects of never-ending public attention. Few mothers are expected to exploit their children for their husbands' professional gain. The few mothers who do are rarely rewarded with children who are well balanced and unspoiled. That Diana and Jackie succeeded in doing so is little short of a miracle.

Adding to their success is that they themselves were both survivors of turbulent childhoods and children of divorce; their early memories were filled with acrimonious battles between mother and father. They both had complicated individual relationships with each of their parents. It's as if their collective experience of being daughters to such complex and demanding personalities taught them how *not* to parent. The results they achieved bear witness to their success.

Certainly for Diana, and to a lesser degree for Jackie, bearing children was a requirement of the job. The monarchy survives because of mothers; American politics may not require its candidates to have a family, but it is strongly encouraged. Diana and Jackie fully embraced that requirement and found their greatest reward as mothers. Diana had the additional responsibility of raising two boys who would have official roles to play. They would never be "private citizens" in the way Caroline and John Kennedy could, ostensibly, be private people. In addition to raising her sons as *persons,* Diana was also charged with raising them as *princes*. The necessary training in protocol, history, and the role of a constitutional monarch infringes on the sort of carefree childhood most mothers would choose for their children.

Both women chose to lavish attention and strong physical displays of affection on their children, quite unlike the way their husbands were raised. Both women insisted that the needs of Buckingham Palace and the White House came second to the needs of their children. Both fought to provide an aura of normalcy to their children's upbringing. Both women acknowledged that their children had loving and attendant fathers, whatever their deficiencies as husbands.

Diana and Jackie differed as mothers in one significant regard. Whatever troubles Jackie had with her marriage, she kept them to herself and a few trusted friends. She never spoke publicly against Jack, understanding that to do so would undermine her children's well-being. Loyalty to the Kennedy family was not a charade; it was a bond that cemented her children's fleeting memories of their father. Diana either did not understand or was unwilling to accept that approach. Perhaps it was a quest for her own sanity that drove Diana to go public with the troubles in her marriage. First by cooperating with Andrew Morton for his book *Diana: Her True Story* and then by her *Panorama* interview, Diana made public the intimacies of her life with Charles, coloring them to achieve the effect she wanted— Diana as innocent betrayed. The fact that in many ways she *was* an innocent betrayed is beside the point. Nor was Diana alone in hanging dirty Windsor laundry out to dry. Charles did his part, through his cooperation with Jonathan Dimbleby's comprehensive biography

They were the two most
famous women of the
twentieth century:
Diana Frances Spencer and
Jacqueline Kennedy Onassis.
(AP/Wide World; JFK Library)

Jackie Bouvier developed a love of all things equestrian at an early age. The poise and control she learned on horseback served her well throughout her life. The young Diana Spencer broke her arm in a riding accident and remained skittish around the animals for the rest of her life. (AP/Wide World; JFK Library)

Frances Shand Kydd, right, had a tumultuous relationship with her youngest daughter but represented Diana's interests at the French inquiry into her death. Janet Auchincloss (seen opposite, between Jackie and Hugh D. Auchincloss at Jackie's debut in 1947) was the one who "forced them to brush their teeth and write thank-you notes." (AP/Wide World; courtesy of Yusha Auchincloss)

Earl Spencer was disappointed when Diana was born a girl. Marrying the heir to the throne was her extreme example of making up for it. Jack Bouvier worshiped his oldest daughter. From him she received a steady diet of "Vitamin P" (for praise). (AP/Wide World; JFK Library)

Charles Windsor and Jack Kennedy. Two men groomed
for success, and success required the ultimate trophy bride.
(AP/Wide World; JFK Library)

Maidens. In their elaborate gowns, Diana and Jackie each found a private moment on her very public wedding day.

The connection between the Kennedys and the Windsors began in prewar 1930s England, where Joe Kennedy served as U.S. Ambassador, and with his wife, Rose, entertained King George VI and Queen Elizabeth. A generation later, their children met as heads of state when the Kennedys dined with Elizabeth II and Prince Philip at Buckingham Palace. The relationship between the two families reached its apogee when Elizabeth dedicated a memorial to JFK at Runnymede in 1965.
(AP/Wide World)

Diana and Jackie each succeeded brilliantly in the most traditional of female roles: mother.

(AP/Wide World; JFK Library)

Their official duties sometimes took them on parallel journeys. But in 1962 there was no public knowledge of JFK's infidelities; when Jackie stood alone in front of the world's greatest monument to eternal love, the irony was lost. Diana's forlorn appearance at the Taj Mahal thirty years later fed into the frenzy of gossip about the state of her marriage. (JFK Library; AP/Wide World)

Both Diana and Jackie were lionized
for their iconographic style.
(AP/Wide World; JFK Library)

Each woman usurped her mother-in-law as the star in the family. Diana and Elizabeth never saw eye to eye. After a chilly start, Jackie grew closer to Rose during the Onassis years and after. (AP/Wide World)

Two different lives, two similar paths. In 1968 Jackie turned to the sensual warmth of the Mediterranean and a second marriage to Aristotle Onassis. In 1997 Diana followed suit, and found summer romance in the arms of Dodi Fayed.

(JFK Library; AP/Wide World)

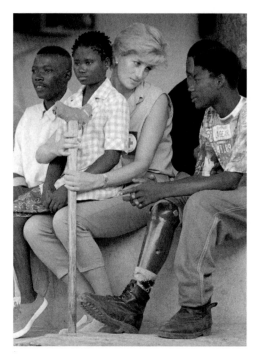

Each was the maker of her own myth: Diana as
the Queen of people's hearts and Jackie as the
keeper of Camelot's flame.

(AP/Wide World; JFK Library)

Diana's death caught the world by surprise. Her funeral was like her life, throbbing with emotion and controversy. Jackie's funeral was graceful, elegant, and reserved, in keeping with her style. (AP/Wide World)

And then there were two...
Diana's boys and Jackie's two children are their greatest legacies. (AP/Wide World)

Elizabeth II bows her head before Diana's passing coffin. It was an unprecedented
gesture of respect for a woman Elizabeth once called "that bothersome girl."
(AP/Wide World)

The temple of Diana at Althorp. Her grave lies unmarked on an island in the middle of the decorative lake on which she played in as a child. Jackie's coffin awaiting burial, high above the city she and Jack dazzled for "one brief shining moment."

(AP/Wide World)

They were England's Princess and America's Queen. (AP/Wide World)

and television interview. Neither Charles nor Diana would con-
sciously do anything to harm their boys. They were both loving
parents. Nonetheless, it's impossible to answer the larger question:
Namely, did their mutual revelations harm their sons' lives?

Jackie's death came when her two children were adults—Caroline,
thirty-six and a mother of three, John, thirty-three and a practicing
attorney. Jackie had been a great influence on the lives of both her
children. She had been there for them from infancy through adulthood. Diana, of course, was not as fortunate. William was fifteen
and Harry two weeks short of thirteen at the time of her death. It's
too early to tell how much of Diana's mothering will influence her
sons' behavior. Physically, both princes favor their Spencer genes,
with William bearing a striking resemblance to his mother. Temperamentally, the boys seem more relaxed than their Windsor relations. The Jesuits say that if you give them a boy for seven years, he
will retain their training. The fictional Scottish teacher Jean Brodie
boasts, "Give me a girl at an impressionable age and she is mine for
life." Whether Diana was able to work that same magic with her
sons is something to be discovered.

London, 1981

Two nights before Buckingham Palace announced that Diana was
pregnant, she and Charles appeared at the Victoria and Albert Museum. Sitting on the dais in a pale blue chiffon ball gown, she looked
just like the princess in a fairy tale—blond, beautiful, serene. Her
head dipped down once or twice, as if the official speeches caused
her to nod off. Two days later, when the news was announced, everyone understood. The reaction was surprise and delight. She had said
that she wanted children, but no one expected her to fulfill her desire
so quickly.

In a way it was a shame that she became pregnant so soon after
her marriage. Her life had changed completely, and there was no
time to adjust. Whereas Jackie Kennedy had a seven-year apprenticeship before she was thrust onto the world stage, Diana had barely

seven months. Whereas Jackie had a few years of marriage to a complicated man before she became a mother, Diana had a few weeks. It was an enormous adjustment for a twenty-year-old to make, and it's not surprising that Diana felt completely overwhelmed.

On one hand, she was "people pleasing," becoming pregnant and providing the dynastic link as one of her very first acts as Princess of Wales. The public story played out beautifully, for the world saw Diana and Charles as happily married newlyweds. When their union was immediately blessed with a pregnancy, it just added to the fairytale quality. A few voices expressed concern that the princess was too young, or too inexperienced, or out of step with the 1980s. But they were isolated criticisms, and if there was something solidly 1950s and old-fashioned about Diana's condition, it was welcomed as being a wholesome antidote to the times.

On the other hand, the pregnancy came at the worst possible time in Diana's life. Surely she needed time to adjust to her new status as royal princess. It was a daunting task. She was suspicious of Charles's relationship with Camilla, temperamentally incompatible with her new in-laws, and unsure of where to turn for help. Getting pregnant fast was one way of drawing attention away from the more significant problems she was facing. People would assume that it was her pregnancy causing the mood swings and ill-tempered behavior. Her pregnancy could be used to avoid dealing with the deeply rooted problems—an "avoidance" technique taken to the extreme.

Like Jackie, Diana started her married life living with her in-laws. The second half of her honeymoon coincided with the family's late-summer retreat to Balmoral, so they were together in Scotland for weeks. When they returned to London, Diana moved into Charles's apartment in Buckingham Palace for seven months while their new home at Kensington Palace was being readied. "Living above the shop" is how Prince Philip characterized Buckingham Palace, and it was an inauspicious place to begin married life. Their rooms didn't even contain a kitchen, so every time Diana wanted tea, she had to ring down to the kitchens a quarter of a mile away.

"Why's she ringing that bell again?" was muttered more than once belowstairs. It only added to the pressures Diana was under.

She felt so isolated and so trapped that she took dramatic measures to get attention. During the New Year holidays at Sandringham, she threw herself down some stairs after an argument with Charles. Elizabeth was the first to discover her lying at the bottom of the staircase. Shocked and frightened, she called for a doctor. Though Diana had suffered abdominal bruising, neither she nor her baby were harmed. According to Diana, Charles was dismissive and scathing, accusing his wife of "crying wolf." Diana later acknowledged that she was acting out of desperation. Sadly, this was not an isolated incident, and in its repetition lay the evidence that it was not the optimal time for Diana to take on the added pressures of motherhood.

Though Charles showed signs of selfishness and insensitivity during this time, he shouldn't be painted as a villain. He went against family precedent and supported Diana's wish to have her baby born in a hospital. On June 21, 1982, Charles became the first royal father to be present at the birth of his child. Though Diana would later claim that the date was selected to accommodate Charles's polo schedule, they were enjoying a rare period of closeness and harmony. Diana told a friend, "I kept saying, 'Charles, come here and hold my hand, hold my hand,' but he kept going to the front of the engine instead." She enjoyed telling the story, as it proved closeness and a feeling of contentment between her and Charles.

Their differences came up again over the issue of the baby's name. Charles wanted to call his son either Arthur or Albert, both names with strong connections to the royal family. Albert was Queen Victoria's loving husband, and "Bertie" was the family's name for Charles's grandfather George VI. Arthur was the name of Queen Victoria's eldest son, the duke of Connaught. Diana had her heart set on the far trendier Oliver. The idea of a royal prince bearing the same name as Oliver Cromwell was outlandish enough to be amusing, but completely out of the question. After a week's debate, the palace announced that the prince would be called William Arthur

Philip Louis. Diana had suggested William, Charles had favored Arthur, and Philip and Louis were to honor Charles's father and great-uncle.

Diana insisted on relaxing the standards by which royal children were raised. While she understood and appreciated their position, and the responsibilities William would acquire as he grew older, she also wanted him to have as close to a normal upbringing as possible. She was much more hands-on in the day-to-day care of her infant than any of the other mothers in the family had been. Diana wanted to create an immediate bond with her son, so William was breast-fed for the first few weeks of his life. It was Diana, and not the nurses or nannies, who changed his diapers and bathed him. She hired a young nanny, Barbara Barnes, over the objection of Prince Charles. He harbored a sentimental spot for his old nanny, Mabel Anderson (who had been one of the handful of nonroyal guests at the wedding reception), but Diana resisted and ultimately won.

A second son, the "spare," was born two years later, on September 15, 1984. He was christened Henry Charles Albert David but was called Harry from birth. Diana would later regard Harry's birth as the turning point in her relationship with Charles. She remembered the weeks preceding his birth as blissfully happy. "We were very, very close to each other the six weeks before Harry was born, the closest we've ever, ever been." After Harry's birth she claimed that the marriage imploded—"just went bang"—and that Charles went back to Camilla.

Diana suggested that one of the reasons for this change was Charles's dissatisfaction with the new baby's gender. Charles had wanted a daughter and made no effort to conceal his dismay in the delivery room. "Oh God, it's a boy" was his first comment, and "He's even got red hair" was his second. Diana was shocked and hurt. She had known the baby's sex from one of her earlier scans but had kept it a secret. And now Charles was disappointed. She felt as if she had failed somehow, that she hadn't fulfilled her obligation to give birth to a daughter. Oddly enough, every other royal mother since Princess Elizabeth had given birth first to a son, then a daughter. Princess Margaret, the duchess of Kent; Princess Alexandra; Princess Anne, the duchess of Gloucester; and Princess Michael of Kent had all followed suit. It was Diana who broke with the royal family's way of doing things, even in the matter of childbirth.

Charles didn't know how painful his offhand remark was to his young wife. The scene at Harry's birth echoed Diana's own, and Charles's dissatisfaction mirrored her own father's the day she was born.

Harry's birth also caused a riff between Charles and his mother-in-law. At the christening, Charles found himself chatting with Frances Shand Kydd and, perhaps unaware of her painful child-bearing experiences, tactlessly said, "I'm so disappointed—I thought it would be a girl." Remembering the tragic death of her infant son John, Frances politely told off her royal son-in-law: "You should be grateful that you had a child that was normal." Charles, unaccustomed to being spoken to in such a manner, backed off. Affronted, he shut the door on their relationship, refusing to speak to Frances after that day. Frances was on shaky ground with the entire royal family, who had come down on Johnnie's side during the divorce. They considered her a "bolter," thinking that Johnnie had had "a very rough time" during their marriage. This contretemps with Charles effectively sealed Frances's fate with her royal in-laws. The rare times Diana mentioned her mother's name, she told a friend, the Windsors came down on her "like a ton of bricks."

During her lifetime, Diana consistently won the public-relations war as the "better parent." Child-rearing experts, the press, and the public applauded her insistence that her boys experience life on both sides of the gilded palace railing. She didn't want them "hidden upstairs with the governess," hence the trips to McDonald's and Disney World, and visits to homeless shelters and hospitals. The palace establishment looked down their noses at her efforts, warning her that the two princes could not be raised as if they were ordinary children. By the mid to late 1980s Diana had seen the results of the Windsors' child-rearing traditions in her husband and his siblings. She fought harder than ever to mix the contemporary with the traditional, to bring a modern perspective to ancient practice.

It was private schools for the boys, not the home tutoring that

Charles had experienced. When the time came, they went to boarding schools far more progressive than the rigorously stark Gordonstoun, where Charles had been so miserable. Both boys took part in official events when it was appropriate—four-year-old William was a page boy at the wedding of his uncle Andrew to Sarah Ferguson, and both boys would appear on Buckingham Palace's balcony after the annual Trooping of the Color ceremony—but more time was made for informal family fun.

The boys' upbringing most closely resembled that of the queen and Princess Margaret. "We want our children to have a happy childhood which they can always look back on," the then–duchess of York had told their governess, Marion Crawford. Like Diana, the duchess had also come to the royal family as a commoner and, like Diana, brought a common touch with her. Lilibet and Margaret enjoyed a childhood free from care and far more relaxed than the one their father and his siblings had experienced. George V's most famous remark about parenting is quite telling and goes a long way in explaining many of the dysfunctional elements in the modern royal family: "My father was frightened by his mother, I was frightened by my father and I'm damned well going to see that my children are frightened of me."

Diana took the opposite tack. "I hug my children to death," she said. "I get into bed with them at night, hug them and say, 'Who loves you most in the whole world?' and they always say, 'Mummy.' " This is lovely, and reassuring to children, but also adds an unspoken sense of competition between parents. If Mummy loves you best, then Papa must love you second best. Given Diana's later efforts to best Charles in a public-relations war, it's hard not to admit the possibility that there was a manipulative edge to her comment.

Diana's natural warmth and her casual and instinctual public persona tipped the scale of public opinion toward the belief that she was the more caring parent. This was unfair to Charles, whom, even in the midst of their divorce, Diana would privately acknowledge as "a wonderful father." Charles loved his children dearly but was restricted by his upbringing from displaying that affection in the media-savvy way that was as effortless as breathing to Diana.

The most famous example of this unseemly competition came in June 1991 when William was hit in the head by a golf club while at his prep school. He suffered a depressed fracture and underwent both a CAT scan and an operation to repair the damage to his skull. Diana stayed by William's side while Charles left the hospital and went to the opera, fulfilling a long-standing obligation. WHAT KIND OF DAD ARE YOU? blazed newspaper headlines around the globe. Charles was battered with unfavorable publicity while Diana was held up to be a saint. Nuance has no place in the tabloids: such a black-and-white story played well in the press, regardless of the facts.

Charles hadn't felt it necessary to stay with Diana during the operation, or to be by William's side when he woke up from surgery. He had been thoroughly briefed by doctors, who assured him that the procedure was relatively normal and the risks involved minimal. Given his behavioral training, Charles conformed to the "reality" of the situation and ignored the "perception" that his leaving William's side would create, namely, that he was a bad father.

That Diana did nothing to alter that impression is understandable yet also unfortunate. Ten years into her marriage, she was desperately unhappy, feeling trapped and under attack. Hurt and embittered by Charles's attitude toward her, Diana lashed out at him in a public way that was anathema to many who felt sympathetic to her plight. Jacqueline Kennedy Onassis was one of those people who felt sympathy for Diana. Jackie was one of a handful of women who had been in Diana's position and understood the pressures that she faced on all fronts.

Jackie's sympathy for Diana turned to disapproval as, in the words of one of Jackie's friends, the Princess of Wales "disemboweled herself in public." Whatever had gone on in her marriage, Jackie presented a unified front in public, chiefly for the benefit of her two children. Some things were just private. "The public has no right to know what went on in the bedroom between Jack and me," she would later say. She understood how the game was played, once telling Yusha Auchincloss that "if you make your living in public office, you're the property of every taxpaying citizen. Your whole life is an open book." Jackie figured out how to circumvent the rules, something Diana never did.

"They were very much alike," Yusha said, comparing Jackie and Diana. "The only character dissimilarity was that Diana went public after the royal family publicly humiliated her." Jackie could not comprehend why Diana would wage her marital battle in the press. The scathing headlines and malicious gossip were damaging to her two sons. Nothing good could come out of a child learning the secrets of his parents' marriage through the press. Jackie had firsthand experience of the pain such revelations caused when her parents' divorce made headlines across the country in 1940. "But then," Yusha Auchincloss adds, "Jackie had never been publicly humiliated."

In 1991 Diana secretly collaborated with the writer Andrew Morton on a book that destroyed the myth that hers was a happy marriage. It was a cry for help that reverberated around the world, giving the monarchy its gravest crisis since the abdication of Edward VIII in 1936. Desperate to tell her story from her perspective, she not only encouraged her family and friends to speak candidly with Morton, but agreed to tape hours of her thoughts and deliver them to Morton through an intermediary.

Consenting to do the book was a rare lapse in maternal judgment that Diana would come to regret. Publication of the book, *Diana: Her True Story,* set in motion a series of cataclysmic events: the couple's official separation, Charles's retaliatory biography and television interview, Diana's *Panorama* interview, the queen's instance on a divorce, Diana's summer fling with Dodi Fayed, and the fatal late-night drive through the streets of Paris.

No child, not even those as sheltered and protected as Princes William and Harry, is unaware of the turmoil surrounding the disintegration of his parents' marriage. But there is a great difference between knowing what is going on behind closed doors and having the entire world aware of every thrust and parry between embittered spouses. It seems as if neither Diana nor Charles ever stopped to consider how their actions or words would affect their boys. Diana was the catalyst in the "War of the Waleses," but Charles gave as good as he got.

What child benefits from hearing his father say that he was forced to marry the child's mother out of duty and resignation? What good comes to a child when his parents make public confessions of their adultery? What bonds of trust are broken when a child sees the safe haven of his home and family smashed in full view of millions of prying eyes?

Jackie understood this, but Diana did not. If Jackie ever spoke of these matters with her children, the world will never know. Diana, the queen of people's hearts, the princess of the media age, succumbed to the tenor of the times she lived in, and told all. What effect this has had on her children remains to be seen.

The two young men, William and Harry, are a credit to their mother. They have inherited Diana's relaxed and natural demeanor, which, when blended with Charles's more conservative influence, promises a future monarchy that is both commanding and caring, duty-bound and compassionate. They are her greatest legacy.

Squaw Island, Massachusetts, August 1963

"Mrs. Kennedy, would you like me to call the President?"

"No," Jackie answered firmly, then turned to her doctor and pleaded, "Dr. Walsh, you've got to get me to the hospital on time . . . this baby mustn't be born dead."

The summer had been perfect. The couple had leased a rambling shingled house on Squaw Island, a spit of land about a mile from the Kennedy compound. They had to separate themselves from the compound, where their house was small and close to the public street. It was always filled with special assistants rushing in with memos and kids running around with beach toys. Jackie told her mother that a weekend in the house was as exhausting as the workweek in Washington and that Jack had to escape to his boat to find any peace and quiet. The house on Squaw Island provided them the privacy she craved and the respite he needed.

In April the White House announced that Jackie was expecting a child in September. It would be the first child born to a sitting

President in many years, and the country was enchanted. Jackie's friends joked that she was having a baby in order to avoid campaigning in 1964. That may have been an exaggeration, but Jackie did announce to her staff that she was "taking the veil." Declaring that she had done quite enough as First Lady and that the restoration of the White House was almost complete, Jackie stated that she wanted to spend more time with her children and that she would participate in only the most important state events.

The White House years had brought Jack and Jackie closer. She remembered thinking that summer, "Let me stay this happy with Jack forever." Their relationship had deepened and they shared great happiness at the thought of expanding their family. Because of her past difficulties, Jackie stayed back in the United States during JFK's last trip abroad, to Germany, Ireland, England, and Italy. The four days in Ireland—"That's exactly what I want, a pleasure trip to Ireland"—had been the most magical in JFK's life; when he left, he promised to return the next spring, "with Jackie and the kids."

It was not to be. On August 7 Jackie went into premature labor. She was rushed by helicopter to Otis Air Force Base, where a wing had been prepared for such an emergency. "I don't want anything to happen to this baby," she cried. The baby was born just before one o'clock in the afternoon, weighing four pounds ten ounces; he was soon discovered to suffer from hyaline membrane disease. They named him Patrick Bouvier Kennedy, honoring his Irish and French heritage. The little boy fought valiantly for his life but died less than two days later. Jack was devastated by the loss, and not just at the death of his son. "I can't bear to think of the effect it might have on Jackie," he told Janet Auchincloss, and he showered Jackie with concern.

JFK moved his base of operations up to Hyannis in order to be closer to Jackie during her recuperation. He made twice-daily visits to her side at the hospital, often bringing the children with him. One Sunday after Mass, JFK and Dave Powers were getting ready to leave Squaw Island to go to the hospital when Jack called out to his daughter, who was outside in the garden, "Caroline, are you coming with us?"

"As soon as I pick some flowers for Mummy!" was her reply.

She soon appeared carrying a bouquet of blue larkspur and black-eyed Susans. JFK looked at the flowers, then at his daughter, and said, "Your mother will be proud of you, and so am I."

As Jackie began to recover, Jack told her, "You know, Jackie, we must not create an atmosphere of sadness in the White House because this would not be good for anyone—not for the country and not for the work we have to do." His remark affected her profoundly, and the private grief that they shared drew them closer than ever.

Seven years earlier, in 1956, they had mourned the death of another baby. The difference in Jack Kennedy's behavior toward his wife shows remarkable emotional growth and deep affection. His insensitivity to Jackie's emotional needs after the stillborn death of Arabella was so callous that Jackie seriously considered ending their marriage. Their friends and Jackie's family were appalled by his behavior but did not understand the reasons for it. JFK's emotional coldness was a protective device self-created as a young boy to deal with his feelings of maternal abandonment. Whether Jackie understood that is unclear. Jack was perplexed by Jackie's childbearing difficulties. His mother had had nine children, his sisters and sister-in-law Ethel all were producing babies without complication. Just two days after Arabella's death, Pat Lawford gave birth to a daughter, Sydney, and asked Jackie to be her godmother.

"I don't think [Jack] ever really understood what went with having babies," Jackie told a friend after his death. After a miscarriage in 1954 and the stillbirth, she feared that she would not be able to bear children. She could not reveal that fear to Jack, could not, at that time, make herself vulnerable to him. They were, she once said, like "two icebergs."

The icebergs thawed a little when Caroline was born. She was a cesarian birth, born the day before Thanksgiving on November 27, 1957. "I'll always remember Jack's face when the doctor came into the waiting room and told him that the baby had arrived and that it was a girl and that Jackie was fine and the baby was fine," Janet Auchincloss said. "I will always remember the sweet expression on his face and the way he smiled." The birth date had been arranged, in part, so that the Auchinclosses could travel to Aiken, South Carolina, to spend Thanksgiving with their ten-year-old son, Jamie, who was in boarding school there. Jackie remembered it as the "very happiest day of [my] life."

Caroline's birth was a joyous event, the happiness dulled only by Black Jack Bouvier's death the previous summer. He had been miffed to learn about Jackie's pregnancy from the newspapers and spent most of the summer stewing in his two-bedroom apartment at 125 East Seventy-fourth Street. He had developed a friendship with Yusha Auchincloss and would complain over dinner about how his two daughters weren't paying enough attention to him. Jackie's life was based in Washington, and Lee's in London with her first husband, Michael Canfield. When he fell ill that summer with cancer, no one suspected how serious it was. Yusha alerted Jackie when Black Jack lapsed into a coma, but she arrived at the hospital too late to say good-bye. Nearly six months pregnant, Jackie took charge of the funeral arrangements—"I want it to look like a summer garden, like Lasata in August"—and tenderly placed in her father's hands a gold bracelet he had given her.

Four months after her father's funeral, Jackie returned to St. Patrick's Cathedral for Caroline's baptism. It was held in the Bouvier Chapel, with Lee and Bobby, who had been matron of honor and best man at the wedding, serving as godparents. The Kennedys were there en masse to celebrate, and Jackie felt, perhaps for the first time, like a member of the clan.

Jackie reveled in the delight her husband took in their new baby. "A man without a child is incomplete," she said. "He is so affectionate with [her]. She has made him so much happier." Jack brought his wife and new baby to their first real home, a three-story Federal house at 3307 N Street in Georgetown. The redbrick house would be their home until the day they moved into the White House. Moving in with them was Maud Shaw, the English nurse who would stay with the family until 1965. Shaw was later banished from the inner Kennedy circle after she published her affectionate memoirs, in much the same manner that Marion Crawford, the governess of Princesses Elizabeth and Margaret, had been exiled from the Windsor circle by writing *The Little Princesses* in the late 1940s.

Motherhood gave Jackie a new focus in life. She stood up to Mama Rose, who considered herself the child-raising expert in the family. When Rose would complain that Caroline shouldn't be outside playing when she was going to have her photograph taken, Jackie insisted that her daughter be allowed to live as normal a life as possible. Children should run and play outdoors, not sit inside waiting for their portraits to be taken. When Rose tried to interfere with the way Jackie was raising Caroline, Jackie stopped her cold. "The difference between us," she told her mother-in-law, "is that you want Caroline to grow up to be like you and I want her to grow up and be like me."

Jackie became an aggressively protective mother after the presidential election and the birth of John F. Kennedy Jr. Joe Kennedy had convinced her to let Caroline be photographed for magazine features and newspaper stories. Joe had recognized, early on, the value of television and the importance of image—perception over reality. He knew that Jack, Jackie, and Caroline presented an attractive package to the country, and he revolutionized the way political candidates were presented to the voters. Photographers Jacques Lowe and Mark Shaw were invited into the Kennedys' private world. Their photographs have become iconographic images of the early 1960s. Never before had the public seen their political leaders photographed in such informal and intimate settings, and they were enchanted.

As distasteful as she found it, Jackie allowed the cameras into Caroline's nursery. She, too, understood the impact of a visual image and was willing to put her personal feelings aside in order to help Jack win the presidency. So the cameras came into the house, and onto the beach, becoming an integral part of Jackie's life until the day she died.

Just as the Kennedys were rewriting the rules of politics, the press rewrote the code of conduct they had maintained toward elected officials and covered the Kennedys as if they were movie stars. It was the birth of modern celebrity journalism, as Jackie was to learn the hard way.

Two weeks after the 1960 election, John F. Kennedy Jr. was born. His birth was a month premature and required Jackie to have a second cesarian surgery. She, Jack, and Caroline had enjoyed a quiet Thanksgiving in Georgetown before he flew to Palm Beach that night. Jackie had hoped he would stay in Washington with her, but since the baby wasn't due for a month, Jack thought it safe to go. When Jackie went into emergency labor that night, he was in the air en route to Florida. "I'm never there when she needs me," he told a colleague, and immediately flew back to be at her side.

It was during her convalescence in Georgetown University Hospital that she discovered how much her life had changed. "You're Mrs. Kennedy, aren't you?" a woman asked while she was resting in the hospital's solarium. "I recognize you from your pictures." "I know," she replied, "that's my problem now."

The problem, from Jackie's point of view, was escalating out of control. Photographers hid in hospital closets, jumping out to take ambush shots of her with the baby. She had to leave the hospital in a wheelchair, and when she saw a pack of reporters and photographers waiting by the entrance, she told Jack to wheel her past them without stopping. He paid no attention to her request, stopping to allow pictures to be taken. Jackie hid her anger and fulfilled her duty, smiling for the cameras and offering short, polite answers to the reporters' questions.

Jackie flew down to Florida that afternoon, after Mamie Eisenhower gave her a tour of the White House, which depressed her so much that "it almost sent me back to the hospital with a crying jag." She had wanted to see the family quarters in order to begin planning the children's rooms. The overall condition of the house offended her keen aesthetic sense. For the next few weeks, Jackie formulated two plans: what she would do regarding the White House and how she would conduct herself as First Lady.

In a memo to Pamela Turnure, her press secretary, Jackie stated her philosophy: "I feel strongly that publicity in this era has gotten completely out of hand—and you must really protect the privacy of me and my children. My press relations will be minimum information given with maximum politeness. I won't give any interviews—pose for any photographs, etc.—for the next four years."

Her attitude was both understandable and frustrating. Understandable in that she wanted to create a relatively normal environment for Caroline and John. In the White House the children were surrounded by fawning servants and omnipresent Secret Service agents, so Jackie had her work cut out for her. But she had firsthand experience in seeing the effects of White House living on children. As a child in New York, she had been a friend of President Roosevelt's daughter Kate. Jackie remembered how the continued presence of the Secret Service made her young friend jumpy and irritable. She was determined not to let that happen to Caroline or John.

Her decision to limit press access to Caroline and John met opposition from all corners, even from her own husband. JFK conspired with his press secretary, Pierre Salinger, to have photographers take pictures of the children when Jackie was away from the White House. Salinger would receive the brunt of Jackie's anger. Referring to photographs of the children playing outside at the White House, she wrote, "I want no more—*I mean this*—and if you are firm and will take the time, you can stop it. So please do. What is a press secretary for—to help with the press, yes—but also to protect *us?*" As hard-line as she could be, Jackie never lost her whimsical sense of humor. At the end of her first year in the White House, she gave Salinger a photograph of her, inscribed, "From the greatest cross you have to bear."

Even if JFK agreed with Jackie in principle, he understood that a charming photo essay featuring his children cavorting about the White House would enhance his image. The three years in the White House were a continuing tug-of-war between father and mother. Jackie's fears were on target, for the more the public saw of Caroline and John, the more they wanted. There was a feeding frenzy that Jackie tried to control with a number of innovative steps.

Jackie articulated her feelings to a photographer who agreed to hold back some photographs of Caroline. "I know that newspapers need to print different—or rather unusual pictures—and there is the conflict of trying to raise one's children fairly normally. So when you—who are torn both ways, respect a little girl's chance to have a happy day with the other children who fortunately treat her as just another 4 year old (this is almost the only public place where she isn't singled out and fawned over)—it's amazing and consoling."

Jackie created a school in the White House so Caroline could attend kindergarten and first grade in relatively normal circumstances. It was an extension of a play group that she had started in Georgetown and was funded as a cooperative venture, with each of the twenty or so families dividing up the costs for the teacher, Betsy Boyd, a Vassar graduate, and supplies. The school was progressive in that it was integrated through the inclusion of Avery Hatcher, the son of JFK's assistant press secretary. The school's prime location offered the children a variety of educational goodies. When a contingent of American Indians came to visit the President, they were invited upstairs to meet the children. The youngsters would stand on the balcony and watch the arrivals of state visitors from a unique vantage point.

In creating a harmonious world for her two children, Jackie achieved her primary goal—that life in the White House not turn Caroline and John into "official" children and spoil them. When those years came to a shattering end on November 22, 1963, Jackie's main objective became to protect her children as fiercely as she could. Pierre Salinger remembered Jackie telling him shortly after the assassination: "There's only one thing I can do now. I've got to take care of these kids. I've got to make sure they move forward in life. Because if I don't do that, they'll totally be linked to their father's death."

She broke many of her own rules on the weekend of President Kennedy's funeral. She kept Caroline and John by her side, exposing them to the merciless glare of publicity under the most trying of circumstances. The children did not have to appear with her on the North Portico that Sunday or stand outside St. Matthew's Cathedral the next morning. But Jackie understood the impact of a visual image. She knew that the sight of her two fatherless children, in their powder-blue coats and red leather shoes, would sear itself into the public consciousness. The images from that weekend were so powerful, conveying so much emotion, that Jackie inadvertently forfeited any chance she had of retiring from the public eye.

When Caroline knelt at her father's coffin and slipped her gloved hand up underneath the flag to say good-bye, and when John raised his hand in salute, they became America's children. As such, America considered them public property. Jackie had hoped to return to Georgetown and raise her children in the neighborhood where she had lived with Jack. But the public turned her home into a tourist attraction, leaving sandwich wrappers on her lawn and stealing the house-number sign. Forced from Washington, she moved to New York in the fall of 1964, again setting her children as her top priority.

"I don't want the children to be just two kids living on Fifth Avenue and going to nice schools. . . . I want them to know about how the rest of the world lives, but I also want to give them some kind of sanctuary when they need it, some place to take them into when things happen to them that do not necessarily happen to other children."

She grew even more intensely protective of her children in her years as a single mother. Her most controversial actions from those years—her attempts to censor William Manchester's official account of the assassination, and the Onassis marriage—were taken to shield Caroline and John from the harshest realities of the world. Manchester was approached to write a family-sanctioned account of President Kennedy's assassination. When his book, *The Death of a President,* was about to be published, Jackie fought to have certain passages she deemed too private removed from the manuscript. "When my children grow up," she said, "I don't want them to read all the gruesome stuff about his brain and the way he looked."

Manchester had conducted almost forty hours of taped interviews. With a pitcher of frozen daiquiris to relax her, Jackie talked and talked and talked, assuming that Manchester would use discretion with her memories. When she found he hadn't, she threatened to take him to court, uttering one of her most infamous statements: "Anyone who is against me will look like a rat unless I run off with Eddie Fisher." In the end, Manchester deleted the sections Jackie objected to, but since they had already been leaked to the press, it was a hollow victory. Her reputation took a hit, as she appeared imperious and demanding, but she had her children's interests at heart.

The Onassis marriage was, in many ways, an escape for Jackie. Coming just a little more than four months after Bobby Kennedy's murder, it was an escape from the insanity that was sweeping America. "I wanted to get away," she said. "They were killing Kennedys and I didn't want them to harm my children." She suffered public indignation over her second marriage, but it brought her freedom and security for her children. They stayed in school in New York, taking summer vacations on Onassis's island retreat on Skorpios. This kept them away from their Kennedy cousins during the turbulent years after Robert Kennedy's assassination, years when the cousins banded together, calling themselves the HPTs, or Hyannis Port Terrors. Drugs and alcohol played a large part of those teenage years, and by removing her kids from that atmosphere, Jackie helped them avoid the troubles that plagued so many of their Kennedy cousins.

Both Caroline and John grew up to become exemplary adults, conscious of their heritage yet not overwhelmed by it. Whereas Caroline inherited Jackie's shy reserve and absorbing intelligence, John inherited her dazzling star quality. She was justifiably proud of both of them. Caroline, a lawyer and author, married in 1986 and had three children, turning Jackie into "GrandJackie," a role she adored. John graduated from law school and worked as a district attorney in New York.

John had neither married nor embarked upon his career as a magazine publisher by the time Jackie died. He married a strikingly beautiful woman in September 1996 and founded a political magazine, *George*. In both endeavors there are signs of Jackie's influence. She would have loved the fact that he hoodwinked the press and was able to be married in total secrecy on an island off the coast of Georgia. His simple wedding echoed her desire for the intimate ceremony she had wanted in 1953 and actually had in 1968. Jackie had come close to working at a magazine in 1951 and would have appreciated John's drive and focus. Here was a way for him to partake in a family calling without having to endure the rigors and pitfalls of being a political candidate.

John Kennedy's death in the summer of 1999, when the plane he was piloting crashed into the waters off Martha's Vineyard, killing him, his wife, and her sister, sent a seismic shock wave throughout the world, on a par with Diana's death two years earlier. The reaction was similar: deep shock and dismay. The only sense of relief came from the unstated but deeply felt sense of gratitude that Jackie was spared this last tragedy. "Thank God Jackie's not alive to see this" was the heartfelt feeling of those who cared for Jackie and knew how the death of her beloved son would have crushed her spirit.

Chapter Twelve

Supernovas

One minute I was nobody, the next minute I was Princess of Wales, mother, media toy, member of this family, you name it.

—Diana, on her fame

JACKIE IS THE TOP BOX OFFICE FEMME IN THE WORLD
—*Variety* headline, 1962

The term *first class* is used to mean "the best," but these days *first class* somehow isn't quite good enough to express the ultimate height, hence the use of *world class* as, for the time being, the definitive superlative. In much the same way, the word *superstar* has become trite and overused. The dictionary definition of *superstar* is "one that is very prominent or is a prime attraction," but that doesn't begin to capture the excitement and glamour generated by Diana and Jackie when they made their debuts on the world stage.

They were more than superstars; they were what *Webster's* defines as an "explosion . . . in which the star may reach a maximum intrinsic luminosity one billion times that of the sun," or, in clearer terms, as "one that explodes into prominence or popularity." That is what happened to Jackie in the spring of 1961, and to Diana exactly twenty years later. They burst onto the scene as supernovas.

Interest in both women was intense and worldwide. People followed their activities, admired them, copied them, even worshiped them. They became leaders in fashion and style, and role models as mothers and young wives. People saw their better selves in Jackie's behavior after the death of her first husband and identified with the darker side of Diana's pain and rage as her marriage to Prince Charles disintegrated.

Diana and Jackie may have had the same effect on the world, but the ways in which they dealt with their stardom were completely different, and in these differences we find a key to their characters. Jackie had the upper hand here. She understood what this fame business was all about. Partly because of her relationship with her father, she was accustomed to being adored, as odd as that may sound. She took it as her due. If someone failed to fall under her spell, the problem was with that person, not with her. Jackie also enjoyed a seven-year apprenticeship as the wife of a public figure. She may have been tossed into the Kennedy maelstrom, but public attention was controlled and limited to events surrounding JFK's political campaigns. When the dam of publicity burst in 1960 and 1961, she understood the ephemeral nature of fame, and its essential meaninglessness. Jackie once summed up her attitude succinctly: "That river of sludge will go on and on. It isn't about me."

Diana didn't get that. She couldn't quite believe that her fame, even her notoriety, hadn't become an intrinsic part of her character. She grew up feeling so adrift, so unmoored, that it became second nature for her to accept the adoration as confirmation of her talents, ability, and self. Diana loved the adulation, and when it slipped away, her life became one increasingly frantic attempt after another to regain it. Jackie, at best, was bemused by her celebrity and used it only when it suited her purposes. She could evade it quickly if she wanted to and didn't miss it when it wasn't there. She was honestly perplexed about her unending celebrity status, telling her friend Jayne Wrightsman two years before her death, "I'm sixty-two now and I've been in the public eye for more than thirty years. I can't believe that anybody still cares about me or is still interested in what I do."

Diana lived for the public's fascination, and came to see it as part and parcel of her life's calling. She continually spoke of the people she came to see as her fan base. She told an interviewer that the "man on the street...matters more [to me] than anything else." Unlike Jackie, Diana had no inner reserve of self-approval. Not being able to find it within herself, she turned to external approbation. The support of her fans sustained her. Diana acknowledged her debt to them in a way that Jackie would have found abhorrent and unhealthy. During her famous BBC interview, Diana spoke to her public with an eerie disconnect reminiscent of *Sunset Boulevard*'s demented movie star, Norma Desmond: "I want to reassure all those people who have loved me and supported me throughout the last fifteen years that I'd never let them down." She was perpetually ready for *her* close-up.

Gloria Steinem once said about Jackie that "part of her uniqueness was an ability to distance herself from her public image, to ignore the obsessive interest of strangers and to refuse to read most of what was written about her." Diana was the polar opposite, finding succor in the kindness of strangers. According to her private secretary Patrick Jephson, she devoured newspaper accounts of her activities and adjusted her mood according to the tone of her daily press coverage. In the early stages of their marriage, Charles understood and sympathized with Diana's predicament, writing to a friend, "How can anyone, let alone a twenty-one-year-old, be expected to come out of all of this obsessed and crazed attention unscathed?"

Despite their different reactions to celebrity, both women's initial impact was dazzling, and very real. They both captivated the world, first through their looks and clothes, then through their public behavior in both good and bad times, then lastly by their innate character. The historian Doris Kearns Goodwin told Jackie's biographer Sarah Bradford that "culturally something happened between [Jackie] and the decade that she lived in, and that is what is really interesting to try and figure out." What applied to Jackie and the 1960s is much the same as what happened with Diana and the 1980s.

Washington, D.C., November 9, 1985

It was as dazzling an evening as the White House had seen in over twenty years, and was Diana's apogee as a supernova. She and Charles had come to Washington in their roles as patrons of the

Treasure Houses of Britain exhibition at the National Gallery—which included a Fabergé letter opener from their private collection—and Ronald and Nancy Reagan held a dinner dance in their honor. It was the most sought-after social invitation of the Reagan presidency. An intoxicating guest list of Hollywood glamour, Washington power, and New York society gathered in the East Room for cocktails as the President and First Lady waited on the North Portico for the royal couple to arrive.

People literally gasped at Diana's radiance as she emerged from the British embassy's dark green Rolls-Royce. As she and Charles took their places on either side of the Reagans, posing for the assembled photographers, she was clearly the center of attention. Diana looked exquisite that night, sophisticated and glamorous in an ink-blue silk velvet gown, statuesque and regal next to Nancy Reagan in a silver white-beaded gown. The Victor Edelstein dress had cap sleeves that gave Diana a subtle sexuality, baring her creamy white shoulders and gently enhancing her breasts. She wore one of her most spectacular pieces of jewelry, an enormous oval sapphire set in a seven-row pearl choker. The gem, mined in Sri Lanka, was a wedding gift from the Queen Mother. It had originally been a brooch, but Diana had it converted into a necklace; that night was one of the first occasions she wore it.

The Reagans took special care to invite a mixture of guests who would appeal to the royal couple. Diana sat between the President and ballet dancer Mikhail Baryshnikov; opera singer Leontyne Price, a great favorite of Prince Charles, was invited to sing; and at the specific request of the princess, John Travolta was there to be her dancing partner. As Nancy Reagan led the movie actor to Diana, he sheepishly inquired, "Is touch dancing permissible?" When assured that it was, he swept Diana onto the marble floor and did a modified swing dance to the Marine band's rendition of "You're the One That I Want." "She's good," recalled the dancing sensation of *Grease* and *Saturday Night Fever*. "She's got style and good rhythm."

While Travolta found Diana "charming, adorable and down-to-earth," another film star enjoyed a more flirtatious moment with her. "You're too old for me," Clint Eastwood told the princess as they danced together. "But I'm only twenty-four," Diana protested with coquettish glee, looking up at the six-foot-four movie idol and batting her eyes. They made a handsome couple, as Eastwood was well matched with the statuesque princess, who stood just over six feet in her medium heels. Using a line made famous in one of his films, Eastwood told reporters that his fox-trot with Diana "made his day."

The four-day trip to the United States had been an enormous success, reminiscent of the state visit of Charles's grandparents in the late 1930s. The Reagans took pleasure in the Waleses' visit as much as the Roosevelts had enjoyed that of George VI and Elizabeth. Nancy Reagan was a favorite of Prince Charles; she was one of the "older, elegant" women whose company he enjoyed. Nancy, who had attended Charles and Diana's wedding, told Diana, "My husband has a sharp eye for a beautiful woman." Diana's canny assessment of the President: "Charm to his hair roots."

The Waleses were featured on the cover of *Time* magazine, where a ten-page story heralded their arrival at the peak of popular-culture celebrity. They were the most famous couple in the world. They didn't quite do anything other than cut ribbons and visit hospital wards, but thousands of people turned up just for a glimpse of the dazzling couple.

Diana's clothes were one of the major reasons people lined up to see her. "What would she be wearing?" was the question most often asked, and her two official dressers would issue daily reports to the press on the details of her ensembles. Diana's influence on fashion was comparable to that of only one other public figure: Jackie Kennedy. Both women revitalized their country's fashion industry, but whereas Jackie had been a longtime devotee of haute couture, Diana literally started from scratch.

"On the day we got engaged," she remembered, "I literally had one long dress, one silk shirt, one smart pair of shoes, and that was it." She had to build up a wardrobe that covered three seasons of active public duty, often requiring a complete change of clothing four times a day. Diana made a very wise choice in seeking assistance from Anna Harvey, the editor of British *Vogue*. Harvey introduced Diana to the best British designers, and under her tutelage Diana developed a keen fashion sense. "It happened before our very eyes," recalled photographer Jayne Fincher, "the transformation from this shy teenager ... into the self-assured woman ... confident in her beauty.... I really saw no evidence of vanity in her, and sometimes I looked pretty hard."

Diana's fashion sense evolved as she created strong working relationships with such designers as Catherine Walker and Victor Edelstein. Her style became simple, pared-down elegance, moving away from the billowing gowns and ruffled sleeves of her early years in the public eye. Her choices are interesting and telling: the romantic look of the early years, the pastels and flounces, replaced by more severe lines and sharp colors of her later public wardrobe.

This shift in Diana's public appearance in the middle years of her marriage, 1985 to 1990, corresponds with the internal struggle she was facing. The contradiction of external perfection and internal turmoil was absurd and cruel; her life was falling apart as her star continued to ascend.

Both Charles and Diana turned outside their marriage to find both spiritual and physical comfort. Charles's relationship with Camilla Parker Bowles was a constant source of dismay to Diana, chipping away at her confidence until she found comfort in the arms of army captain James Hewitt. Diana described Hewitt as "a great friend of mine at a very difficult time," which is almost identical to Charles's description of Camilla as a "very close, very good friend." Diana had met Hewitt on the polo fields, where he often played for the army team opposing Prince Charles and the navy squad. Hewitt became Diana's riding instructor, helping her overcome a fear of horses that stemmed from a childhood accident in which she broke her arm.

The dashing Hewitt was no stranger to London society. A single, well-born officer in the Life Guards, the most prestigious army regiment, is perpetually welcomed at the dinner tables and cocktail parties of London's smart set. "God gave him piercing blue eyes, wavy russet hair, and an enormous dick," an ex-girlfriend told *Tatler,* "but He didn't give him much of a brain." Hewitt had the easy relationship around the royal family that grew out of shared equestrian interests. He fell into a comfortable teacher-mentor relationship with Diana, who came to trust him, sharing many confidences about her life and the troubles in her marriage. They became lovers and carried on an intense romance for several years, ending when Hewitt's regiment was sent to the Gulf War in the early 1990s.

The risks Diana took in having an adulterous affair were enormous, much more perilous for her than for Charles. Society held a double standard whereby men's infidelities were tacitly condoned, but women's were roundly condemned. A man could have an affair and be considered a fit, if wayward, father; a woman under the same circumstances was branded a bad mother and an immoral harlot. Diana had seen firsthand the treatment her mother endured, the banishment Frances Shand Kydd received from her own family as a result of her extramarital affair. Such was her despair that she took the risk, which in the end cost her dearly, as Hewitt would come to betray her as surely as Charles did.

Part of the reason for the difficulties in Charles and Diana's marriage comes from the very nature of their jobs. The life of Prince of Wales is one of perpetual anticipation, waiting for one's parent to die so one can assume the only job one will ever have. With nothing to do but wait, the endless rounds of official visits, polo matches, and country weekends drone on and on. With few shared interests and less in common on an intellectual plane, it's no surprise that the couple ran into difficulties. They were supporting characters in the monarchy pageant, and troubles grew as Diana continued to steal the show.

The royal family came to regard Diana as a loose cannon and an outsider. She was not what she had appeared to be, hardly the docile young creature they thought they could mold into a partner for Charles. The introduction of Sarah Ferguson into the family in 1986 caused further feelings of isolation in Diana. "I wish you could be more like Fergie—all jolly," Charles would tell her. "Why are you always so miserable?" Diana admitted to being "terribly jealous" of the welcome Sarah received. Ruth Fermoy had seen it coming, warning her granddaughter, "Darling, you must understand that [the royals'] sense of humor and their lifestyle are different. . . . I don't think it will suit you."

Diana came into her own within the marriage in 1988, during a skiing holiday in Klosters, Switzerland. Suffering from the flu, Diana was resting in her chalet with Fergie when word came that there had been an avalanche and that one of the skiing party, which included Charles, had died. For a tense forty-five minutes the two sisters-in-law waited, anticipating the worst, until Charles telephoned Sarah to say that he was unharmed. Major Hugh Lindsay, the queen's former equerry and close friend of Charles, had died. Diana took charge in the ensuing shock and confusion, telling Charles, "We're going home . . . we owe it to [Lindsay's wife] Sarah to take the body home." Charles at first wanted to stay and continue the vacation, but despite "tremendous arguments," Diana prevailed.

Diana recognized it as the turning point in her life with Charles. "I took charge there," she said. "My husband made me feel so inadequate in every possible way that each time I came up for air he pushed me down again." She fought back, and the newfound inner strength enabled her to control her bulimia for the first time in years. "When my bulimia finished," she told a friend, "I felt so much stronger mentally and physically . . . able to soldier on in the world."

She was able to move beyond the crippling fear and insecurity and began to establish her own identity as Princess of Wales, and as the 1980s came to an end, she began to map out her own destiny.

There's a long tradition in the royal family of its members' giving their support and patronage to various worthy causes, the military and charitable institutions being two of the most notable. Hospitals, children's wards, and shelters for the poor are among the most traditional arenas where the royal family earns its keep. In the late 1980s Diana became patron of the first British AIDS ward. Her association with the deadly disease would bring her as much personal reward as anything she had done in her life. The images that flashed around the world, of Diana shaking hands with a gay man dying of

AIDS—gloveless, despite the fact that Buckingham Palace suggested she wear gloves to protect herself—was of immense public service. "It made a tremendous impact," recalled Dr. Mike Adler, the ward's head doctor, "a member of the royal family *touching* someone. It was a colossal impact. It shouldn't have been, but it was."

In tackling as controversial an issue as AIDS was in its early years, Diana was both a traditionalist and a rebel. While visiting hospitals was a time-honored royal role, embracing those struck with what was then called "the gay plague" was a brave and commendable choice. It indicates her newfound level of confidence. Her work with AIDS patients recalls the tender interest of the nineteenth-century Princess of Wales, who later became Queen Alexandra, consort of Edward VII, in John Merrick, the Elephant Man. Alexandra befriended the grossly disfigured Merrick when others shunned him. Diana embraced those suffering with AIDS at a time when society was fearful and disapproving.

Her interest ran more deeply than visiting sick wards and shaking hands. She offered real comfort to those suffering from AIDS and also to their loved ones. She had an uncanny knack of being able to anticipate their feelings of guilt and anger, and offered moments of friendship and understanding. Diana spent over five months helping care for her friend Adrian Ward Jackson as he succumbed to the disease. She brought her son William, then age nine, with her when she visited Jackson, helping to dispel any fear her son might have had either of the disease or of death in general. When Jackson's conditioned worsened, Diana drove through the night from Balmoral to sit with him, stroking his hand and resisting pressure from the royal family to pay a token visit and return to Scotland.

Diana did as much as any other public person to raise AIDS awareness around the globe, as much as anyone outside of the medical profession did to destigmatize the disease in the eyes of a suspicious world. There was a mystical connection between her and those suffering from AIDS, some inner sense of suffering that she identified with. When Diana would hold an AIDS baby, she took on the aura of a neo-Madonna, a pietà in Prada. Yet there was honesty in that connection, and Diana benefited greatly.

She found an inner peace, telling a friend, "I'm much happier now. I'm not blissful but much more content than I've ever been. I've really gone down deep, scraped the bottom a couple of times and come up again." On the upswing, she was ready to face life with an honesty and sense of purpose she hadn't felt before.

Washington, May 11, 1962

Nearly a quarter century before Diana's triumphant evening at the White House, Jacqueline Kennedy was hostess to an equally splendid party that signaled the apex of her career as chatelaine of the White House. André Malraux, the French minister for cultural affairs, came for dinner, and Jackie used the evening to further many of the causes she championed. Malraux was a war hero, a member of the French resistance, and a highly regarded author. Jackie had met him the previous year during her triumphant visit to France, when he had escorted her through the Jeu de Paume museum a few days after his two young sons had died in a car accident.

One of Jackie's goals upon entering the White House was to foster an appreciation for American culture and art. Inviting Malraux to the White House, and according him all the honors of a state visit, was a brilliant and effective use of her position to promote her agenda. The Kennedys gathered an impressive array of American creative artists at the White House that night: painters Andrew Wyeth and Mark Rothko; composer Leonard Bernstein; playwrights Thornton Wilder, Arthur Miller, and Tennessee Williams; directors Elia Kazan and Lee Strasberg; choreographer George Balanchine; actresses Julie Harris and Geraldine Page: writers John Hersey, Robert Lowell, and Saul Bellow; and the great American aviation hero Colonel Charles Lindbergh and his wife, writer Anne Morrow Lindbergh.

In bringing the best American artists together in the president's home, the Kennedys signaled their approval of the arts in American life. In his after-dinner toast, JFK told his guests that "we do not manage our cultural life in this country . . . but it is an important part. It is one of the great purposes. And I would hope that this tremendous energy obtained in the intellectual life of America could be communicated not only to people in this country but all around the world."

This was part of Jackie's plan. She remembered how "my step-uncle Wilmarth Lewis once told me, 'There were three geniuses of the eighteenth century, and two of them were American—Jefferson, Franklin and Diderot.' Why shouldn't the White House represent that tradition to the nation and to foreign visitors of state? Why should it not inspire people, make them proud of their country's heritage?"

Malraux was so charmed by the Kennedys, and by Jackie in particular, that at the end of the evening he promised to send Leonardo da Vinci's masterpiece, the *Mona Lisa,* to Washington on loan from the Louvre. It was a spectacular evening from start to finish. Jackie was more dazzling than any of her guests. Her pink silk shantung Christian Dior gown set off her cocoa brown tan. The strapless dress left her shoulders elegantly bare and in her hair she wore an eighteenth-century diamond starburst pin.

It was through her clothes that Jackie made her first impact upon the world. Never one to seek personal publicity, she essentially stopped talking to reporters once she entered the White House. The press, unable to interview her, wrote about her clothes. Jackie was lionized for her youthful fashionable appearance. She revolutionized the American fashion industry, breaking the stronghold that Paris and Rome had enjoyed as centers of couture. Jackie made it possible for American women to wear American clothes and be considered well dressed. Her fashion influence was global and pervasive. When she wore a leopard-skin coat, demands for the pelt grew to the point that leopards were placed on the endangered species list, where they remain to this day.

She didn't enjoy the fuss made over her wardrobe. "She hated all the attention and the asking how much this cost and how much that cost," her social secretary, Tish Baldrige, remembered. "She just wanted to be well dressed and not have people asking all those questions." Nor could she understand why people considered her beautiful. "She was very modest, she thought she was ugly, she always said Lee was the beautiful one," Yusha Auchincloss recalled. "She would always say, 'I have big eyes, a pug nose and great big lips.' "

The first hints of her international stardom came during a short trip she took with JFK to Canada in May 1961. JFK began to regard his wife with renewed appreciation as the crowds cheered her. Their triumphant state visit to Paris later that month and his summit with Khrushchev in Vienna both benefited from her dynamic presence. The two of them, Jack and Jackie, were a picture of youthful vigor, the perfect representatives of the leading democracy in the world.

One major difference between Diana and Jackie is that Jackie knew who she was before this massive public adulation was thrown at her. She used it to benefit the causes she found important, and the cause she found most important was supporting her husband. There may have been a subtle tug-of-war with JFK at certain points in their tumultuous relationship, but she never once sought to publicly undermine his stature. Regardless of the state of her marriage, she never used her personal popularity against her husband, as Diana did against Charles. Jackie knew that public acclaim was fickle, and it never became an important part of her life.

In September 1960 Jackie told the *Today* show, "I have always thought the main duty [of the First Lady] is to preserve the President . . . so he can be of best service to his country, and that means running a household smoothly around him, and helping him in any way he might ask you to." One way she helped Jack was by creating a relaxing atmosphere for him, both in the White House and away from it. She went so far as to ask Janet and Hughdie to vacate Hammersmith Farm so that the first couple could spend a relaxing weekend there in October 1961. Jack was "laughing and full of jokes and sunburned and healthy" after a short vacation, not "preoccupied and exhausted the way he has been all winter." She complained that the Hyannis Port house was cramped and lacked privacy, as opposed to Hammersmith, where they sat on the terrace "just looking at the bay and drinking in the beauty" for hours. She thanked her mother for doing a patriotic service, letting the President find rest and comfort at the home she had loved for twenty years. Whatever feelings

Jackie may have had about JFK's extramarital activities, she had made her peace with them and was willing to move forward as her husband's helpmate.

The wife of one of Jackie's male friends, with whom she shared a polite if not warm relationship, offered this observation of Jackie during her White House years: "She's a very interesting person. A *jeune fille, bien élevé*, not particularly an intellectual but with a good deal of intuitive cleverness. At least that is my impression of her— bright, interested in art and literature and with a wicked sense of humor and irony and a satiric eye."

Humor was a godsend, with her living in the public fishbowl of the White House. She kept it well guarded, never offering a glimpse of her wicked tongue in public. Thanking a friend for a gag Christmas present, she told him, "Just as Jayne Mansfield wants to be admired for her mind—so I—the recipient of many art books this Christmas—am delighted with a red plastic bathing suit cut to the navel. I will wear it to the opening of the National Cultural Center."

In private she could toss off zingers to those who weren't on her wavelength. She thought that the man heading the commission to preserve Pennsylvania Avenue had "interesting ideas—but he does sound like a conceited little snot!" She instructed a friend to "make it quite clear that he can't behave [like] a little tyrant and throw his T-square on the floor and leave in a huff." She asked for the man in question's height, adding that "all my theories will be blown up if he is over 5'2"."

Even her friends weren't immune to her scathing tongue. Planning a guest list for a state dinner, Tish Baldrige sent Jackie a note suggesting she include her Vassar classmate Scotty Lanahan, the daughter of Jazz Age writer F. Scott Fitzgerald. "I know you're mad at her," Tish wrote, "but golly, gee, Scotty has been bearing the torch for you all over Washington." Jackie's response was swift: "I'm not mad anymore but the 2 times I've seen Scotty she has gotten tight & really made a slight spectacle—some other time."

The public never saw this side of Jackie; it was kept as firmly under wraps as her smoking. Bill Walton, the artist and close friend of both JFK's and Jackie's, remembered that "at an official luncheon at the Commodore in New York City, Jackie took Mayor Wagner's place card and sent it to me." She wrote, "That boy with the crew cut, very young, 3 to your left—keeps taking pictures of me smoking—he just got one—can you get it—also Jack with beer." Walton remembered that "she worried so about such photos. I, of course, was unable to seize the young man's film."

When Jackie entered the White House, her plans included both a physical restoration of the Executive Mansion and an aesthetic restoration of Washington as a cultural hub, with the White House at its epicenter. She had learned from Janet Auchincloss the skills needed to run a great house; she knew how to supervise a staff of servants and get the maximum effort from them. JFK was skilled at this as well. Tish Baldrige said that JFK "was like a wonderful department store manager who goes through the store and knows everybody's name and knows how all the departments work and knows how to wrap packages better than the wrappers do."

Jackie started restoring the White House on her first full day in residence. Working first with her decorator, Sister Parish, and later with the French head of Jansen, Stephane Boudin, she was able to turn what had been a sadly shabby interior into a first-rate museum of American presidential and decorative history. Within two years the State Floor had been restored to its early-nineteenth-century splendor. As attendance for the public tours of the White House skyrocketed, Jackie created a guidebook whose profits funded the restoration. She would host a televised tour in February 1962 that won her an honorary Emmy. Jackie also used her influence to have Congress designate the White House a museum so that its interiors and contents were protected in perpetuity.

Just as she created a lavish setting for the presidency, Jackie set about revolutionizing White House entertainment. The Kennedys introduced what Harold Macmillan called "a casual sort of grandeur." They relaxed White House entertaining, following the rules of economist Bernard Baruch, who said, "I don't have any protocol in my household. Those who matter don't mind, and those who mind don't matter."

From exchanging the large U-shaped banquet table for small circular tables for ten that would make for livelier conversations, to having Jerome Robbins create jazz dance ballets for after-dinner entertainment, Jackie's innovations made the White House an exciting, vibrant place. For the first time in many years, the First Lady was the premiere hostess in Washington, D.C. The Kennedy parties were legendary, entertaining Nobel Prize winners and African emperors, European duchesses and Iranian shahs.

The Kennedys also entertained privately, holding five or six large dinner dances during their White House years and small dinner parties for six or eight on average twice a week. "One of the few nice things about being here," Jackie told Hughdie's former stepson Gore Vidal, "is we can get to meet everyone we've ever wanted to meet." They invited screen legend Greta Garbo to a small dinner in the second-floor private dining room. Garbor enjoyed herself, later telling Vidal, "The President took me into his bedroom. So romantic. Then he gave me a whale's tooth and we went back to Mrs. *Jah*-kee, who said, 'He never gave *me* a whale's tooth.' "

Another friend was able to see a private side of the Kennedys' relationship. "I remember going there to dinner . . . and Jackie coming into the room in a very good-looking suit that she had obviously paid a lot of money for—Chanel, I remember—and his drawing attention to this and saying, 'Well, how much did you pay for that, Jackie?' You know, half kidding and half mock irritation at how much she had paid, and at the same time there was an element of showing off. It was sort of cute and fun . . . this kidding was a form of communication."

Jackie worked hard at creating a life for her family in the White House. In June of 1962 she told a friend, "Now my life is the way I want it—though deadly little details always do crop up, but not enough to spoil the atmosphere I want for Jack + me + our children. . . . If I can do it, so can you."

Having perfected a domestic life, Jackie took her act on the road, traveling more than any other previous First Lady. She made state visits to France, Austria, England, Columbia, Venezuela, and Mexico, semi-state visits to India and Pakistan, and private trips to Italy, Greece, and Morocco. She was feted all over the globe. Everywhere she went, more and more was demanded of her, a visit to a school, a tour of a museum, a reception for local dignitaries.

Jackie learned to pace herself and was not shy about saying no. The schedule for her trip to India and Pakistan was in danger of overwhelming her with activities until she put her foot down. "Exhaustion is a factor men can't understand," Jackie told Pamela Turnure. She understood the impact of her public appearances. "If I do big things well," she said, "[the] trip will be a success. If I get tired, it will all be ruined."

Jackie set her own course and did the things she wanted to do. She was admired all over the globe. After her first year in the role of First Lady, she warmed to it, telling a friend, "Think of this time we're living through. Both of us young, with health and two wonderful children—and to live through all of this."

Chapter Thirteen

Smashing the Archetypes:
The Rebels Within

*I think I'm going to cut a very different path from everyone else;
I'm going to break away from this set-up and go and help the man
on the street.*

—Diana, 1991

*I just told Tish . . . that I would NEVER go out—lunches, teas,
degrees, speeches, etc. For 2 months there was a flap—now it is a
precedent established.*

—Jackie, 1962

Diana and Jackie share a legacy—each took an archetypal role and
smashed it. Both women married into situations in which their roles
were clearly defined, and surprisingly similar. Though they entered
married life thirty years apart from each other, the expectations for
the wife of an American politician in the 1950s were no different
from those of the wife of the Prince of Wales in the 1980s. You stood
behind your husband, both literally and figuratively, lent your name
to charitable causes, and steered clear of controversy.

The women who were Diana's and Jackie's immediate predeces-
sors are excellent illustrations of the archetype: the Queen Mother,
as duchess of York; Princess Marina, the duchess of Kent; Bess Tru-

man; and Mamie Eisenhower. Whatever the private circumstances of their marriages, whatever the strengths and weaknesses of their husbands, these women accepted their roles without question. They found happiness and maintained equilibrium despite the pressure of public life, despite marriages to men who could be difficult husbands (Prince George, the duke of Kent, Dwight Eisenhower) or men who inherited power under stressful circumstances (King George VI and Harry Truman). Nancy Reagan is regarded as the epitome of the ideal official spouse. But even she couldn't get it quite right. Mrs. Reagan's über-wife persona—the adoring gaze and unwavering loyalty to her husband—was offset by revelations of fierce behind-the-scenes power struggles and her inability to tap into the mood of the country. By appearing insensitive to those less fortunate while displaying a craving for imperial trappings, she wound up having as many detractors as admirers.

Both Diana and Jackie possessed a keen awareness of the tenor of their times. This understanding enabled them to make radical changes in the way they performed their jobs. Whereas Diana eagerly sought entry into the whirl of the royal family through her marriage, Jackie, for the most part, merely tolerated the political life that came with hers. Diana came to the role of Princess of Wales eager to fit in, do a good job, and make her husband proud of her. Over time, despite the disappointment and disillusionment of a marriage turned sour, Diana came to understand that she had both the skills and the unique position to change the way the monarchy conducted its business. As she started to carve out an individual role for herself, she selected causes that would benefit from her support. The fact that these causes were far removed from the royal norm only focused more attention on them. Diana received acclaim from most quarters. Only the palace establishment, which felt that hugging babies infected with the AIDS virus reflected badly on the monarchy, were critical. Diana gave the royal family the humanity necessary to ease its passage into the twenty-first century.

Jackie approached the White House with trepidation. She "dreaded" the thought of life there, fearing it would take her away from her children and her husband. To her surprise, she quickly learned that she saw more of him, and they spent more time together as a family, than she had throughout her seven-year marriage. Unlike her Kennedy mother- and sisters-in-law, Jackie was not a natural politician. Once she had completed her obligations as a political wife by helping elect JFK President, she limited the amount of time she would spend on anything that a "traditional" political wife considered an essential part of the job. Her attitude was due in equal parts to her natural shyness and her wide range of interests in everything but politics. The areas to which she devoted her considerable talents and power were projects that appealed to her interest in history and the arts. She ran into opposition from everyone, from JFK on down, but her vision was backed by clearly stated arguments, a strong sense of patriotism, and sheer determination. She did the things she wanted to do, the way she wanted to do them. Jacqueline Kennedy was the wife of the President for only thirty-four months, but her power changed the White House forever and influenced the nation's attitudes toward culture and the arts.

London, 1995

Fifteen years into her job as a royal princess, Diana was in a unique position. As the wife of the heir to the throne, she was the ultimate insider. But as a commoner who married into that position, she was also the ultimate outsider. What was the norm for the other members of the family—a life lived according to rigid protocol, prescribed modes of behavior, being surrounded by sycophantic advisers—was a life that Diana could not help but question. It would never occur to Charles or Anne to ask why something was done a certain way, because it had *always* been done that way. If Diana observed something that didn't make sense to her, she questioned it. When her questions fell on deaf ears, she changed the way she conducted her public life. She learned to trust her instincts more and the palace advisers less.

Because of her unequaled stature, Diana was capable of being of real service to the monarchy. She had the common touch; her instincts rarely failed her in public. Like the Queen Mother, Diana brought warmth to a monarchy that often seemed cold and emotionless. But unlike anyone else in the family, she had a contemporary outlook that brought relevance to the way the royals conducted business. The Windsors often seemed out of step with modern life. For the monarchy to thrive in the twenty-first century, it would have to be flexible and adapt to the times. No one was better suited than Diana to help the monarchy achieve this.

Where Diana created a problem for herself, a problem that led to her eventual failure, was that, unlike Jackie, she did not play the game by the rules. Jackie may not have liked, or even respected, the rules, but she understood the way the game was played. Jackie subtly manipulated the rules, whereas Diana ruthlessly ignored them. She was a renegade, a royal rebel. Her eating disorder gave Diana an addict's mind-set: she judged herself by her intentions, but the royal family judged her by her actions. In her eyes she was helping modernize the monarchy; in their eyes, she was a loose cannon.

It didn't have to be that way. The Palace hadn't given much, if any, thought to what role the Princess of Wales might play. "No one sat me down with a piece of paper and said: 'This is what is expected of you,'" Diana told Martin Bashir during her BBC interview in 1995. There hadn't been a wife to the heir for four generations, since Charles's great-grandmother Queen Mary became Princess of Wales in 1901. The most recent addition to the senior branch of the royal family had been Philip in 1947. The palace was out of practice indoctrinating new members into the "firm," and their viewpoint could hardly be called progressive. Diana was expected to do nothing more than accompany Charles on his rounds, cut ribbons at hospital dedications, and bear children.

Her first exposure to this sort of life came three months after the wedding during a three-day trip to Wales. Diana was two months pregnant, but the news had not been made public. In addition, she had begun to harbor doubts about her marriage: the past two months had been emotionally difficult. To top it off, it did nothing but rain in Wales, and she was continually soaked. Nonetheless, she was a triumph. She responded to public life with a natural skill, making easy personal contact with the crowds who lined the streets waiting for her. The crowds cheered for Diana and ignored Charles. At first the novelty of playing second fiddle amused him, but soon his bruised ego and a sense of self-pity emerged. "They don't want to see me" was a frequent complaint, and several times he barked at the crowd when they asked about Diana, "She's over there. Do you want your money back?"

Diana's star continued to rise, and her popularity came to dwarf that of her husband and the rest of his family. Charles was so annoyed that after the first few years, he insisted that they maintain separate schedules of public engagements. Diana understood that the lopsided attention was hard on Charles: "It [the press attention on her] made it very difficult... basically we were a married couple doing the same job, which is difficult for anyone, and more so if you've got all the attention on you. We struggled a bit with it; it was very difficult."

The tensions in their marriage and Diana's inability, or unwillingness, to hide her emotions did not endear her to the royal family. She once said, "Maybe I was the first person ever to be in this family who was ever openly tearful. And obviously that was daunting, because if you've never seen it before, how do you support it?" No one in the royal family seemed willing to help her; perhaps they were incapable of giving her the help she needed. During the tour of Wales, she saw photographer Ken Lennox and asked, "How am I doing, Ken?" The photographer laughed and gave her a thumbs-up. She would later say that there were never compliments when she had done a good job, only complaints when she made a mistake. For a young woman barely out of her teens, such negative feedback was devastating.

Diana dealt with those negative feelings both inwardly and outwardly. She internalized them by battling her eating disorder. She externalized them by embracing those whose lives were engulfed in pain. The external manifestations of her feelings led to her greatest success in the public arena. Her brother recalled her telling him that "it was her innermost feelings of suffering that made it possible for her to connect with her constituency of the rejected." Diana opened doors that the monarchy had kept closed. She wore her emotions on her sleeve. Her career as "queen of people's hearts" (a title that first appeared in a newspaper headline during the trip to Wales) came at the same time as the start of the "let it all hang out" wave of television programs (*Oprah, Donahue,* et al.).

Diana's spontaneity was in direct contrast to her mother-in-law's buttoned-up self-control. When people complained that the queen seemed cold and remote in emotionally trying circumstances, they failed to grasp that Elizabeth had been trained from childhood to hold back her emotions. She kept them firmly in check while on duty and in the presence of anyone but her family and trusted friends. Though Diana was most often compared with the Queen Mother, the member of the royal family she most closely resembled was the Danish princess Alexandra, who married Queen Victoria's son, the future Edward VII, in 1863. Alexandra was known for her beauty, charm, and gaiety. She moved with ease among all manner of people, as opposed to her mother-in-law, who essentially retired from public life after the death of her husband, Prince Albert. In one regard, however, Diana differed greatly from Alexandra. When Edward VII was on his deathbed, Alexandra welcomed his mistress, Alice Keppel, and brought her in to say good-bye to her royal lover. In a curious twist that seems to happen only in the world of the British aristocracy, Alice Keppel, mistress of this late-nineteenth-century Prince of Wales, was the great-grandmother of Camilla Parker Bowes, mistress of the late-twentieth-century Prince of Wales. Both Diana and Alexandra were commended for the compassion they brought to their position.

Diana's compassion was the tool she used to revolutionize her role. Her emotional scars gave her the power to empathize with people in need, and they, in turn, recognized her interest as genuine and deeply felt. She made an extraordinary emotional connection with people, and the people she chose to champion, those suffering from AIDS or leprosy or land-mine injuries, were often viewed as life's rejects. Diana became a champion of the underdog.

The result on the public psyche was electrifying for two reasons. First was her exalted position as a royal princess and a future queen.

Second, and equally important, was her external perfection. She was beautiful, tall, blond, and thin. She had every attribute prized in Western society. A person in her position had no need to be kind, compassionate, and generous. But because she was all of these things, she acquired an almost saintly aura that was augmented by the clear authenticity of her compassion. She was a woman who appeared perfect, yet she experienced real suffering and spoke publicly about her pain.

Diana did an extraordinary service to women by speaking openly about her personal problems. She spoke of experiences common to many women but rarely discussed openly, as they are often cloaked in shame. Bulimia, depression, spousal rejection, suicide attempts, adultery, sexuality—each one is an explosive issue. Not only did Diana experience them all, she spoke about them with pain and honesty. In doing so, she shattered the icon that trapped her.

She reached out to people without condescension. She felt homeless and alone, and could talk to a homeless man or a battered wife on their level. Speaking out about her troubles let other people feel less ashamed of theirs. Smashing that divide between people was Diana's true gift to the world.

Washington, D.C., February 1961

"First tell me, what is the least you will do?" the man asked Jacqueline Kennedy.

The man asking the question was Angier Biddle Duke, the Kennedy administration's chief of protocol. The man who wanted to know the answer was his boss, the new President. JFK enlisted his protocol chief to find out just how willingly the new First Lady would embrace the myriad obligations that came with the role.

Jackie explained that her family came first. She said she was willing to do as much as possible within the confines of her primary role as mother. Her point was understandable—after all, Caroline was three and John was barely ten weeks old. But she answered Duke in plain English: "I want to do as little as I have to."

Duke worked out a system that Jackie approved and largely honored during her tenure in the White House. When heads of state, prime ministers, and chiefs of governments came to Washington with their wives, Jackie's presence would be required. If they came solo, it would not. She agreed in principle, partly because it got her off the hook for many of the obligations she had no desire to participate in, and partly because she knew she could count on her mother, mother-in-law, and sisters-in-law to fill in for her.

During her first few weeks in the White House, Jackie was coerced into making a few appearances she found "corny," including welcoming the Heart Fund Twins, six-year-old sisters bearing heart-shaped corsages, and hosting a buffet luncheon for the Washington Women's Press club. The creamed chicken and carved ice swans were as little to Jackie's liking as sitting down to lunch with women she considered "harpies."

She quickly put her foot down and foisted off most of these sorts of engagements on Lady Bird Johnson, her mother, or her sisters-in-law Ethel Kennedy and Eunice Shriver.

Jackie came to the White House with a strong sense of individuality and a will characterized as "the steel beneath the silk." She would do what she considered important and ignore everything she did not. When JFK insisted she attend some event or other, she would negotiate with him: a horse show in exchange for a Democratic Party rally, a ballet for a senators' wives' luncheon. She was the first wife of a President to operate completely independently of her spouse. Yet she framed everything she did with a respect for the presidency and loyalty to the President.

She took control of the situation, telling a friend that organization was the key. "I like to live in a disorganized or free way ... but I spend about 1 week organizing things as well as Field Marshall Rommell [sic] ever did—and now my life is the way I want it." She came to the White House with a plan, and on her second day there she went to work. Her first priority was to create a warm and comfortable environment for her family in the cavernous and chilly second-floor rooms that served as the President's private residence.

Jackie's second priority would grow to become one of her enduring legacies. She planned to turn the White House into a grand home befitting its stature as the President's House. A decade earlier the entire building had been gutted and rebuilt; cost overruns had left little money for furnishings and decorations. The great staterooms were furnished with reproduction antiques from B. Altman. To Jacqueline Kennedy's eye, the house was an abomination. She had been raised in well-run households and had a keen appreciation for beauty and art.

With the help of her interior decorator, Mrs. Henry Parish II, known as Sister, Jackie assembled a committee chaired by Henry Francis du Pont, the leading authority of early-American decoration, and including a dozen wealthy benefactors. She told *Life* magazine, "All these people come to the White House, and they see practically nothing that dates before 1948. Everything in the White House must have a reason for being there. . . . It must be restored— and that has nothing to do with decoration. That is a question of scholarship."

Jack Kennedy was concerned. The White House was as big a sacred cow to him as it was white elephant to Jackie. Harry Truman faced tremendous controversy when he added a balcony to the South Portico in the late 1940s. The last thing JFK needed was for his wife to bring unwanted attention with a costly redecoration. He asked his private attorney, Clark Clifford, to talk her out of it. Clifford tried and failed. As Jackie's star began to rise, the White House restoration became incredibly popular with the American public. Housewives were sent scurrying up to their attics and off to flea markets in search of the American antiques that Jackie had made fashionable. Public approval of her restoration reached its peak in February 1962, when she hosted a tour of the restored White House staterooms that was broadcast on two networks. She was awarded an Emmy for her performance. JFK's brief appearance on the show gave his official blessing to her pet project.

She broke another taboo by introducing commerce within the White House walls. The restoration was expensive, and Jackie was savvy enough to know that the public would appreciate it more if it weren't paid for with their tax dollars. Soliciting funds was time-consuming, so she came up with the idea of a guidebook. It was a way to mix scholarship and fund-raising, and once again Clark Clifford was called in to dissuade her. Once again he failed. Jackie essentially created the guidebook; she devised the format and size, edited the text, and chose the photographs. She specifically edited out any reference to her contribution, writing in the notes of the first draft of the text, "Don't want to pat me on the back." The guidebook was published in the summer of 1962 and continues to this day to be a major source of funding for the White House Historical Association.

Jackie then turned her attention to saving the nineteenth-century town houses ringing Lafayette Square, across the street from the White House. They were scheduled to be demolished and be replaced by nondescript 1950s government buildings, whose design, Jackie complained, resembled "some state school for the deaf." In the early 1960s little attention was paid to historic preservation. It took the razing of the McKim, Mead & White Pennsylvania Station in New York City to draw national attention to the issue. Jackie used her influence to get the government to stop its plans for Lafayette Square. She told one friend that she feared that "lovely buildings will be torn down and cheesy skyscrapers go up."

Jackie was disturbed to learn that the Federal Arts Commission had opposed the destruction of 133 buildings but that 131 of them were still torn down. "Perhaps saving old buildings and having the new ones be right isn't the most important thing in the world—if you are waiting for the bomb," she said a few months before the Cuban missile crisis. "But I think we are always going to be waiting for the bomb and it won't ever come and so to save the old and to make the new beautiful is terribly important."

On March 6, 1962, she wrote to Bernard Boutin, head of the General Services Administration. Taking a hint from her favorite fictional heroine, Scarlett O'Hara, she opens with a buttery flirtation: "Bobby says you are the most wonderful head of GSA there ever was or will be," and goes on to lay out her case for preserving the early-nineteenth-century square. Boutin capitulated, and the Kennedys had family friend John Carl Warnecke devise a plan that saved the row houses by placing the redesigned government buildings behind them.

Having accomplished two of her major goals, Jackie contemplated pulling back from her already limited public schedule. Just after the election, she had insisted that Jack rent a weekend retreat so they could get away from the White House and she could hunt. Using the White House as a base, she would go to Middleburg, Virginia, each weekend, Cape Cod in the summer, Newport in September, and New York frequently for shopping and the theater. She spent weeks traveling on her own, to Greece, England, Italy, India, Pakistan, and Morocco. Her absence from Washington became a running joke—radio announcers would sign off by saying, "Good night, Mrs. Kennedy, wherever you are."

She didn't really care what they had to say. She understood how the game was played: that by making big bold strokes—restoring the White House, hosting a state dinner at Mount Vernon, dazzling the President of France—she could pretty much do what she pleased the rest of the time. Charles de Gaulle wasn't the only one dazzled by Jackie; she was the darling of the people. Everyone wanted to be like her, dress like her, entertain like her, or be entertained by her.

The pressure on her staff was unbelievable. Jackie hired a small but efficient team to run her offices in the White House. Letitia "Tish" Baldrige was her first social secretary. She had known Jackie for nearly twenty years; her father was a Republican congressman and a friend of Hughdie and Janet Auchincloss's. Tish brought an outstanding résumé to the job. She had been social secretary in two of the most prestigious U.S. embassies (Paris, under David and Evangeline Bruce, and Rome, under Clare Boothe Luce) and came to the White House from Tiffany and Co., the Fifth Avenue jeweler, where she had been the first female executive. Imaginative and with indefatigable energy, Tish was in charge of all White House entertaining; she directed the great evenings that came to symbolize the glamour and style of the Kennedy years. It was Tish's idea to invite the Nobel Prize winners to dinner, and to have Pablo Casals return to the White House after a sixty-year absence.

Tish listened to Jackie's complaints about White House entertaining. "We used to come to the White House when Jack was a Senator and the Eisenhowers were here. It was just unbearable," Jackie told her. "There would be Ike in one chair and Mamie in another . . . and everyone stood and there was nothing to drink. We made up our minds . . . that nobody was ever going to be bored like that." She relaxed many of the outdated formalities of state dinners, making them looser, jazzier, and more fun.

Pamela Turnure was Jackie's press secretary. Her appointment, in hindsight, was a controversial one. Not only did she lack experience as either a press secretary or a reporter, she was a former lover of JFK's. She had been a secretary in his Senate office, and he had been photographed leaving her Georgetown apartment in the middle of the night. JFK had met her through his navy friend Red Fay, who had been on the lookout for an "eager, attractive typist" and proclaimed Pam to be as "nice as she was lovely."

She bore more than a passing physical resemblance to Jackie. When it came time for Jackie to hire a press secretary, she was offered a choice between Pam and another woman, a former reporter who worked for the Democratic National Committee. Jackie found the DNC women too aggressive and "tub-thumping" and hired Pam. Pam tuned into Jackie's wavelength immediately, understanding that her job was to protect Jackie and her children from the press. In June 1962 Jackie gave Pam an unqualified rave, telling a friend, "Look how Pam helps me—because she answers every question exactly as I would—I know she will do it correctly—so we don't even communicate for weeks on end."

The third key member of Jackie's team, Mary Barelli Gallagher, had been her private secretary for three years, after having worked in JFK's Senate office and for Jackie's mother. Mary had the closest day-to-day contact with Jackie and organized the Kennedys' personal bookkeeping. Though Jackie had once praised "the loyalty which Mrs. Gallagher has show me and my family" as being "most gratifying," she was furious when Mary wrote a gossipy tell-all book shortly after the Onassis marriage. *My Life with Jacqueline Kennedy* details down to the penny Jackie's spending habits and the ire her never-ending consumption caused her husband. Rife with barely disguised bile, the memoir reads like a guilty pleasure.

The last member of Team Jackie was the man who ran the White House. J. Bernard West, the chief usher, had worked for every President since FDR, succeeding in part thanks to his ability to "manage up," to interpret the wishes of the family he served. He was quick to discover that Jackie's whispered requests "Do you think . . ." or "Would it be possible . . ." were firm commands, identical to any general's shouted order.

Together they created an efficient environment for Jackie to work in, giving her "the happiest time I have ever known—not for the position—but for the closeness of one's family—the last thing I expected to find in the White House." Her priorities had been clear from the start: her children first, Jack's comfort second, and her sanity third.

She was the first First Lady to create a "cause," though that was not her intention; she was, in the words of Joseph Conrad, "following her bliss." But every First Lady who came after her has felt the need to focus her energy on a special project: beautification or literacy or the ERA or an anti-drug campaign. Historians say that there were two significant First Ladies of the twentieth century, Eleanor Roosevelt in the political arena and Jacqueline Kennedy in the social arena. But First Ladies aren't compared with Eleanor when they host state dinners or travel to foreign countries or refurbish the White House.

Jackie didn't have any hidden agenda or subversive goals. Motivated by a love of history and a sense of patriotism, she elevated Americans' pride in their culture and heritage. She put to optimal use her intellectual, social, and administrative abilities, nurtured by her parents, honed by Vassar and the Sorbonne, and inspired by the can-do ethics of the Kennedys. Jackie Kennedy revolutionized the role of First Lady.

Chapter Fourteen

The End of the Dream

I should have known that it was asking too much to dream that I might have grown old with him and seen our children grow up together.

—Jackie, summer 1964

I heard [the announcement of our separation] on the radio, and it was just very, very sad. Really sad. The fairy tale had come to an end.

—Diana, 1995

"Can anyone understand how it is to live in the White House, and then, suddenly, to be living alone as the President's widow?" Jacqueline Kennedy wondered a few weeks after the assassination. Though there is no comparison between the shocking and violent end of Jackie's marriage and the drawn-out, tawdry soap opera that ended Diana's, Diana is perhaps the one person who could understand what had happened to Jackie's life. The end of a marriage is a painful thing; the end of a marriage to a public figure, and with it the loss of status and position, adds a different kind of pressure. Diana and Jackie were similar in that, if possible, they became *more* famous after their marriages ended.

Jackie had expected the public's interest in her to cease after she left the White House. She did not welcome the intrusion into her life and into the lives of her children. She felt that they deserved a decent amount of privacy. Jackie had two young children and struggled valiantly for a semblance of normalcy. Diana, on the other hand, saw public adoration as a validation of self. Though at times frustrating, it was her lifeblood. Her situation as a mother was different, too. William and Harry had not lost their status, as she had. Diana's children were older than Jackie's had been, their father had not died, and their privacy was well protected by the Palace.

Nonetheless, the effect of the end of their marriages on their psyches was brutal. Jackie's dream ended just as all the pieces were beginning to fit together. "I know I held a very special place for him," she told a friend after she had moved out of the White House, "a unique place." Diana's dream suffered a long, lingering death. Everything about the marriage was falling apart, so a divorce seemed inevitable. "I don't want a divorce," Diana told an interviewer, "it's not my wish." But her actions helped ensure that divorce would be the only solution to an untenable situation.

Diana and Jackie each became an icon with the death of the dream. In 1963 Jackie became "America's queen"—a majestic figure whose personal courage and dignity held together a wounded country in one of its darkest moments. In 1996 Diana became a different sort of icon— the "queen of people's hearts." She was the idealized representative of what her brother called "her constituency of the rejected."

Dallas, November 1963

That she was even in Dallas with him that day was an indication of how everything was finally pulling together in their ten-year marriage. The death of Patrick that August had awakened a feeling in Jack Kennedy, and he treated Jackie with such tenderness and concern in the last three months they had together. Pamela Turnure recalled that after Patrick's death, "suddenly it was all out in the open . . . the President's real devotion to Mrs. Kennedy . . . it was a new side that had never been seen . . . before." Jackie returned the devotion, writing to Jack a month before his death, "I've loved you from the first day I saw you, and if I hadn't married you, my life would have been tragic because the definition of a tragedy is a waste. But ten years later I love you so much more."

Jackie had accomplished many of her goals in her three years as First Lady. The White House was running smoothly and was truly the "grand house" that she had envisioned, with wonderful food, beautiful flowers, and exquisite entertainment. The restoration of the executive mansion was largely complete. (One of the last projects waiting for completion was redecorating the Oval Office, but the painters and carpenters needed two days when the President would be out of the office. The short trip to Texas was perfect. When JFK returned on Monday, he would have a newly painted office with a bright red carpet and white draperies with red trim.) The nineteenth-century character of Lafayette Square had been saved, spearheading the historic preservation movement. Plans were well under way for a National Cultural Center on the banks of the Potomac (it would be renamed the John F. Kennedy Center for the Performing Arts).

With time on her hands and a new joy in married life, Jackie made a decision that surprised many of her friends—she jumped wholeheartedly into the 1964 campaign. She instructed Pam Turnure to tell the press, "Yes, I am going out with my husband on this trip and that it will be the first of many that I hope to make with him. I plan to campaign with him . . . I will do anything to help my husband be elected President again."

She was enjoying the trip to Texas, telling her husband, "Campaigning is so easy when you're President," despite the fact that the second day of the trip, Friday, November 22, had a grueling schedule. Air Force One arrived in Fort Worth shortly after midnight. There was a speech and a breakfast there in the morning, a short flight to Dallas, a motorcade and lunch there, another short flight to Austin, a reception and a formal dinner, and then finally another flight to the vice president's ranch, where Lady Bird Johnson was planning a warm display of Texas hospitality.

According to biographer Edward Klein, who attributes as his source a closed portion of Janet Auchincloss's oral history at the

Kennedy Library, Jackie began her menstrual cycle that morning in the Fort Worth hotel. It was the first time she had menstruated since Patrick died. Klein says that Jackie was filled with joy. She would later say that JFK had wanted a large family, but spread out, so that as one child reached two or three years old, another came along. "Remember," she said, "I gave him four children in seven years." This news meant that they could start again.

If true, this story brings an anguished dimension to the events in Dallas—life ending just as the promise of life was renewed. It adds an element of grief too private to share. The public could never know: she would keep the secret loss locked in her heart.

Jackie's last moments with her husband were spent in the glare of the Texas sun, surrounded by adoring crowds, but even there evidence of the new closeness between the couple was apparent. Thirty years after the assassination, the Dallas CBS affiliate television station discovered footage long thought discarded. The film shows mostly the arrival at Love Field, but what is interesting is that Jack is filmed walking hand in hand with his wife as they approached the crowds waiting to greet them. His concern for her comfort and well-being was evident to everyone, and his Murphia—the group of Irish men who were his top aides—were amazed to see this previously hidden side of him.

The murder on Elm Street resonated around the world, affecting people and politics for many years. But the horror of the act on a political level was one thing; the personal horror Jackie experienced in the back of the open car was grotesque. Her husband's head exploded in front of her eyes, covering her in blood and gore. While she was sitting there, holding his shattered head, some primitive survival instinct took hold. Jackie scrambled up onto the back of the Lincoln, looking for an escape, any escape. She was pushed back to safety by her Secret Service agent, Clint Hill, who pounded his fist in frustration on the trunk of the car.

From that moment on, and throughout the next four days, Jackie regained her monumental self-control. From the corridors of Parkland Hospital to the harrowing flight back to Washington, through three days of ceremonies, Jacqueline Kennedy did not make one false step. She was blessed with an unerring and instinctual sense of rightness.

"I never saw her cry, even in the White House," Yusha Auchincloss remembered. "On the day of the funeral, I saw tears in her eyes, but never really crying." Of the funeral, Auchincloss said, "Jackie loved history; she loved, for example, the history of Joan of Arc. She had this sense of herself, that she had been some sort of military heroine."

Jackie planned her husband's funeral with the bravery and bold strokes of a great military leader. It was her last great tribute to him in her role as First Lady, and her efforts had a profound effect. The four days of the Kennedy assassination and funeral are the defining event that turned television into a global means of communication. In *The Death of a President,* William Manchester reports that a Gallup poll in Athens, Greece, reported that by noontime on Saturday, 99 percent of all Athenians knew of the slaying. People around the globe were focused on the events in Washington. The visual images that the weekend provided—from Jackie in her bloodstained suit at Andrews Air Force Base to John's salute to the flickering tongues of flame at the gravesite—became, thanks to television, indelibly etched on the national psyche.

Those four days were touched with a sense of majesty that had been lacking in the American landscape. They restored a sense of dignity to the United States, which suffered badly from JFK's barbaric death and the shooting, two days later, of the accused assassin, Lee Harvey Oswald. But the four days were also graced with small, personal details that put Jackie's stamp on what was the largest state event in American history.

When Air Force One returned to Washington, the President's casket was removed from the plane by a mechanical lift that didn't lower all the way to the ground. The casket was awkwardly lowered by hand. Jackie had to be helped down the five-foot gap. When Taz Shepard and Ted Clifton, two of JFK's military aides, helped her down, she could be seen looking up at their grief-stricken faces and saying, "Thank you"—an example of innate courtesy functioning in a time of shock.

Jackie asked her friend Bunny Mellon to do the flowers for the funeral. "I don't want the church to look like a funeral," she told Mellon, with "awful purple wreaths and gold ribbons all around." Mellon had designed the Rose Garden for JFK, who took great delight in showing it to visitors. "Jack loved flowers . . . [and there's] one thing I want at the grave. A straw basket with just the flowers he had in the Rose Garden. Only those flowers and nothing else at the grave." Bunny had anticipated Jackie's wishes. For the funeral at St. Matthew's she had created simple arrangements of daisies, white chrysanthemums, and stephanotis in a pair of blue vases from the White House. For the gravesite, Mellon took a fifteen-inch-long wicker basket and filled it with blue salvia, chrysanthemums, white roses, and branches from hawthorn and crab apple trees she gathered from the Rose Garden.

The three most stunning visual images from the funeral were of Jackie's making. The walk on foot from the White House to St. Matthew's Cathedral was her idea. She was insistent and fought everyone, from her own family to the Secret Service, who envisioned a security nightmare as representatives from more than a hundred nations converged on Washington. Jackie flatly refused to ride "in a fat black Cadillac." Her will was iron, and all opposition ceased. There was precedent, planners discovered, at the funerals of Washington, Lincoln, Grant, and Theodore Roosevelt. With her posture tempered by years of equestrian training, Jackie cut a moving figure as she strode up the eight blocks of Connecticut Avenue, leading a gathering of world leaders, including Charles de Gaulle, Queen Frederika of Greece, the duke of Edinburgh, and the emperor of Ethiopia.

After the funeral, as the family stood outside St. Matthew's waiting for the coffin to be secured to the caisson, Jackie leaned down to her son and whispered, "John, you can salute Daddy now and say good-bye to him." John, who turned three that day, lifted his arm with the precision of a West Point cadet and crisply saluted his father's coffin. Jackie did not witness the moment. Later, looking at photographs, she was surprised—he had never mastered the motion; when playing soldier with his father, his salutes had always been, in

Jackie's words, "kind of droopy." Those who did witness John's salute were devastated. Friends, who knew how much JFK loved his son, as well as those around the world watching on television, were thunderstruck.

After she returned from the Capitol Rotunda on Sunday afternoon, where JFK's casket would lay in state overnight, an idea "just came to my head." Jackie blurted out, "And there's going to be an eternal flame." Those with her, including her brother-in-law Sargent Shriver, tried from the start to dissuade her. Shriver told her, "People might think it's a little ostentatious."

"*Let* them" was her response.

In addition to questions of appropriateness, there was also a question of time. There was barely twenty-four hours before the burial at Arlington. Presidential assistant Dick Goodwin was put in charge of the project, and he went head-to-head with army bureaucrats who kept telling him that it was impossible. Goodwin silenced them. "Listen," he said, "if you can design an atomic bomb, you can put a little flame on the side of that hill, and you can make it so she can light it."

They did fabricate it on time, and Jackie was able to light it. The eternal flame remains to this day one of the most enduring symbols of the Kennedy story.

After the burial Jackie played official hostess one last time in the White House. There was a reception for all the foreign representatives—the most illustrious gathering the house had ever seen. Though, as her former social secretary recalled, "she really should have been allowed to give in long ago . . . this was a great show of strength on her part." She met privately in the yellow oval salon with Prince Philip; Charles de Gaulle; Haile Selassie, the emperor of Ethiopia; and Eamon De Valera, the President of Ireland. She later went downstairs and received all the guests in the Red Room, offering a personal word to each.

Tish Baldrige spoke for many when she said, "Mrs. Kennedy carried through under the greatest amount of strain with more dignity than any woman in public life has ever shown in a moment of tragedy, and this was her last great tribute to him in her role."

Jackie stayed in the White House for two weeks after the assassination, moving out on December 6. When reporters asked Lady Bird Johnson about her own plans to move into the executive mansion, she answered with white-hot compassion: "I would to God I could serve Mrs. Kennedy's comfort; I can at least serve her convenience."

On her final day in the house she loved so much, Jackie was too emotional to attend a ceremony in which Lyndon Johnson awarded his predecessor the nation's highest award for peacetime service, the Presidential Medal of Freedom. Bobby Kennedy accepted the posthumous honor on his behalf. Later, as the family was about to leave, they were joined by Lee Radziwill and Dave Powers. Powers gave young John a small American flag that he had kept in his office. He knew that John loved flags and thought it would be an appropriate gift for the young boy. Jackie watched as John waved the flag back and forth. She smiled sadly and handed her son the black leather case containing the Medal of Freedom.

"John, here's something else that you can carry out of the White House," she whispered to her son. "Keep it, and be proud of it always."

Taking her children's hands, Jacqueline Kennedy walked out of the house and got into the long black limousine, never once looking back as the car drove off.

London, February 1996

Queen Elizabeth's study is a large square room with a bow-shaped wall arching over the monarch's private entrance to Buckingham Palace. The walls are covered in pale blue damask, and the furnishings are comfortable rather than grand—down-stuffed chairs, silk lampshades, and a handsome eighteenth-century desk, where Elizabeth spends much of her workday. The room faces north, as do most of the royal family's private apartments, overlooking the palace gardens, with Green Park beyond. With no direct sunlight and on a rainy Wednesday afternoon in mid-February, the room was cold and dismal.

More than just the weather was contributing to the chilly ambience. Diana had been called to a private audience with her mother-in-law, and as the two women sat down, Diana shuddered in apprehension. To have an unpleasant confrontation with an angry in-law, regardless of how well mannered all parties are, is difficult enough. For the in-law also to be your sovereign, the titular head of your country, brings with it an additional pressure that very few can understand.

For Elizabeth, the meeting was an unwanted necessity. The battles between her son and daughter-in-law had gone on for too long and been far too public, damaging the monarchy.

Elizabeth had reached the limit of her patience and had decided that divorce was the only solution to the War of the Waleses. This decision came with great reluctance, but the tasteless disintegration of Diana's marriage had to stop. The *Panorama* interview, which Diana had conducted in total secrecy, had been the last straw in a nearly five-year conflict. Elizabeth Windsor wasn't requesting that her son and daughter-in-law divorce; Her Majesty the Queen was commanding it.

Diana later referred to that day as the saddest of her life. What she seemed unwilling to accept was that it was her passive-aggressive behavior that had led to this moment. She may have felt justified in all her actions, refusing to "live the lie" as the Palace preferred, but her actions had an element of self-sabotage that greatly reduced the "victim" aura she liked to project. How did things fall so far?

When, in November 1993, Prime Minister John Major announced to Parliament and the world that Charles and Diana were separating, there was almost as much relief as there was disappointment. What wasn't expressed was much surprise. The royal couple had just returned from an official visit to Korea, where their antipathy toward each other was on full public view for all the world to see. There was no hiding the very obvious fact that neither Charles nor Diana could bear to be near the other. Diana looked tortured and depressed just riding in a car with Charles. At an official banquet, her eyes red-rimmed and downcast, she glowered at the tablecloth for two and a half hours. If the couple's personal problems were going to destroy the effectiveness of their professional obligations, something had to be done.

What was surprising about Major's remarks was his statement that despite the official separation, the couple's constitutional roles would remain intact. Therefore, if sometime between December 1992 and August 1996 (when the divorce was legalized) Queen Elizabeth died, Charles would become king and Diana queen. Though there was precedent for such a scenario (George IV's coronation in 1820 was interrupted when his estranged wife, Queen Caroline, tried to force herself into the ceremony by screaming and banging on the locked doors of Westminster Abbey), the idea of rival royal establishments was ludicrous in the modern age.

The course of Diana and Charles's separation was marked by bitter fighting and petty jealousy from both parties. The private betrayals, the infidelities with Camilla Parker Bowles and James Hewitt, escalated into the public backstabbing of the Andrew Morton and Jonathan Dimbleby biographies. Both Charles and Diana allowed their friends to lob hand grenades of gossip. Details of Charles's insensitivity and Diana's unstable behavior were spewed across the pages of both books.

Just when it seemed that the stories couldn't get any more tawdry, there were the explosive revelations based on two tape recordings of private cell phone conversations, one between Diana and her friend James Gilbey (of the gin family) and the second between Charles and Camilla. These, of course, have become known as the "Squidgy-gate" and "Camilla-gate" tapes and serve as a reminder to all to be careful of the topics discussed on a cell phone: you never know who's listening and recording.

The Squidgy-gate tape (so named because Gilbey repeats his pet name, Squidge or Squidgy, more than a dozen times) reveals an unhappy woman who felt lonely and isolated within her marriage and within the royal family. Charles made her life "real, real torture," and the rest of the family wasn't helpful. She received a "strange look" from the Queen Mother. "It's not hatred, it's sort of interest and pity." The tenor of the conversation is playful and affectionate rather than passionate. Diana talks of visiting her old home, Park House, which had been converted into a rest home for the disabled, and how she stayed for an hour and a half, chatting, hugging, and taking photographs with the patients. She talks ruefully of James Hewitt ("Cost me a lot, that one") and calls Gilbey "the nicest person in the whole wide world." Diana's tone is adolescent and self-centered—when Gilbey proffers his adoration, Diana responds, "I love it"—I love *it,* not I love *you.* The tape (which was released as a pay-per-call moneymaking venture by the *Sun*) reveals a side of Diana that runs counter to the "victim" role she was so eager to portray. The release of the transcript in August was devastating to Diana, although her shame was mitigated somewhat four months later by the Camilla-gate tape.

The Camilla-gate tape proved that Charles had been unfaithful to Diana, and it did so in the most flamboyant manner possible. In and of itself, the conversation is the sort of pillow talk that many couples share, full of intimacies and private jokes. But the language and the imagery—his fantasy to be Camilla's "Tampax . . . forever swirling round," his macho boast that "I fill your tank," and his sheer arrogance ("Your great achievement is to love me")—were deliciously salacious. The tape created one of the great scandals in the history of the royal family. Diana's popularity soared while Charles's plummeted. Camilla received death threats and was terrified to leave her house. She was blamed for having ruined the fairy tale and ridiculed for her looks—the "ugly witch" to Diana's "beautiful princess." Soon the world knew Diana's name for her—"the Rottweiller"—and roared its approval.

By 1995, having been betrayed by her husband, her lover (Hewitt sold his story to writer Anna Pasternak, whose *Princess in Love* reveals the details of their affair), and then her brother (Charles Spencer reneged on a promise to let Diana have a house for weekend use on the Althorp estate), Diana may have felt that she had nowhere to turn but the press to fight her battles. If the Jonathan Dimbleby biography of Charles and its accompanying television biography threw down the gauntlet, Diana picked it up by agreeing to the *Panorama* interview. That ended up being one indiscretion too many for the queen.

Elizabeth then resolved to do what neither Charles nor Diana seemed willing or able to. A few weeks after the *Panorama* interview aired, she wrote separately to both Charles and Diana, telling them that she wanted them to divorce. The marriages of Elizabeth's three eldest children had fragmented under the pressures of living within the royal family. It was truly a last resort for Elizabeth, one that she must have deeply regretted on a constitutional, as well as a personal, basis.

The divorce negotiations were complicated by Diana's continuing insistence on playing the game by her own rules. She bypassed the Palace to issue a press release regarding the divorce. "The Princess of Wales," she announced, "has agreed to Prince Charles's request for a divorce. The Princess will continue to be involved in all decisions relating to the children, and will remain in Kensington Palace, with offices at St. James's Palace. The Princess of Wales will retain the title and be known as Diana, Princess of Wales." The problem was that the queen had not approved any of this, and it was conceit on Diana's part to present it as a fait accompli.

In the end, though, what Diana announced is exactly what she received. Stripped of her royal status, the *HRH* that preceded her name, she kept the Princess of Wales title, though amended, as it would be for a divorcée or widow.

She received a lump-sum payment of $27 million (which Elizabeth had to pay for, as Charles didn't have access to that much cash) and over half a million dollars a year for her official expenses. Custody of the two boys would be shared, but Charles was responsible for all of their expenses.

Diana also signed a clause agreeing never "to write, speak or communicate any further information concerning the monarchy, the House of Windsor, Prince Charles, her marriage or her divorce settlement." She had no need to divulge any more than she already had. On August 28, 1996, fifteen years and one month after it began, her marriage ended, and, as she told a friend, "my acting career is over."

Chapter Fifteen

Myths

I think that I should have known that he was magic all along.
—Jackie, November 1964

The size of the crowds—if that doesn't make me seem like a pop star; people thanking me for bringing happiness into their lives.
—Diana, 1991

Both Diana and Jackie were the perfect creators of their own myths, and although the creation of any myth is a tapestry woven of many threads, it is possible to examine the instruments that created the two most identifying pieces of fantasy that touched their lives: the Camelot legacy and the Queen of People's Hearts identity. Thanks, in part, to both women's expert manipulations and their empathetic understanding of the pulse of public opinion, and because there is ubiquitous media to assume the role of ancient storyteller, eagerly spreading the legend far and wide, we are the lucky beneficiaries of the actual blueprints of these myths.

What compelled both Diana and Jackie to enter the mythmaking business?

In Jackie's case, her motivation is fairly clear. In the two or three days after JFK's funeral, her extraordinary radar had picked up hints from historians and news commentators that her husband's truncated term as President would result in the history of the Kennedy era being cloaked in the *promise* of what might have been, rather than the pride of actual accomplishment. Newscasters were actually saying that his brief tenure disqualified him from being a great President. Despite her shock and exhaustion, her energies went into remarkable overdrive as she devised a way to cement JFK's legacy and enshrine it for her children's heritage. Could she have known that the public, its emotions rubbed raw after the harrowing televised display of national disgrace and national courage, would seize on her misguided rereading of history so that the Kennedy years would forever be known around the world as Camelot?

For Diana the reasons are more complex, more personal, and much more psychologically driven. She was feeling under attack on all fronts in the fall of 1995. It had been a year since the twin humiliations of the adulterous revelations in Charles's television interview and the in-depth biography that essentially reduced her role in the monarchy to that of a bought-and-paid-for uterus, necessary only to provide the dynastic link from monarch to monarch. Two years into her official separation, she was battle-scarred from the incessant bickering and jostling for position in the public arena. She felt a strong need to take her case directly to the public. She wanted to tell her story in her own way. In secretly contracting with the BBC to do a tell-all interview, Diana was frantically attempting to further several impossible-to-reconcile agendas. In a true bulimic mind-set, she wanted to have her cake and eat it, too.

Both Diana and Jackie were the focal points of world interest when their marriages ended. The shocking and sudden death of JFK provided Jackie with a precise time frame in which to respond to that interest, something that Diana, thanks to the slow and steady implosion of her marriage, didn't enjoy. Events dictated the timing of Jackie's response; Diana was on her own to pick the most advantageous time to address the public's interest, and the results are illuminating.

The enduring myth that comes out of the BBC interview, for all its mixed messages and cluttered agendas, is that of a young maiden betrayed. It is how Diana is remembered, and even as the revelations of her own behavior are brought to light, it is how popular thought perceives her. For all her talk of what's best for her children, and what's of most benefit for the country and the monarchy, the heart of the interview is egocentric—this is how I want people to think about me. Poor, brave, unselfish me, soldiering on despite the many, many hardships I've had to bear. There is no search for a greater meaning, no sacrifice for a great goal, and, sadly, no thought for the best interest of her two children and their futures. This conversation is all about Diana, and its success is in fashioning her role as martyr in a very grim fairy tale.

Jacqueline Kennedy, who was equipped with a much stronger sense of self and self-worth, used her moment at the apex of public focus to fuel a much greater goal—to create, for her children and for her countrymen, what she considered a fitting legacy for her slain husband. And yet, much to her annoyance, she became a martyr as well. A brave, valiant figure, the symbol of tragic loss, one whom the country would fixate on for the rest of her life. She was never able to "crawl into the deepest retirement," as she wanted to.

In creating this myth, Jackie was able, in an odd way, to get on with her life, living in the persona of the "national widow." Diana, on the other hand, did not have enough time, and certainly not the commanding sense of self, to sort out all the ramifications of her mythic creations.

What we are left with, then, out of the twin creations of the queen of Camelot and the people's princess, are two modern-day fairy-tale heroines. Their stories are based partly on fact, partly on fable, and were shaped by their own hands, but the romantic imagery of these two queens—uncrowned, yes, but brave and unbowed—is a permanent part of the popular narrative of our times.

Hyannis Port, November 1963

It was the day after Thanksgiving, and the sad, cold rain beating down on the cedar shingle roofs was a fitting coda to the joyless holiday. Jackie had not been expected to travel up to the family compound. But where else was she to go? The White House was no longer her home, the staff there was in a whirlwind, busy dismantling the home that she had so lovingly created, the only home where the four Kennedys had lived together as a family, and she had to escape. To go to her mother was the obvious choice, as Janet and Hughdie lived close by. But the Auchinclosses had given up Merrywood the year before and had moved to Thirty-first and O Streets in Georgetown. Merrywood, tucked away in the woods above the Potomac, would have given her the privacy she needed, but the Georgetown house sat just off the street, too available to prying, if well-meaning, eyes.

But Hyannis Port meant Jack. The four-bedroom cottage on Irving Avenue was actually the first house they had ever owned, and she treasured her memories of their time there together. Hyannis Port would soothe her, if indeed anything could offer solace to her wounded soul.

In addition, Hyannis Port meant Joe Kennedy. Joe Kennedy, the original "master of the universe," felled by stroke and powerless even to attend the funeral of his son, could comfort Jackie in a way that no one else on earth could. Alone among the Kennedy clan, Joe had instantly taken to Jackie, seeing in her a rare spirit, the perfect match for his mercurial son. He had long been her emotional touchstone in the turbulent Kennedy family, so she made the journey north, late on the night before Thanksgiving, to come back specifically to tell him about Jack's death, to seek comfort in his withered and useless arms, to gain strength from his unwavering love.

"I'm here to see Grandpa . . . I'll rest after I see Grandpa . . . please, please leave me alone," she pleaded as the rest of the family tried to keep her from going upstairs in the main house, up the stairs to Joe's bedroom. With aggravation and determination in her voice, she firmly told her in-laws, "I'm fine. I just want to see Grandpa." She went up the stairs, holding the furled flag from her husband's casket tenderly in her arms. Rita Dallas, Joe Kennedy's case nurse, took the flag from her and escorted the young widow into the room, watching as Jackie embraced the frail old man and rested her head on his shoulder. Mrs. Dallas witnessed an extraordinary scene.

"Oh, Grandpa, I'm so glad that at last I'm here with you," Jackie said in her soft, whispery voice. "I've been so worried. Are you all right?" She sat, holding his hand, and in a voice dredged with emotion, said, "Jack's gone, and nothing will ever be the same for us again. He's gone, and I want to tell you all about it." Starting with the drizzly Thursday morning they had departed Washington for Texas, she continued in exacting detail through the final burial in Arlington Cemetery, never faltering, knowing that this proud man deserved to hear the truth in its unadulterated brutality. When she finished, she kissed him good night on both his eyelids and turned, exhausted, to the nurse.

"Did he see it on television? Did he read the newspapers?"

"No," Mrs. Dallas answered. "He didn't want it that way."

"Perhaps he was waiting to hear it from me. Oh, thank God, thank God I came."

She walked slowly down the hall toward the stairs. "I'm so tired, so very tired," she said as she slipped off into the night.

Such were the tensions of that post-assassination week that Robert Kennedy couldn't face the emotional challenge of Hyannis Port; he took his family to a borrowed house in Florida far away from the compound. The Kennedys pulled the cloak of normalcy around them as much as humanly possible, playing a vigorous game of touch football on the wide lawn after Thanksgiving dinner and holding a wake that continued late into the night. It was an Irish wake, full of laughter and whiskey and outlandish stories about the slain President, so much so that the governess of Ted and Joan's children resigned in disgust the next day. She was, perhaps, unfamiliar with the Irish use of laughter as an antidote to unbearable sorrow. Laughter was one of the coping mechanisms with which the Kennedy family dealt with this tragedy.

But Jacqueline Kennedy had a singular way of dealing with her grievous loss: she spent a quiet Thanksgiving Day, lost in thought and planning an effective memorial to her husband, a memorial that would create a myth out of a man and live on for forty years as the enduring legacy of those thousand days of the Kennedy presidency.

Theodore White was sitting in a dentist's chair on Friday morning, November 29, when a call came to him that Jacqueline Kennedy was looking for him. White, a journalist and historian, was the author of *The Making of the President, 1960,* the popular and critically acclaimed account of JFK's presidential campaign. He had covered the President's funeral for *Life,* the great photojournalism weekly magazine, and had returned to New York, exhausted and saddened. When he reached Jackie by phone, she told him, "There's something I want to say to the country. I want to say it in *Life,* and I want you to write it." Was there any man alive who wouldn't have moved mountains to comply with such a request? And it took almost as much strength out of White.

Jackie had told him that she would send a Secret Service car to ferry him to the Cape, but the Secret Service had moved on, curtly informing White that the widowed Mrs. Kennedy no longer had jurisdiction over them, that the cars were not hers to order about, so he was left to make his own travel arrangements in the midst of a raging nor'easter. Then White's elderly mother, who had answered Jackie's first telephone call, suffered a heart attack and was rushed to the hospital. *Life* magazine, eager to learn what the former First Lady wanted to say, agreed to hold the presses at a cost of thirty thousand dollars an hour. In a hired car, with a driver unfamiliar with the route, White made his way up the New England coastline to a rendezvous he later described as more compelling than "a talk with Mary Todd Lincoln a week after Lincoln's assassination" would have been.

Ushered into Joe Kennedy's living room, White took note of Jackie's "composure ... beautiful ... dressed in black trim slacks, beige pullover sweater ... eyes wider than pools ... calm voice ..." His notes, madly scribbled on fifteen pages of plain white typing paper, begin with Jackie's defiant pronouncement of her future plans—"I'm not going to be the 'Widder Kennedy' in public; when this is over I'm going to crawl into the deepest retirement"—and continue in an extraordinary vein, sometimes rambling and oddly poetic, like Tennessee Williams dialogue ("In Dallas they gave me red roses ... how funny, I thought, red roses for me"), often razor-sharp ("I'm not going to be accepting plaques. I don't want medals for Jack. I'm not Mrs. Medgar Evers"), but always tightly focused on her main objective, to memorialize her husband's brief shining moment as a modern-day Camelot.

When you look at the notes, you can see that she refers to Camelot again and again over the course of what was a three-and-a-half-hour conversation, returning to the theme five or six times. When White had finished his first draft of the piece (originally titled "For One Bright Shining Moment" but eventually called "A Conversation with Jacqueline Kennedy"), Jackie painstakingly edited it, inserting the Camelot reference by hand several times. You can see it in her spiderweb handwriting: "For one brief shining moment there was Camelot ... and it will never be that way again!" and her plaintive ending, "And all she could think of was to tell people there will never be that Camelot again."

Jacqueline Kennedy's motives were beyond admirable: she wanted to both honor her husband and provide a context for her children to understand and appreciate their father's legacy. She spent a lot of time talking with White about history and its role in shaping JFK's character. "Jack loved history so.... History made him what he was... this lonely sick boy... in bed so much of the time... reading history.... He devoured the Knights of the Round Table."

Jackie then goes on to make a startling pronouncement, one that White never published, and refused to release until a year after Jacqueline Kennedy's death. She states: "His mother didn't really love him.... She likes to go around being the daughter of the mayor of Boston or [talk about] how she was an ambassador's wife.... She didn't love him."

So it is from whispered intimacies between husband and wife, where Jack confessed the boyhood hurt that led him to substitute history stories for emotional nourishment, that forged Jackie's connection between the sickly young Jack Kennedy, suffering from scarlet fever, and the urbane President listening to a Broadway show album before going off to bed. In doing that, she created the enduring myth of Camelot.

Jacqueline Kennedy, in effect, *branded* the Kennedy administration in much the same way advertisers brand consumer products—

"Things go better with Coke" or "GE brings good things to life." It was a stroke of pure genius, for she was able to perfectly capture the national mood and the desire to have a coda, a final word, a romantic and hopeful ending to the sordid events in Dallas. The Camelot analogy, regardless of the fact that it was a misreading of history and would most likely have caused JFK to chortle in amused derision, brought a sense of history and romance and high ideals and majesty to the Kennedy saga, cloaking those three short years in purple velvet and ermine.

White was, by his own description, the "inadvertent . . . instrument" in tailoring this myth. He knew that it was romantic hooey but considered himself a friend and it his particular duty to hear her out. Her monologue drifted from the gruesome details of the previous week's events to tributes to her Secret Service agent ("Clint Hill, he loved us, he made my life so easy") to a scathing denunciation of writers she didn't care for ("a lot of bitter old men like Merriman Smith") but always centered on her dead husband's love of history and what she perceived to be his rightful place in it. She confessed that the Camelot analogy made her "ashamed of myself . . . all I keep thinking of is this line from a musical comedy, it's been an obsession with me." So much of an obsession that she waited, patiently, as White spent two hours shaping his story. When it was done, he turned the pages over to her for her approval.

Her handwritten edits are insightful, for she carefully traverses the line between drama and history. She is precise in her political obligations—"The Johnsons are wonderful, they've been wonderful to me"—yet relentless in driving home her point—"but there'll never be another Camelot again." Where White had written, "But this was the idea she wanted to share," she crossed out the last four words and inserted "that transfixed her." A reference to the Kennedys as "they're such wonderful people" is changed to "they're my family." Her relationship with her husband is strengthened with intimate references to "a month after the death of their baby" and a token left in Patrick's casket "that was from them both."

It was spin control before spin control was even invented, prac-ticed under the most extraordinary circumstances after the most excruciating week in postwar America. Jacqueline Kennedy is singularly responsible for the creation of the most popular metaphor in American political history. The Kennedy presidency will forever be viewed through the romantic filter of the Camelot myth. Indeed, it crumbles only to be rebuilt, and lives on in the legacy of the entire Kennedy family, bringing a magical connection to such diverse enterprises as the global reach of the Special Olympics and the neighborhood goodwill of Boston's Citizens Energy Corporation, from the museum retrospective of Oleg Cassini dresses to the NBC News reports of Maria Shriver. Far from being "one brief shining moment," the Camelot legacy is well on its way to its golden anniversary and shows no sign of ever fading away.

London, November 1995

Pity Sir Robert Fellowes. He was really at the top of his game, professionally speaking. As private secretary to Queen Elizabeth II, he was one of the most influential people in Britain, solely responsible for whom and what she saw. Every letter she receives, every request for an audience, every member of her extended family who wants to speak with her, goes through the hands of the private secretary. Fellowes had had the top job for five years. He was respected for both his diplomatic skills and his CEO abilities, and was known to demand tough, exacting results from the royal household.

He was also in a very curious position, thanks to his marriage to Lady Jane Spencer, one of Diana's two elder sisters. They had married in 1978, three years before the wedding of Diana and Charles. Fellowes was the son of the queen's land agent at her private retreat, Sandringham, and he both knew and relished the form, the "correct" way of behaving and, indeed, thinking that surrounds the queen's inner circle of advisers. His rise in the royal household had been swift, and in a dozen years he had moved from an assistant private secretary to his current position as the queen's right-hand man. With an outstanding record, his background in finance (he had been a broker in the City), and his successful marriage to Diana's soft-spoken sister (their three children were first cousins to William and Harry), Fellowes was in an ideal position to segue, at the appropriate time, from the service of Elizabeth II to Charles III.

But Diana threw a monkey wrench into that scheme. Her rebellious streak, her independence, and her unwillingness to toe the royal line made her a source of continued irritation and a severe test to Sir Robert's patience. It was enough that he had to deal with the wayward duchess of York, Sarah Ferguson (and in the slightly incestuous way of the British aristocracy, Fergie was also a relation, a second cousin). Fellowes was not the source of the infamous quote "The knives are out for Fergie at the Palace," but he surely was there in the background, sharpening the blades. Diana presented an altogether different set of problems. She was, after all, the wife of the heir to the throne and, therefore, Fellowes's future queen. She was the daughter-in-law of his boss, and the baby sister of his wife. Diana had point-blank lied to him about her cooperation with Andrew Morton, which caused Fellowes to tender a letter of resignation to the queen (who was disinclined to accept it). The Waleses' separation was unprecedented in modern English history and presented no end of tension. Furthermore, their public bickering was doing little in the way of enhancing the image of "the boss," either as a monarch or as a mother.

So when Diana phoned her brother-in-law in late November to announce that she had arranged an interview, in total secrecy, with the BBC program *Panorama* (sort of a British *60 Minutes*), he must not have believed his ears. It was unthinkable behavior; something that simply was *not done* in the royal family. And if it was done, it was cleared through proper channels and not sprung upon Her Majesty at the last possible moment, a mere forty-eight hours before broadcast.

"Oh, Robin," Diana cooed, using the family's nickname for him, "I just want to let you know that I've done an interview with *Panorama,* and it is going to be broadcast Sunday next."

"Does Her Majesty know of this?" Fellowes asked her.

"No, I've rung you first" came the suspected reply.

For not the first time in the past few years, Fellowes coldly informed his sister-in-law that she was making his life "unbearable." He hung up the phone and began a fruitless effort to cancel the broadcast. When that task proved impossible, he tried to get a preview screening of the tape. But the BBC refused and held firm, going so far as to conceal the interview's very existence from the company's board of directors. That Diana had perpetrated this travesty of royal behavior was completely unfathomable to Fellowes, and now it was his job to break the news to the queen, who would be equally perplexed by Diana's brazen flouting of royal convention.

The *Panorama* interview, conducted by Martin Bashir, seen in Britain in mid-November and broadcast in the United States a week later, is a truly remarkable piece of theater, in the purest form of the word. It is Diana at her most magnificent and most manipulative, clearly articulating her goals and presenting her perspective of the past fifteen years. Her desire to control, her need to control, is evident in every word she utters, every sound bite that passes her lips, and continues through to the props, setting, makeup, and costuming she chose on her own.

A woman celebrated for her fashion acumen, Diana dressed for the interview with precision and clarity. Her objective was to look serious, somber, and slightly mournful, as if sad for the dream that had long ago died. She wore a simple black suit, with a glimpse of virginal white underneath the jacket. Her eyes, ringed with jet black kohl, were piercing and sad, even if at times somewhat mischievous. Her only jewelry was a pair of gold button earrings and her plain gold wedding band, the last ring created from the nugget of 22-karat Welsh gold that had supplied three generations of royal brides.

Sitting in the formal drawing room of her Kensington Palace apartments, Diana appears neither comfortable nor overly confident. Yet she displays complete mastery over the range of subjects discussed, neither wavering in her conviction of the wrongs perpetrated upon her nor willing to admit to anything that didn't jibe with her version of the story. It is an extraordinary interview, bordering on the revolutionary, as she discusses with astonishing candor her psychological history, her eating disorders, her adultery, her husband's betrayal, and her opinions on his fitness for the top job.

Her performance is riveting, and explosive, and canny. The conversation starts at the beginning of her public life, and the special problems faced by a newcomer adapting to life within the royal family. She sets the tone in her first reply, when she states, in reference to the pressures she was facing at the time of her marriage, "At the age of nineteen, you always think you're prepared for everything...but although I was daunted at the prospect...I felt I had the support of my husband-to-be." In other words, "I was just a child, I thought I could handle it, my husband was supposed to help me, but as we all know now, he failed to do so."

She shoots, she scores, with her first shot, and the hour then wends it way through a dozen distinct and yet interwoven themes.

Alternately disarming ("It took a long time to understand why people were so interested in me, but I assumed it was because my husband had done a lot of wonderful work") and sparring (in response to a question about being flattered by the public adulation: "With the media attention came a lot of jealousy, a great deal of complicated situations"), Diana uses the early part of the interview to underscore her innocence, her modesty, her willingness to learn the ropes. As the public and the media singled her out for special acclaim, she didn't understand it, claiming that her self-image was that of "a fat, chubby twenty-year-old." She felt the attention to be "isolating" and yet she was astute enough to realize that the higher the pedestal, "the bigger the drop."

She tells how the birth of her first son ("I had actually known that William was going to be a boy, because the scan had shown it") led her to a severe bout with postpartum depression, and targets the royal family as unfeeling and mean-spirited, labeling her "unstable" and "mentally unbalanced" because they were daunted by the fact that she "was the first person ever in this family who ever had a depression."

She admits to deliberately trying to injure herself, claiming that she had so much internalized pain that striking out against herself with knives and scissors was "actually crying out because I wanted to get better." She immediately ties this startling confession to her current workload, in which "I see women doing similar things and

I'm able to understand completely where they're coming from." Then she accuses Charles of not taking the time to look beyond her actions for the underlying causes.

She talks openly about her bulimia and how she suffered, in secret, for a number of years. She speaks with remarkable frankness about the shame and dismay her eating disorder caused her, and again paints Charles as an unfeeling, unenlightened lout ("I suppose you're just going to waste that food later on?" was his taunt at the dinner table).

The subject then turns to her marriage and the pressures that would eventually cause the couple to break apart. When asked to agree that she and the prince had different outlooks and interests, Diana plainly lies in order to further her own version of the story: "We had a great deal of interest—we both liked people, both like country life, both loved children." She carefully lays the groundwork for the big payoff—"I don't think I've ever been given any credit for growth," "Whatever good I did nobody ever said ... 'Well done' "—and when the subject of Camilla Parker Bowles comes up, she is ready and loaded for bear.

"Oh, a woman's instinct is a very good one," she says about her knowledge of the affair between her husband and Camilla. She knew from his behavior and her instincts and was warned, as well, by staff and friends who cared about the state of the marriage. It wasn't just that her husband was having a relationship with someone else that bothered her, it was that she was left "with a husband who loved someone else." That betrayal devastated her, leaving her to feel "useless and hopeless and failed in every direction."

With rueful bemusement, Diana then utters one of the most famous lines in the history of the monarchy: "There were three of us in this marriage, so it was a bit crowded." Those fourteen words permanently cast her in the role of royal martyr, the blameless pawn of the heir to the throne and his married mistress, the two elders conniving and plotting against the innocent maiden. Another brilliant score for Diana, bringing fairy-tale folklore into what was essentially the mundane breakup of a marriage—the love between the fairy princess and her handsome prince ruined by the evil witch, or in modern terms, the maiden becoming the martyr thanks to the crone. Not since the duke of Windsor's "without the help and support of the woman I love" has royal phrasemaking entered the public lexicon.

Then the talk turns to Andrew Morton's controversial bestseller, *Diana: Her True Story*. When asked if she had either met or personally helped Morton with the book, she cagily answers the first part of the question truthfully, that she had never met Morton. But Bashir presses on. "Did you ever personally assist him with the writing of the book?" Diana deftly parries with "A lot of people saw the distress that my life was in, and they felt it was a supportive thing to help in the way they did." She fails to divulge that she supplied Morton, through an intermediary, with hours of taped responses to his questions. She admits that the book, thanks to its candor and intimate knowledge of her relationship with Prince Charles, "shocked and horrified and . . . disappointed" the royal family. But when asked if she understood why they would feel that way, Diana goes on the defensive, refusing to answer, and, instead, pushes Jonathan Dimbleby's biography of Charles as equally disappointing to the family.

Diana then continues to strengthen her own case, articulating that she now felt she had "enemies" who were waging a campaign against her because she was a problem who wouldn't go away. She lays the blame squarely at the feet of her husband's official household, as they were both jealous of her publicity and personal acclaim and also fearful of a strong woman "doing her bit"—which was such anathema to them that they had to strike out at her. She then fires off a resounding salvo—"I'm a great believer that you should always confuse the enemy"—as if she were one of Winston Churchill's cabinet, offering advice from the underground war room bunkers near 10 Downing Street, and not a royal princess, the third-highest-ranked woman in the land, sitting in her drawing room, surrounded by silk pillows and gilt-framed paintings. It is unbelievable stuff.

And it only gets better. Bashir then turns to Charles's disclosure of his adultery in the Dimbleby interview. Diana bashes Charles for the devastating effect it had not only on her but also on their two boys, then goes on to state that she *admires* him for having the honesty and character to come forward with such a confession. Picture Charles, watching this on his telly; he must have felt sucker-punched.

Having presented herself as the innocent maid, the wronged wife, and the protective mother, Diana then frees herself to accept some of the responsibility for the breakup of her marriage. "We both made mistakes," she readily admits. The scene has been set perfectly for her to make still another startling revelation, that of her own adultery with James Hewitt. She, with more than a little justification, presents Hewitt as a cad who betrayed her friendship to make money off of her. When asked, directly, if she had been unfaithful to her marriage vows, she answers immediately, "Yes, I adored him. Yes, I was in love with him. But I was very let down."

Slam-dunk brilliant. Emotionally ravaged, betrayed by her handsome prince, she turns to the gallant knight (he even came on horseback) to rescue her and receive her adoration, her love. But he betrayed her as well. This was as masterful a piece of public relations as had ever been pulled off, and in a way, it's a shame that the Camelot legacy had already been co-opted, as Diana could have played the perfect Guinevere to Charles's Arthur and Hewitt's Lancelot (*C'est moi, c'est moi,* Hewitt was forced to admit; although being paid handsomely to admit would be more accurate). Diana then closes this section with equal deftness, saluting the thousands of single women among her public, by talking about being very much on her own these days: "I don't mind that actually."

The press is then taken to task for making her life impossible, as she again states that she has no desire to be the center of attention, and that although she can understand that she's a product that "after fifteen years [still] sells well," she can't tolerate the press's unceasing attention, calling it abusive and harassing, and referring to her life as "a soap opera really ... it goes on and on and on."

Diana then makes her case for her future directly to the public. "I'd like to be an ambassador for this country. As I have all this media interest, let's represent this country and the good qualities of it abroad." It was a plan that the duke of Windsor, the last great loose cannon of the royal family, had envisioned for himself half a century earlier. He, like Diana, was engaging and charismatic, hugely popular in foreign countries. But George VI and his Queen Elizabeth would have none of it then, and neither would their daughter, Elizabeth II, have any of it now. By thumbing her nose at royal convention, Diana had effectively ruined any chance to serve in any official capacity of Her Majesty's government.

And then she metamorphoses into Oprah Winfrey. "I think the biggest disease this world suffers from in this day and age is the disease of people feeling unloved, and I know I can give love for a minute, for half an hour, for a day, for a month. . . . I think the British people need someone in public life to give affection, to make them feel important, to give them light in their dark tunnels." She knew, like a champion prizefighter, just when to land her punches and when to pull back. The rhythm of the fight was in full play now. Diana may not have hoped to win any converts to her side, but in proposing this role of an angelic "ambassador feel-good," she knew that her public, which at that time was the majority, would eat it up and that public demand would put this plan over.

On one hand, it seemed so rational and well thought-out: "I've been in a privileged position for fifteen years. I've got tremendous knowledge about people and how to communicate. I've learned that, I've got it, and I want to use it. . . . Let's now use the knowledge I've gathered to help other people in distress." And yet on the other, it is a fantastic backhand slap to the very monarchy she professed to respect. The monarchy needed to be "sorted out" because people had become indifferent to it. They didn't care, and the establishment was too frightened to effect the changes necessary, changes she perceived would alleviate the doubt that people had about the concept of monarchy and would sort out the "sometimes complicated relationship between monarchy and public." Diana foresaw the solution: a monarchy with a more in-depth understanding of the people's needs.

She then comes in for the kill. Stating firmly that she didn't want a divorce and that Charles would have to throw down that particular gauntlet, she goes on to deny that divorce would bring the closure, provide the clarity in her tattered marriage that she craved. She offers

the two young princes as an excuse not to divorce—"our boys—
that's what matters, isn't it"—while refusing to elaborate on how this
continuing barrage of sniping from rival camps could possibly benefit
them.

Before Bashir can follow up with a more probing question, Diana
proposes her tender offer for her future role: "I'd like to be a queen
of people's hearts." She doesn't see herself as ever becoming queen
of England and puts a maddening question mark over Charles's
desire and fitness to be king.

"Who knows what fate will produce. . . . There's always conflict
on that subject with him when we discussed it. . . . It's a very demanding role being Prince of Wales, but it's an equally more demanding role being king." She then skates on some very thin ice:
"Being king would be a little more suffocating. And because I know
the character, I would think that the top job . . . would bring enormous limitations to him, and I don't know whether he could adapt
to that." As far as the establishment was concerned, this statement
was the last straw. Charles had been educated and trained his entire
life, close to fifty years by then, to assume the throne, and here was
his estranged wife calling his dedication, purpose, readiness, and willingness into doubt. She even opens the door for William superseding
his father in the line of succession, couched in the gentle terms of
wishing that Charles "finds peace of mind."

She then closes the interview, "sitting here with sadness because a
marriage hadn't worked."

It's as if she stood on the front steps of Kensington Palace and
sang out, "I am woman, hear me roar."

The dichotomies at work here are amazing. It is an unbelievable
interview, something a fiction writer would be chastised for invent-
ing, yet every word is captured on videotape. On one hand, it was
a monumental success; Diana pushed forward her agenda with the
public, creating her persona as the "queen of hearts" whose own
heart, shattered beyond repair, could help her feel the pain of her
public. It was simultaneously a colossal failure, as it destroyed any
chance of achieving her stated goal of an official role in British public
life. It is also classic passive-aggressive behavior, because for all her

posturing that she didn't want a divorce, Diana's behavior forced her monarch's hand. Within a matter of weeks, Elizabeth had written to her son and daughter-in-law, advising them in no uncertain terms that they must divorce.

In a very real way, Diana in the interview was fighting for her emotional sanity, avidly seeking the approbation of the world by playing to the cheap seats in the balcony. The media pounced on the interview, which was rebroadcast across the world. The revelation of her adultery was cushioned by the "There were three of us in this marriage" quote, which effectively set the scene that she was practically forced into Hewitt's arms. Her "I'd like to be queen of people's hearts" became her moniker and the cornerstone for her later coronation as the "people's princess."

The more serious elements of the interview, her attack on Charles's fitness to be king and her desire to be a roaming ambassador for the country, were downplayed. Even though they were sensational claims, in this context, they were perhaps not sensational enough—although they may have been her true intent in giving the interview in the first place, to give Charles some of his own back and to ensure her future in what would essentially be a rival royal court. After all, wasn't she a princess for the people of contemporary Britain? Wasn't she the one who understood the people in a way her royal in-laws couldn't even guess at?

Chapter Sixteen

Two Ladies, Alone

You know, people think that at the end of the day a man is the only answer. Actually, a fulfilling job is better for me.

—Diana, 1995

I have always lived through men. Now I realize I can't do that anymore.

—Jackie, 1975

Diana and Jackie each went through two distinct phases in their lives as post-marriage single women. Phase one was inexorably tied to the lives of their first husbands. Diana's separation years, between 1993 and 1996, made her a ghost figure to the royal family—there but not there—and a powerful threat to Charles's position as heir to the throne. The five years between Jackie's two marriages, 1964 to 1968, cast her in the role of national widow. Her life was seemingly devoted to a glorification of Jack's thousand days in the White House. "He changed our world," she told America, "and I hope people will remember him and miss him all their lives."

Diana's wish for her husband at the end of her marriage was, needless to say, quite different. "If I were to write my own script," she told an interviewer as her marriage was falling apart, "I would hope that my husband would go off, go away with his lady and sort that out and leave me and the children to carry the Wales name through to the time William ascends the throne."

Jackie treasured the years she lost, while Diana was glad to be rid of them.

Society didn't easily accept a woman on her own in the 1960s when Jackie was first widowed. By the 1970s attitudes had changed. Popular opinion, thanks in part to pop-culture landmarks like *The Mary Tyler Moore Show,* accepted, if not embraced, the idea of a woman's existing happily without the "benefit" of being attached to a man, and working women were making inroads. By the 1980s divorce had lost most of its stigma, and unmarried women—widowed, divorced, and single by their own choice—were a force in society and in the workplace.

This cultural shift eased the way for the second phase of their single-woman status. The year after Diana's divorce and the period after Aristotle Onassis's death gave each woman a level of independence and self-reliance that she had not known previously. During this time both Diana and Jackie found the work that gave them, after motherhood, their greatest joy. Diana's work on the anti-landmine campaign was a brilliant and effective use of her worldwide celebrity to bring attention to a controversial topic. Jackie's years as an editor led to the creation of dozens of books, ranging from huge bestsellers to lavish art books to literary novels.

"How many of us would have the strength," the writer Gloria Steinem asked in reference to Jackie, but the question is equally applicable to Diana, "to choose work over derived influence? In the long run, her insistence on work that is her own may be more helpful to other women than any use of the conventional power she declined."

London, 1997

"I need someone like Aristotle Onassis."

The first-year anniversary of her divorce was a few weeks away as Diana sat in her yellow silk drawing room at Kensington Palace, sipping instant coffee with Ingrid Seward, editor in chief of *Majesty* magazine. They had been talking about her plans for the future, and what kind of man might figure into it. On second thought, Diana giggled. "No, perhaps Fergie needs him more." Interestingly enough, in three weeks' time, Diana would become involved with her own version of a wealthy Mediterranean playboy, Dodi Fayed.

Seward had come to "KP"—as the royals referred to Kensington Palace—at the invitation of the princess. Diana wanted to give her an off-the-record update on life as a divorced ex–royal princess. Seward told her that she had the same qualities that made Marilyn Monroe a star, a combination of vulnerability and glamour.

"I'm not like *her* at all," Diana responded with a tinge of resentment in her voice. She told Seward that the woman she identified with most was Jacqueline Kennedy Onassis, the wife of Monroe's most famous lover. Diana had read a *Vanity Fair* story on Jackie that described her sometimes turbulent relationship with the Kennedy family. "I know all about being treated like that," Diana told Seward, rolling her eyes heavenward for emphasis.

Certainly a man with wealth comparable to Onassis's would do for Diana what the Greek shipowner did for Jackie, namely, free her from the financial and emotional constraints of the royal family. True, Diana had received a large lump-sum payment upon her divorce, but her housing and official expenses were still provided by the Windsors. So even though she was legally free of the Windsors, they still had control over a large part of her life.

Diana and Charles legally separated in December 1992 and divorced in July 1996. The three-year separation was fraught with anxiety and was really an untenable way to live. Charles's relationship with Camilla was out in the open; though he endured abundant criticism for the adulterous liaison, it continued in its low-key fashion. Diana, despite her confessed affair with James Hewitt, was in a different position. For Diana to be seen with any other man would have provoked outrage, regardless of the fact that she had been rejected by Charles and branded an outcast by his family. Fergie found this out with the notorious "toe-sucking" incident. She had been separated from Andrew, on a private holiday at a rented villa, sunbathing topless with a male friend and her two daughters. Her efforts at discretion were spoiled by an aggressive paparazzo scrambling through the brush, trespassing on private property, and snapping photographs that, while titillating, were hardly indecent. Yet the public indignation she faced was straight out of *The Scarlet Letter*.

Is it any wonder, then, that in the first years of her separation Diana referred to herself as "the biggest prostitute in the world," whose main objective was "to get out of this hellhole!"?

Diana turned to two avenues to cope: alternative medicine and a determinedly solo public career. To salve her wounded soul, she sought out a small army of advisers, including psychics, acupuncturists, colonic-irrigation specialists, faith healers, fitness trainers, and energy healers. She engaged a vocal coach and a speechwriter to help her improve her public speaking.

To salve her wounded ego, Diana embarked with obsessive zeal on a life of public duty. She made her first overseas trip after the separation in March to Nepal. When Diana arrived at the Nepalese airport, her hosts had been instructed by Buckingham Palace to refrain from playing the national anthem. Playing "God Save the Queen" is routine protocol when any member of the royal family makes an official overseas visit; the Palace's instructions were petty yet indicative of what was to come. Diana's name was taken out of the *Court Circular*, which lists the daily activities of the royal family. She was denied permission to make trips that would cast her in a more favorable light than Charles (visiting British peacekeeping troops in Bosnia, visiting Northern Ireland).

The upside of the visit was that it connected Diana with a powerful ally in Lynda Chalker, the government minister in charge of overseas development. Chalker was well placed within Prime Minister John Major's government to use Diana in the sort of "roving ambassador" role the princess had envisioned for herself.

Whereas Jackie spent the early years of her widowhood solidifying JFK's memory, Diana spent hers trying to solidify her own position as a quasi-member of the royal family. It was a stressful period, and not just for Diana. Elizabeth was having a difficult time coping with Diana's passive-aggressive behavior. A member of her staff commented, "It was the martinis and Princess Anne that kept her going." Anne, a no-nonsense woman who never had a warm relationship with Diana, would discuss the situation with her mother without mincing words, something the queen's advisers could never do. As for the martinis, Elizabeth was known to ask for an extra cocktail or two, and was seen at Christmas 1992 walking shakily down the hall at Sandringham. "The previous year she would complain that the drinks were too strong," another staff member revealed. "After the separation she never complained."

Though Diana once confessed, "I would never rattle their cage, the monarchy," she seemed to be doing nothing but knocking it. In April 1993 she personally asked Elizabeth if she could attend the state dinner for the President of Portugal. The queen agreed but was caught unaware when Diana chose the same day as the dinner to make a headline-grabbing speech at an international conference on eating disorders.

"I have it on very good authority that the quest for perfection in society can leave the individual gasping for breath at every turn," she announced to the group, who sat in stunned silence as Diana went on to describe circumstances and feelings that were very obviously her own. "From early childhood many felt they were expected to be perfect but didn't feel that they had the right to express their true feelings to those around them—feelings of guilt, of self-revulsion and of low personal esteem, creating in them a compulsion to dissolve like a Disprin." When she described bulimia as "the illness they developed [that] became their shameful friend," people understood her confessional tone to be a tacit admission.

Needless to say, the President of Portugal's state visit was largely ignored in the next day's newspapers, except for a brief mention of Diana's presence at the state banquet. "What is *she* doing here?" the Queen Mother asked her daughter. "I can't understand it. Why *have* you allowed it?" Elizabeth must have asked herself the same question, as she was outmanipulated by Diana yet again. State visits are serious business, an important part of the monarch's job. Diana's willful interference undermined Elizabeth's ability to get her job done. That was a very real threat to the future of the monarchy. It would not survive if it was turned into a popularity contest between a media-savvy, photogenic princess who tapped in to the nation's pop psyche and the staid, starchy, slightly out-of-sync Windsor family.

Charles decided to become proactive and agreed to an in-depth documentary and authorized biography to coincide with the twenty-fifth anniversary of his investiture as Prince of Wales. His office took pains to let it be known that the book was not retaliation for the Andrew Morton book that had rocked his marriage, but Charles and his allies couldn't help but see it as an opportunity for an offensive strike. It was a major rehabilitation job for the prince, whose image had been badly tarnished over the past decade. The Dimbleby biography *The Prince of Wales* caused a bigger stir than the Andrew Morton book had, largely because it was known to be an authorized work. (Diana's active participation in the Morton book wasn't revealed until after her death.)

The *Prince of Wales* presents Charles's version of his love-deprived childhood and a whining admission that he was forced into marriage with Diana, primarily by his father. It discusses his loveless marriage and admits to an adulterous relationship with Camilla Parker Bowles.

The night the Dimbleby interview aired was one of Diana's greatest public-relations victories in her war with Charles. She had been invited to attend a *Vanity Fair* gala at the Serpentine Gallery in Hyde Park. She arrived dressed to kill in a flirtatious off-the-shoulder black silk dress (it would be called the "F You" dress, acknowledging its effect). She looked glamorous, sexy, and confident, as if she had not a worry in the world. The assembled crowd, including media heavyweights like Graydon Carter, Dominick Dunne, and Bob Colacello, was dazzled. Dunne wrote about the encounter in his fictionalized retelling of the O. J. Simpson murder trial, *Another City, Not My Own*. Using the character name Gus Bailey, Dunne allows that "although Gus was not unused to being in the presence of august beings, he suddenly found himself beset with shyness in front of the princess. He had not expected her to be so warm and friendly. He wanted to tell her how much he admired her but he was momentarily speechless. As if she understood his dilemma, she asked him more about the trial."

The guests were savvy enough to realize that her appearance was calculated down to the last sweep of her mascara brush. Said one guest present that night: "It occurred to me that what she was thinking was, If I do this right, my ghastly hubby's interview with Jonathan Dimbleby will not be on page one tomorrow and instead it will be 'Di Knocks 'em Dead at Serpentine Bash.'" Colacello, the former publisher of Andy Warhol's *Interview,* agreed. "When she came down the line, I noticed that she was wearing *a lot* of makeup," he said. "The next day, when her picture was in every paper in the world, I understood why."

Christopher Hitchens, the writer well known for his antimonarchy stance, sidled up to Diana and said, "It's delightful to meet you. We republicans must stick together." She giggled but said nothing. Hitchens knew she got his joke, later adding, "She's done more to subvert the monarchy by accident than I have been able to accomplish on purpose."

Diana's love life continued to be complicated. Though separated from Charles, she knew that she had to be circumspect in her behavior. Charles's relationship with Camilla Parker Bowles drew controversy but fell under the same "boys will be boys" tacit public approval that had been in place for generations. Diana couldn't risk being branded an "unfit mother" by being seen with other men while still legally married to Charles. However, her choice of companions did her no favors. She had affairs with married men, including rugby star Will Carling (whose wife blamed Diana in the press for the breakup of her marriage) and art dealer Oliver Hoare (whose wife complained to the police about crank callers who would hang up when she answered the phone; police traced the frequent calls back to Kensington Palace before the investigation was dropped). Her most serious romance was with a Pakistani doctor, Hasnat Khan. They met in September 1995 and conducted a secret romance for almost two years, until he ended it in July 1997. In the interim, Diana made two trips to Pakistan to convince his family that she was worthy of him. His family was skeptical and wanted him to marry within his Moslem faith. Khan's final breakup with Diana coincided with her vacation with the al-Fayed family in Saint-Tropez. Some of Diana's friends are convinced that her relationship with Dodi Fayed was, or at least started out as, an attempt to make Khan jealous. Even if her love life wasn't working out, her working life was.

Soon after the divorce became final in July 1996, Diana dropped her patronage of more than one hundred different charities. She kept the six that most closely aligned with her interests: the Great Ormond Street Hospital for Sick Children, Centrepoint, the National AIDS Trust, the English National Ballet, the Leprosy Mission, and the Royal Marsden NHS Trust. She told friends she wanted to streamline her life, but the move was seen as a petulant response to losing her HRH status. What it did do, however, was open the path for her connection to the last, and greatest, humanitarian concern she would be involved with: the anti-land-mine campaign.

Diana's brief association with anti-land-mine work would crystallize her public-service persona, in much the same way that land-marks preservation did for Jackie in the later years of her life. Diana's was a moral stance on an issue shrouded by political controversy. She was able to cut through the red tape of political opposition and focus the white-hot glare of world attention on the suffering wrought by land mines. Her fame was put to good use, in much the same way it had been for AIDS awareness. Patronage of the ill had long been an "approved" royal activity, so Diana's work with AIDS, while controversial because of its ill-perceived status as a "homosexual" disease, was not revolutionary. What was revolutionary about her land-mine work was that she was a former royal princess and the mother of a future king, and she was going against the current government's expressed policy.

Diana was vilified in the press back home. She had the worst of both worlds: she wasn't royal anymore but was expected to live under the strictures that forbade the royal family from engaging in controversial behavior, in this case, taking a strong moral stance. When Tony Blair's Labour government ended a nearly two-decade stretch of Conservative Party leadership, it also offered Diana hope for some sort of government-sanctioned official role as roving ambassador.

Blair understood the connection between Diana and the people of England.

The divorce had even drawn Diana and Charles together, as if playing the final notes on their discordant symphony enabled them to reach a place of mutual affection. Charles continued to use the helipad at Kensington Palace for short trips around England and stopped in for tea with his ex-wife on several occasions. He invited Diana and William to join him in Hong Kong in December 1999, when he was due to turn over control of the British colony to the Chinese. She hadn't decided whether to accompany him but was flattered and at ease with him in a way she had never been during their marriage.

Divorce had given her her sea legs. She was on her own now— more confident than she'd been in years, happy and, as the summer of 1997 began, looking for adventure. "I'm happy now," she told Ingrid Seward just two months before her death.

New York, 1964

Jackie returned to New York in September 1964, moving into an apartment in the same chic Upper East Side neighborhood as the home she had shared with her parents on Park Avenue. There were many reasons for her return; chief among them, according to her friend William vanden Heuvel, was that "Washington wasn't for her. Washington is the President's town, and she knew that." She had become a freak show, her house a tourist attraction nestled in the quiet side streets of Georgetown. The move to New York wouldn't stop people from thinking of her as public property—the national widow, as it were—but it would provide her with a buffer from the endless stares. The Fellini-esque spectacle of tourists littering her front lawn with their discarded sandwich wrappings would thankfully end. She told a friend that living in New York made her feel "like a human being—I can walk the streets and not be singled out."

She purchased a $200,000 cooperative apartment at 1040 Fifth Avenue (which would be sold after her death for $9.5 million). To avoid press leaks, Nancy Tuckerman played the role of potential buyer, with Jackie disguised in a trench coat, head scarf, and glasses accompanying her as the nanny. The apartment she chose occupied the entire fifteenth floor of the building; it had been designed by the same architect, Rosario Candela, who had worked with her grandfather James T. Lee on her childhood home at 740 Park Avenue. Typical of the grand prewar Fifth Avenue apartments, the sweep of public rooms—dining room, living room, and library—as well as the master bedroom faced Central Park. Jackie's apartment was unique in that, thanks to building setbacks, she had a long, narrow terrace off her living room and library. Her bathroom also faced the park; it was a large square room the size of many Manhattan apartment bedrooms. There were four other main bedrooms; two additional, smaller terraces; four servant's bedrooms; and a large kitchen with a pantry and living room for the servants in the back. Jackie referred to her home as "1040" and lived there for the rest of her life.

Safely ensconced, she went about her life as a young widow with two goals in mind: to provide her children with as normal an upbringing as possible and to commemorate her husband's memory. The day after JFK's funeral, Jackie told Pierre Salinger that her life would be dedicated to raising her two children. To help ease their third move in less than a year, Jackie had her decorators replicate the children's White House bedrooms, pink-and-white-rose-patterned chintz for Caroline, blue and white stripes for John. Maud Shaw went to New York with them, as did Nancy Tuckerman and Pamela Turnure, who had run Jackie's government-funded office. Private secretary Mary Gallagher and personal maid Provi Parades, both young mothers with families, did not go to New York. Second-grader Caroline was enrolled in the Convent of the Sacred Heart, which she attended with two of her Lawford cousins, Sydney and Victoria. Jackie rented cottages, first on Long Island and later in Peapack, New Jersey, so they could ride on the weekends.

A pair of JFK memorials occupied much of Jackie's time during the next few years. Of paramount importance was a permanent design for the gravesite at Arlington. She would bring Patrick and

Arabella to Washington to be interred alongside their father. John Carl Warnecke was selected to design the 3.2-acre plot. Warnecke, a friend of Red Fay's, had been the chief designer of the Lafayette Square project. In the midst of the three years of design and construction on the gravesite, Jackie and Warnecke enjoyed a discreet but passionate eighteen-month-long affair. They traveled together with their families to Hawaii, where, joined by Peter Lawford and his children, they enjoyed a seven-week vacation in the summer of 1966. Warnecke later said that they discussed marriage, but Jackie told him, "Bobby says it's too soon."

Bobby and Jackie grew incredibly close during these years. Bobby had replaced Joe Kennedy as Jackie's strongest supporter within the family, telling friends who questioned him about her future plans: "Jackie has always kept her own identity and been different." Over the years there has been much speculation as to the precise nature of their relationship, but there's no doubt it derived from a shared desire to perpetuate an idealized memory of JFK. Bobby inherited the Kennedy political crown with the death of his elder brother; Jackie's gift to him was to "class him up" the same way that she had Jack. It was Jackie who suggested the moving stanza from *Romeo and Juliet* that Bobby used to introduce a filmed memorial to his slain brother at the 1964 Democratic National Convention:

> When he shall die,
> Take him and cut him out in little stars,
> And he will make the face of heaven so fine
> That all the world will be in love with night,
> And pay no worship to the garish sun.

The moving lines, with an oblique reference to the "garish" usurper to the Kennedy throne, Lyndon Johnson, brought the audience in Atlantic City's convention center to tears. Jackie also gave Bobby her copy of Edith Hamilton's *The Greek Way*. The book was his introduction to the Greek philosophers, and their writings struck a resonant chord deep inside him. He was profoundly grateful to Jackie. As for the gossip that they had an affair, no physical relationship could have brought them closer than the spiritual bond they now shared.

The other memorial that Jackie concentrated on was the John F. Kennedy presidential library. She sent a collection of memorabilia, including his famous desk, a coconut shell that he had carved an S.O.S. message on during World War II, and other personal mementos, on a fund-raising tour. It would take more than fifteen years for the building to be completed, during which time the Kennedy myth was badly damaged by an endless projection of unseemly revelations. In the end, however, the I. M. Pei–designed structure rose majestically over Columbia Point, close to the Dorchester neighborhoods where Rose Kennedy played as a young girl. Today the Kennedy Library is the most popular of all the presidential libraries, attracting more than 4 million visitors a year. The John F. Kennedy Library Foundation furthers the goals of the Kennedy presidency, in part through the yearly awarding of the *Profiles in Courage* Awards.

The years between her first and second marriages saw Jackie assume the role of professional widow. It was not a role solely of her own choosing. Gloria Steinem said, "We behaved as if she could not (or should not) create any future independent of the powerful Kennedy image." That image is one Jackie helped create and one she fought to maintain.

Jackie displayed intense interest in the multitude of Kennedy books that were published in the years after the assassination. She selected William Manchester to write the Kennedy-sanctioned account of JFK's death, *The Death of a President* (Manchester was the third choice, after Theodore White and *A Night to Remember* author Walter Lord). Both the process and the publication of Manchester's book caused Jackie much anguish. Her seemingly high-handed behavior with Manchester led to the first suggestion of public disapproval since the assassination. She was accustomed to being the arbiter of Camelot's literary legacy, and her sword cut both ways. Both Arthur Schlesinger's *A Thousand Days: John F. Kennedy in the White House* and Ted Sorensen's *Kennedy* were shown to her for approval and editorial suggestions. The family welcomed both books, as they did Ken O'Donnell and Dave Powers's *Johnnie: We Hardly Knew Ye* ("I know it will bring a great deal of pleasure to Caroline and John, as they always love your stories about their father," Jackie wrote, thanking Powers).

Other writers were not so lucky, with the family restricting access to sources and adopting a passive-aggressive noncooperation strategy. If you were an insider writing a book that the family disapproved of, the Kennedy reaction was frigid disdain. Red Fay's *The Pleasure of His Company* annoyed her so much that she returned his three-thousand-dollar contribution to the library. Both Maud Shaw's affectionate memoir and Mary Gallagher's bitter tell-all, *My Life with Jacqueline Kennedy*, earned their authors Jackie's lasting enmity. In some regards the Kennedys' attitude was understandable; no one welcomes friends and former employees writing "warts and all" stories, and people were coming out of the woodwork to write these books—the presidential dog handler, Joe Kennedy's nurse, the White House housekeeper, et al. But on the other hand, it was a piece of our history, and the Kennedys had worked very hard throughout the 1950s to capture the public imagination. They succeeded beyond their wildest dreams, and perhaps beyond their wildest desire.

Jackie was the keeper of the flame, ensuring that it burned brightly until Bobby was ready to take Jack's place in the Oval Office. And yet shortly after Bobby entered the presidential race in the late winter of 1968, Jackie confessed her fear for Bobby to Arthur Schlesinger: "They will do to him what they did to Jack." When Bobby was killed three months later, Jackie was devastated, telling a friend, "I have a tendency to go into a downward spiral of depression or isolation when I'm sad." She wasn't allowed to, though, for there were public expectations of her conduct.

Jackie was the national mourner. She was the public widow. It was a tough role to play, but she had done it once before—and we knew how brilliant she was at it. The American public could not see her as anything but a living memorial to her dead husband and, now, his slain brother. "It was this refusal," Gloria Steinem said, "to see her as a separate woman that increased the public shock when she married Aristotle Onassis. Without an understanding of her own problems and daily life, not to mention the penalties of just existing as the most famous living symbol of the Kennedy era, her second marriage just didn't make sense."

New York, 1975

Jackie once told a reporter for the *Scranton Times,* of all places, "Why do people always try to see me through the different names I have had at different times? People often forget that I was Jacqueline Bouvier before being Mrs. Kennedy or Mrs. Onassis. Throughout my life I have always tried to remain true to myself. This I will continue to do as long as I live."

From 1975, after Onassis's death from myasthenia gravis, until the end of her life almost twenty years later, Jackie finally found an identity apart from any connection to a man. Though Maurice Tempelsman would spend more than half of that time as her last, and closest, companion, Jackie came into her own upon her return from Skorpios.

"What," she exclaimed over lunch, "me . . . *work?*"

But that's just what Tish Baldrige had in mind for her old friend. They met a month or so after Onassis died, and Tish had a plan in mind for Jackie. That the two women remained friends for so long is a testament to Tish's loyalty and Jackie's good sense. They'd been friends for almost twenty years before Tish became Jackie's first social secretary in the White House. Two and a half years of nonstop stress nearly ruptured their relationship. "There are stories of what happened during those years that I will never repeat," Tish wrote in her revised memoirs, *A Lady, First.* Tish recognized the power that Jackie wielded as First Lady and forever tried to convince her to take on more. "You've just *got* to do it," she would beseech Jackie. "I don't *have* to do anything," Jackie would respond. She had never allowed herself to be pressured into anything, by either family or friends. Jackie would once confide to a friend, "Mummy and Tish prefer frenzy—but that is all they have to fill their lives." Tish sensed

Jackie's growing resentment of her nudging but kept on plugging. Jackie would rail at her, "Not everyone has your energy, you know. I certainly don't. I don't want to do all those things. Keep it away." But Tish had been responsible for some of the most memorable White House events during the Kennedy years. A dozen years had passed, and Tish felt confident enough in her idea to bring it up over lunch. She suggested that Jackie become a book editor, volunteering to act as a go-between with a few publishing houses.

So began Jackie's career as an editor, one that she enjoyed tremendously and that earned her wide respect. The news that she would be joining Viking Press as a consulting editor drew skeptical comments around the city. "It's not as if I've never done anything interesting," Jackie said in retort. "I've been a reporter myself and I've lived through important parts of American history. I'm not the worst choice for this position."

It was, Arthur Schlesinger would say, "a job for which her critical eye and flawless taste admirably equipped her." She would stay at Viking for almost two years, until a controversy arose over the house's 1977 publication of a novel that featured an assassination attempt on Ted Kennedy. When the *New York Times* book reviewer made a pointed allusion to Jackie in his review—"Anyone associated with its publication should be ashamed of herself"—Jackie left Viking, moving over to Doubleday, where she stayed for seventeen years, until her death.

"She reveled in her books becoming moneymakers," Stephen Rubin, Doubleday's publisher and Jackie's boss, remembered, but "making money wasn't what fueled her passion; publishing good, interesting books motivated her." Jackie's work as an editor allowed her to delve into her varied interests: "I'm drawn to books that are out of our regular experience.... To me a wonderful book is one that takes me on a journey into something I didn't know before."

Her tastes were catholic, as evident in an aside she once made to a publishing colleague: "I would give up food to publish Hunter Thompson." Thompson, the gonzo journalist for *Rolling Stone* and author of *Fear and Loathing in Las Vegas*—a first-person psychedelic account of the author's attending a law-and-order convention in Las

Vegas in 1971—is the complete antithesis of the kind of author that, given Jackie's genteel upbringing, one would expect her to embrace.

She would enter a new relationship with New York society. She could easily have become the leader of the wave of society that came to New York in the 1980s, when brash and hugely wealthy upstarts joined old-money families. But she remembered Black Jack's lessons from childhood—hold something back, be a little mysterious, a little hard to get—and carefully chose those events that she would patronize. Again, she stayed true to herself and supported causes that she had long been involved with, the American Ballet Theatre and the Municipal Art Society. Her involvement sparked commitment and, if not capable of moving mountains, was, in the latter case, sufficient to put fear into the hearts of commercial real-estate developers.

Grand Central Terminal was saved from desecration thanks primarily to the very visible support Jackie threw behind efforts to thwart plans for a tower on top of it. "They're stealing the sky" was her battle cry when it was discovered that a building plan for New York's Columbus Circle would cast a long shadow across the southern end of Central Park. She took on God, in the form of Park Avenue's St. Bartholomew's Church, which wanted to tear down its rectory to make way for a huge skyscraper that would cantilever over the church's byzantine dome. Neither project materialized.

Her social life in the mid-1980s was far different from her social life twenty years earlier, which was ridiculed in a chapter in Truman Capote's unfinished novel, *Answered Prayers,* a malicious gem called "Le Cote Basque, 1965." Calling Jackie and Lee "a pair of Western geisha girls . . . their heads inclining towards each other in whispering Bouvier conspiracy," Capote takes elaborate pains to present a life of languid self-absorption. He caps his story, which was fueled by personal animosity toward Jackie, with a tale that rippled with campy scorn: "A drag queen contest held in a Harlem ballroom: hundreds of young queens sashaying in hand-sewn gowns to the funky honking of saxophones: Brooklyn supermarket clerks, Wall Street runners, black dishwashers, and Puerto Rican waiters adrift in silk and fantasy, chorus boys and bank cashiers and Irish elevator boys got up as Marilyn Monroe, as Audrey Hepburn, as Jackie Kennedy. Indeed Mrs. Kennedy was the most popular inspiration: a dozen boys, the winner among them, wore her high-rise hairdo, winged eyebrows, sulky, palely painted mouth. And, in life, that is how she struck me—not as a bona fide woman, but as an artful female impersonator impersonating Mrs. Kennedy."

Even in the eighties, however, Jackie couldn't escape camp. One night in the late 1980s she was invited to the home of her friends Brooke Hayward and Peter Duchin for an informal dinner. Informal, yes, but it required both a touch of redecoration and the services of that particular breed of Manhattanite known as the cater-waiter—a young person, usually male, usually an actor, who subsidizes his creative life by waiting tables at private parties large and small. The redecoration was necessary out of tact to the former First Lady; a large Andy Warhol painting of Jackie Kennedy at President Kennedy's funeral dominated the Duchins' foyer. Walking in on it would hinder the start of an enjoyable evening. With the artwork rearranged and the offending painting hidden in a back bedroom, the cater-waiters hovered around the door waiting to see which one would be called upon to take Jackie's coat when she arrived. It didn't matter really who took her coat: throughout the evening each would slip into the bedroom where they were stored and slip it on, posing in front of the mirror like the would-be actress Phoebe at the end of *All About Eve*.

Jackie-spotting became a New York sport; the author Dominick Dunne recalled, "I saw her standing on a long line for the ladies' room at Radio City Music Hall." He remembers being impressed by her demeanor, thinking of "a whole list of people far less famous than she who would have found a way to get to the head of the line." She went to the theater, ate in hamburger shops as well as five-star restaurants, and jogged around the reservoir in Central Park. Her ubiquitous sunglasses became her shield—she could see but not be seen.

Caroline and John both graduated from college and moved out on their own during these years, leaving the big apartment empty. Jackie built a home on Martha's Vineyard, inviting the Kennedys over to see her for a large family picnic once a summer. She moved with grace into her middle years; in the words of William F. Buckley, "She gave more time to consolidating friendships that especially appealed to her than to quick processing fresh friends." A burgeoning romance with Maurice Tempelsman would bring contentment to the third act of Jackie's life.

Chapter Seventeen

Owning a Piece of the Myth
Two Sales of the Century

*The inspiration for this wonderful sale comes from just one per-
son . . . our son William.*

—Diana, June 1997

*Because these things she collected link her with history, and because
she cared about them, they represent more than just a record of her
life and travels. As they go out into the world, we hope that they
bring with them not only their own beauty and spirit, but some of
hers as well.*

—Caroline and John Kennedy, April 1996

The 1980s and 1990s saw the celebrity auction rise to dazzling
heights, turning what was essentially a high-priced tag sale into an
art form. Starting with the 1987 sale of the jewels of the duchess of
Windsor, there seemed to be a "sale of the century" with every celebrated death. Andy Warhol's quickly followed the Windsor sale,
and the ranks were enlarged by Marilyn Monroe, Pamela Harriman,
Sister Parish, et al., but the trend reached its apogee with the 1996
Sotheby's sale of the estate of Jacqueline Kennedy Onassis.

Auction houses like to say that they are driven by the three D's—
death, divorce, and debt. It was the death of Jacqueline Onassis and

the substantial tax debt that her children faced that led to the massive auction of her belongings, and it was divorce that would lead Diana to divest herself of some of the trappings of her former life, the ball gowns and evening dresses she wore before and during her tenure as a working princess.

The Windsor sale was the first of these mega-auctions, and the jewels collected over a forty-year romance were expected to bring in $7 million. People in the know were amused that Sotheby's would discount the associative value of the pieces, and place the price estimates firmly at the actual value of each piece. "I'd be satisfied taking home the difference between the estimates and the final bids," joked financier Malcolm Forbes at a charity cocktail party held at Sotheby's during the preview week. Forbes knew his business; the estate sold for more than $53 million. The romance of the Windsors, whether real or imagined, plus a whole lot of hype, fueled these incredible prices. The hammer came down and eyebrows went up when an emerald, ruby, and diamond brooch, valued at $7,500, sold for close to $275,000, more than thirty-six times its estimate, or when a mismatched set of blazer buttons, valued at one hundred dollars, sold for six thousand.

The Warhol sale was the next big one on the scene, and the acquisitive nature of the artist, whose town house on East Sixty-sixth Street was chockablock full of his flea-market finds, Art Deco furniture, and those ubiquitous cookie jars, raised more than $25 million for the Andy Warhol Foundation for the Visual Arts. People once again shook their heads in wonder as the series of ceramic cookie jars, valued at thirty or fifty dollars apiece, sold for tens of thousands of dollars each.

What was the appeal? What would drive a person to such mad heights of overspending? There was little chance that any of the items would retain much of their associative value once the fever had died down. Why then? To touch something that your favorite celebrity had touched? To listen to a record or read a book that he or she had enjoyed? To have communion with a celebrity though a tangible asset? It's hard to say. Steve Martin, the comedian and film actor, once said that when a fan comes in contact with a celebrity, that meeting doesn't put the fan in touch with his fantasy; instead, it puts him in touch with his reality. That, Martin found, was distressing. ("He's right about that" was Jackie's comment.)

The sale of Jackie's possessions in April 1996 and the following year's auction of Diana's wardrobe raised millions, which if nothing else, validated their celebrity. Celebrity auctions were hardly a new phenomenon. The lesser-known houses had always had these sorts of sales, at which it was possible, for example, to buy a pair of Joan Crawford's false eyelashes or one of Ruth Gordon's Chanel suits. But the A-list celebrity sale became more than an auction: it became a cultural event, offering those with the money (and the desire to spend it wildly) the opportunity to own a piece of ephemera that would give them a tangible connection to the person they fantasized about.

Few who bought Diana's dresses actually wanted to wear them, if they could even fit into them. But those who bought Jackie's possessions were eager to incorporate these inanimate articles into their day-to-day life, looking at the paintings or sitting on the chairs or wearing the diamond earrings. In that regard it's easier to see the Jackie sale as being the more intimate and personal of the two, despite the fact that Diana actually wore each of the items sold at Christie's. Jackie may never have actually opened the presentation copy of Roger Bye's *How Christmas Came to Hawaii,* but it had been inscribed to her and most likely found a home in the bookshelves she had built into her dining room. She may have run her fingers over the bindings, or used it to prop up a wobbly table leg. And that was enough.

One footnote: in donating the proceeds of the sale of her dresses to two charities, Diana joined that other pariah of the royal family, Wallis Windsor, to become one of the two most philanthropic members of the Windsor clan. The duchess's estate was sold to benefit the Pasteur Institute at the American Hospital in Paris, while the AIDS Crisis Trust and the Cancer Research Fund for the Royal Marsden Hospital were the recipients of Diana's largesse. Together the two women endowed these charities with more than $50 million.

London and New York, Spring 1997

The idea came from fourteen-year-old William. Telephoning Diana at Kensington Palace one day, he boldly announced, "I've had a brilliant idea, Mum.... Why don't you have a sale of your dresses for charity?" Before she could answer, he impishly added, "And I'll take ten percent."

Her divorce settlement, ironed out the previous year, strictly forbade Diana from profiting from her former life as a royal, but there were no provisions to bar a sale of her belongings to benefit charity.

"It is brilliant!" she replied. "I love it."

"The Americans would go wild for this," William reminded her, and rang off to finish his schoolwork.

Diana went into her dressing room, large enough to be a bedroom (which it once had been), and spent over three hours combing through her collection of ball gowns, evening dresses, and cocktail suits. She had amassed a collection of formal wear that numbered well over one hundred different outfits, most of which wouldn't be necessary in her new, simplified life.

She had, of course, been admired for her style and fashion sense, but her stature as a royal princess often took precedence over her personal taste. Skirts had to be a "correct" length, and strict design attention had to be paid to the cultural climate and expectations, especially in the Middle East. Her evening clothes sometimes incorporated elaborate embroidery and embellishment that made the garment seem more appropriate for an older woman. Bodices often had to have protective backing, so that the honors and medals she would wear to state dinners didn't ruin the lines of the dress or pull at the delicate fabrics. There were a lot of clothes that she just wouldn't need again; others, perhaps, she just wanted to get rid of.

Diana contacted Christie's auction house to help her dispose of her dresses in a dignified, and profitable, manner. From its first sale on December 5, 1766, Christie's had been accustomed to dealing with fascinating women. James Christie, the company's founder and namesake, himself negotiated the sale of Sir Robert Walpole's collection of paintings with Catherine the Great of Russia, the collection that would form the base of the Hermitage Museum in St. Petersburg.

Christie's jumped at the idea of the sale, agreeing with Prince William that the United States was the proper venue, both for the high level of interest expected from American buyers and also to remove the sale from under the nose, and expected criticism, of the "establishment." It was decided to hold the event in New York City at the end of the social season, the last week in June, with special preview showings in London and New York. Additional money would be raised through several charity cocktail parties and through the sale of the catalog. As large as an art book, the catalog featured a series of photographs by Lord Snowden of Diana wearing the gowns. Proceeds from the sale of the catalog would be divided among three American charities: AIDS Care Center at the New York Hospital–Cornell Medical Center, the Harvard AIDS Institute, and the Evelyn H. Lauder Breast Center of Memorial Sloan-Kettering Cancer Center.

The dresses Diana chose to include in the sale spanned her entire royal career, from a romantic pale blue ball gown she wore as Prince Charles's fiancée at a state dinner a month before their wedding to the sleek lilac crepe dress with a delicately embroidered bolero jacket from the disastrous visit to South Korea when their marriage was publicly falling apart. The dresses represented the crème of British design, and many of the couturiers enjoyed their success largely because of Diana's patronage. Most of the dresses came from her favorite designer, the French-trained Catherine Walker, but the collection included such stalwart British labels as Hartnell, Emanuel, Bellville Sassoon, as well as the design stars Zandra Rhodes, Bruce Oldfield, and Jacques Agzaury.

Organizing the sale was a means by which Diana could, literally, shed the past and all its unpleasant associations, and face the future with few of the royal trappings that had made her so unhappy. She could be herself, the new Diana.

When Diana swept into the charity cocktail party, held in Christie's Park Avenue galleries, it was clear she was firmly ensconced in her postroyal megawatt star persona. In a short and clinging ice blue dress, she turned on her million-dollar smile and charmed everyone within a ten-block radius. The evening placed Diana at the apex of New York society in the 1990s, when extravagant private parties had been replaced by charity benefits (where one could be simultaneously benevolent *and* chic).

Launched in society, Diana next conquered two of the most powerful media divas in town. Joining Tina Brown, then the editor of *The New Yorker,* and *Vogue's* Anna Wintour at the ultra-chic Four Seasons hotel, the trio talked of the problem of raising a famous child in the media age. During what she described as a "lunch between friends," Diana spoke of William, telling Brown that she had given him advice "about the media—the dangers, and how he must understand and handle it."

"I think he has it," the princess said. "I think he understands. I'm hoping he'll grow up to be as smart about it as John Kennedy Jr. I want William to be able to handle things as well as John does."

The next morning's *New York Daily News* reported on the public exhibitions: "Christie's Auction Gallery yesterday turned its tony halls on Park Avenue into a royal walk-in closet. They go on the block Thursday after a week of scrutiny from perhaps the only audience in the world that could be tougher than Britain's royal family: New Yorkers."

And the New Yorkers who viewed the exhibition were not shy about expressing their opinions: "I'd say about ten percent of what's here is exquisite," said one. "About thirty percent is really tacky, and the rest is in between."

"You can see where she went bulimic," said another. "Some of these dresses, you could put your hands all the way around the waist."

And the clincher: "The really tacky ones, some drag queen should buy them, put elastic panels in the side, and wear them out on the town. That's absolutely where they belong."

There was a phase in the collection, the mid to late 1980s, where the "Dynasty Di" influence could easily be seen in the sequins and big shoulders made popular by Joan Collins and Linda Evans. Many of the dresses had eye-catching details better suited for the cameras and for crowds than for up-close viewing. They were overly fussy and unnecessarily complicated.

But some of the dresses were stunners. The ice blue "Grace Kelly" dress, strapless and made from diaphanous silk chiffon, the pearl-encrusted "Elvis Dress" with its distinctive turned-up collar, and the sexy black "F You" dress by Christina Stambolian that Diana wore to the *Vanity Fair* dinner the night Charles divulged his infidelity on national television were three of the stars of the collection. None of the dresses were sized, as they had all been custom-made for Diana, but experts judged them to be the equivalent of an American size six or eight. Hundreds of eager fans braved the summer heat to view the dresses.

The sale took place on the night of Wednesday, June 25, with admission limited to ticketholders who had purchased one of the catalogs. Lord Charles Hindlip, Christie's chairman, took the gavel that night and conducted a lively auction, to the great amusement of the crowd, which did not include Diana. (She had returned home the day before the sale.) The first offering, a white silk chiffon sari-like dress, sold for $85,000, getting the proceedings off to a quick start.

The famous "F You" dress was up next, selling for $74,000; then the bidding settled down. With a few exceptions, most of the eighty dresses sold for between $25,000 and $35,000. Hindlip gave an inspired performance, cajoling and joking with the audience, which was packed into the main auditorium and an adjacent hall. He even mildly admonished an overexuberant woman in the side room, who starting bidding before the dress she wanted had come up for sale.

The highlight of the sale was the ink blue velvet gown Diana had worn the night she danced with John Travolta at the White House. The elegant gown, Edwardian-inspired with a slight bustle, sold for $222,500, making it the highest price ever paid at auction for a piece of clothing. The second highest price? One hundred forty-five thousand dollars for the three-piece white polyester suit Travolta wore in *Saturday Night Fever*.

When the last dress was sold, between the auction, the two benefits, and the sale of the catalog, the total amount raised for the charities was $5.76 million. "We are thrilled with the results...it was more than we expected to raise," Hindlip said. "We were in new territory with this sale and we didn't know how generous the audience would be."

The buyers were both generous and thrilled. They included the Romance Classics cable television channel (now WE TV), which bought the princess's favorite gown, a Victor Edelstein design in oyster duchesse satin whose bodice and matching bolero jacket were embroidered with simulated pearls and white and gold bugle beads. The Franklin Mint also bought several of the gowns, but most went to private owners.

Back in London, Diana called William at boarding school and squealed with delight, "Isn't it wonderful? Millions of dollars for some old frocks!"

"So," William responded, "where's my ten percent?"

New York, 1996

There were rumors at first, whispers from auction-world insiders that were soon picked up by the gossip columnists. The columns turned the whispers into a buzz, and so when it was announced in the press that Caroline and John Kennedy would be selling off their mother's estate through an auction at Sotheby's, Jackie fans from the Upper East Side to lower Slovenia were thrilled. Jackie represented many things to her admirers—class, courage, dignity, style, luxury, history. There were many who wanted to look, and live, like the queen of Camelot, and now they would have the opportunity to do just that.

There were others who were aghast at the very thought of having the personal items of this very private woman gaped at and pawed over by the masses, well heeled though they might be. Was it greed on the part of her children? they wondered. If they had to have what one friend of the former First Lady called "that dreadful auction," couldn't it have been handled in a more dignified, quiet manner without the attendant monsoon of publicity? After all, Jackie had been quietly selling her personal objects, even her clothes, for years. A quick phone call to a discreet East Side shop, a protracted discussion over price, an unmarked van pulling up to the Eighty-fifth Street service entrance to 1040 Fifth, and some lucky New Yorker would soon be donning a gently used Valentino suit or using a wineglass engraved THE PRESIDENT'S HOUSE to sip a chilled Pouilly-Fuissé.

What nobody realized, though, was that Caroline and John were merely following the instructions clearly laid out by their mother's will. Section E, paragraph 2, states: "I direct that the balance of said tangible personal property shall be sold and the net proceeds of the sale shall be added to my residuary estate, thereafter to be held, administered and disposed of as a part thereof." After a provision stating that all the items relating to the life and work of JFK be donated to his presidential library in Boston, the children were invited to take the items they wanted for themselves and then sell the rest.

Jackie herself, a shrewd observer of the celebrity world she abstained from, knew what was in store and told an antique-dealer friend, "They're going to make a *lot* of money." As for her own feelings, she had once told a reporter (who asked if her point of view had changed about the propriety of examining the private lives of public figures) that "when it's past, it becomes history" and that "I won't be here to mind" if history focused on her after her death.

Sotheby's had been called in to take on the huge task of sorting through the thousands of personal items that Caroline and John wanted to dispose of. There was the Fifth Avenue apartment, the home on the Vineyard, the weekend house near Peapack, New Jersey, and the cottage in Virginia's hunt country, as well as three warehouses filled with the tangible reminders of her extraordinary life. "The estate involved is of extraordinary importance," announced Sotheby's senior vice president David Redden. "Jackie was a marvelous woman who had a unique role in our political and cultural history."

It took nearly two years of planning for the auction to come about. Sotheby's first had to meticulously catalog each item. The scope of

Jackie's collection—from pieces of furniture rich with historic association to fabulous jewelry, a private library consisting of thousands
of volumes, and such ordinary things as couches, pillows, and foot-
stools—required the participation of nearly every department at
Sotheby's. When all the items had been cataloged, valued, and photographed, it was time for the public exhibition of Jackie's goods and
chattel.

Curiosity about the sale reached a fever pitch, and the event was
a publicity department's dream—a famous name, keen interest, a
public peek inside a private life, items priced for every budget. The
sale was given extraordinary coverage on television and in print media. The catalog cost one hundred dollars, and it was necessary to
purchase one in order to enter a lottery to win admission tickets to
the preview exhibition. More than a hundred thousand catalogs were
sold; the profits, said to be close to a million dollars, were donated
to the John F. Kennedy Library Foundation.

What was most interesting to the Camelot anthropologists who
descended upon the items displayed throughout Sotheby's York Avenue headquarters was the choice of items included in the sale. It
was not surprising, perhaps, that Aristotle Onassis's stepchildren
would engineer a wholesale dumping of anything associated with
their mother's involvement with him. Almost all of the fabulous
jewelry he gave her—the 40.42-carat Lesotho III diamond engagement ring, ropes of emeralds and rubies, the extraordinarily vulgar
Lalaounis "moon" ear clips (literal representation of the 1969 lunar
landing, complete with gold spaceships and ruby craters)—was displayed in all its eye-popping opulence.

What raised questions in some quarters was the inclusion of items
with special association to either Jackie or the Kennedy family.
Among these was an Empire-style mahogany desk with ormolu decorations (ormolu is brass lacquered to look like gold) from the late-
nineteenth or early-twentieth century. Neither a historical piece nor
a valuable antique, the slant-front desk's estimate of $1,500 to $2,000
belies its sentimental value. It had been Jack Bouvier's, and not one
but two of Jackie's biographers had written specifically about her
deep attachment to it. Both Mary Gallagher's *My Life with Jacqueline*

Kennedy and J. B. West's *Upstairs at the White House: My Life with the First Ladies* chronicle Jackie's desire to honor her father's memory. She used the desk as her workstation in the private quarters' living room and was compulsive in her care of the piece, scrutinizing it for any scratches or defects when it was moved. She clearly treasured the desk, and its sentimental value was realized in a sale price of $68,500, but there were those who wondered if it could have found a home in the Kennedy Library.

Other pieces with strong family ties included an elaborate pair of eighteenth-century diamond earrings that had belonged to Annie Burr Auchincloss, an aunt-by-marriage of Jackie's. She and her husband, Wilmarth "Lefty" Lewis, the Walpole scholar, lived in Farmington, Connecticut, and had befriended Jackie during her days at Miss Porter's. Jackie had been left the earrings in Mrs. Lewis's will, and instead of returning them to the Auchincloss family, they too went up for sale. There was also a George III silver dinner plate, signed by Paul Crespin, London 1732, that bears the arms of the Cavendish family, dukes of Devonshire, which Kathleen Kennedy had married into during World War II. Jackie had proudly displayed the solid silver plate in the foyer of her home at 1040 Fifth Avenue. It's likely that JFK took the plate as a souvenir during a 1947 trip to Ireland and England to see Kick; they had stayed at a Cavendish estate in Ireland. Instead of being returned to the Devonshires, it was purchased for $13,500, reportedly by Eunice Shriver.

Shriver's son-in-law Arnold Schwarzenegger would also be a successful bidder, spending $772,500 for a set of JFK's golf clubs. Baseball star Roger Clemens, then with the Boston Red Sox, was an underbidder for the clubs. He had received special permission to leave the dugout during a game so he could bid by phone from the office of the team's doctor. Schwarzenegger also successfully bid $134,500 for a Norman Rockwell portrait of JFK and $189,500 for some Hermès leather desk accessories bearing JFK's monogram, spending well over a million dollars for a remembrance of wife Maria Shriver's illustrious aunt and uncle.

Part of the appeal of the sale was that many items were priced at seemingly affordable levels, starting at $25 for a wooden stool. Where some two hundred of the twelve hundred–plus lots were estimated to sell for less than $200, in fact only four sold for less than $2,000. Six books on Asia, selling for $1,437, took the honor of being the least expensive items in the sale. Many lots went for ten times or more their estimated price. After the Windsor and Warhol auctions, this came as no surprise, but it did cause some disappointment when people realized that they couldn't afford a piece of the dream.

Even if one left Sotheby's empty-handed, one could still partake in the voyeuristic ecstasy of leafing through the catalog, with its clues to Jackie's style and taste. It came as a shock that her famous pearls were fake, and a thrill to see that she owned a leather jewel case that was once Marie Antoinette's, as well as a pair of Thomas Jefferson's chairs. Her books, collected over sixty years, revealed a wide range of interests, as did her collection of paintings and sketches. There were formal portraits, equestrian paintings, animal studies, and even some modern art (a major Rauschenberg and a couple of minor Warhols). There was a pirate's treasure in precious jewelry and an even larger cache of the fake stuff. There was her furniture for the city and the less formal furniture for the country. There were bales of magazines featuring her and her family that she had saved, much to the amazement of people who thought she didn't pay any attention to her press coverage.

In truth, the Sotheby's catalog reveals more about the real Jackie than any of the scores of other books written about her could hope to. One can see the items she chose to surround herself with, whether it was the graceful oval mirror she sat in front of while applying her makeup or the Louis XVI obelisks that she had lent to the Red Room in the White House and then used in her own dining room, where the red-fabric-covered walls echoed her favorite room in the White House. It was a surprisingly intimate look into her inner life, complete with photographs of the public rooms of her home at 1040 Fifth Avenue, filled with flowers and candles, which she loved (thanking a friend for a Rigaud candle, she said, "There's nothing I like more. I put it on the table in the living room at Christmas and it made the room smell delicious").

When the five-day auction ended, the only items that had not sold were the few that the family had withdrawn, including a collection of Civil War memorabilia that had come to Jackie from her Bouvier grandfather and was returned to the Bouvier family. Not only did each of the 1,265 items sell, Sotheby's was inundated with calls from unsuccessful bidders eager to buy something, *anything,* from the sale. Immediately after the auction there was a flurry of private sales between those who had made successful bids and those who hadn't. Many items changed hands at a substantial profit even before they had been packed up by Sotheby's.

The aura surrounding Jacqueline Kennedy Onassis had long been considered priceless, but it was now possible to attach a very specific price to her mystique: the $34,461,495.34 that the auction brought in. After fees, expenses, and taxes, it was estimated that Caroline and John netted in the neighborhood of $5 to $7 million each for the "sale of the century."

Chapter Eighteen

Second Loves

Seeking with the soul the land of the Greeks...
—Goethe, *Iphigenia in Tauris*

It's impossible to compare the seven-year marriage of Jacqueline Kennedy and Aristotle Onassis with the seven-week summer romance of Diana, Princess of Wales, and Dodi Fayed, except to note that both women chose men who were the antithesis of their former husbands. Jack Kennedy and Charles Windsor were Celtic, Anglo, WASP, cold, undemonstrative. Aristotle Onassis and Dodi Fayed were Mediterranean, warm, earthy, passionate, sensual. In making such public alliances with men so different from their first husbands, both women declared their independence from others' expectations, moving from the conventional to the carefree, from sensibility to sensuality.

There is the cynical view that both the Onassis and al-Fayed business interests would benefit from their association with the two most famous women of their day. But that discounts the real attraction that Aristotle Onassis and Dodi Fayed held for Jackie and Diana. Each in his own way was perfectly cast for the role he was to play: Ari as the father/protector figure, whisking Jackie away to safe harbors far from the turmoil America was facing in 1968, and Dodi as the charming lothario who brought summer love to the unhappy princess.

Each man could offer the escape that Diana and Jackie needed—escape from a life that they had outgrown, escape from the control of others, escape from the image that society had imposed on them.

Skorpios, October 1968

"Nobody could understand why I married Ari," Jackie later told a close friend. "But I just couldn't live anymore as the Kennedy widow. It was a release, freedom from the oppressive obsession the world had with me."

For five years she had been venerated like some sort of chic national nun. Her decision to step off the pedestal she had been unwillingly placed on sparked shock and outrage. Public reaction to the Onassis marriage was universal condemnation: Jackie was vilified around the world. The Vatican labeled her a public sinner, newspaper headlines denounced her, and she became the object of vulgar jokes. People couldn't understand *why* she had to remarry. And if she had to remarry, we asked, why did it have to be *him*?

What people failed to see was that Aristotle Onassis was the perfect man for Jackie to marry at that moment in her life. She later praised Ari for having "rescued me at a time when my life was engulfed in shadows . . . for which I will be eternally grateful." It was an extraordinary public statement from a person who treasured her privacy as much as she did.

Robert Kennedy's murder the previous June delivered a near-fatal blow to Jackie's psyche. The pair, always close, had become soul mates since Jack's death. Jackie had broadened Bobby's aesthetic sensibility, introducing him to the classical poetry and philosophy that help shape part of his spiritual growth in the intervening years. Now Bobby was gone, shot down like Jack. Jackie had legitimate reason to fear for the safety of her children. She told friends that she was nerve-racked with worry because "if they're killing Kennedys, my kids are number one targets. . . . I want to get out of this country."

During a private vacation in Greece in 1961, Jackie told her hosts,

"I am literally enchanted with your clear blue sky, as well as your beautiful sea. . . . My dream is to have a house here to spend vacations with my children." Little did she know the tortuous route that her life would take before that wish was fulfilled.

Jackie first met Aristotle Onassis in the late 1950s, when he invited her and Jack to a cocktail party aboard his yacht *Christina*. The lure for Jack was the opportunity to meet Winston Churchill, Onassis's frequent guest and a hero of JFK's. The elderly statesman barely took note of the young U.S. Senator, causing Jackie to twit her husband's choice of a white dinner jacket: "Maybe he thought you were a waiter, Jack." Where Jack failed to make a significant impression, Jackie succeeded. Fascinated by Jackie that night, Onassis remarked to a close associate, with obvious approval, "She's got a carnal soul."

Onassis's modus operandi was simple—charming those in power while keeping his eyes focused on his ambitions. When his "good friend" Jack Kennedy was elected President, Onassis saw an entreé to JFK's inner circle through Lee Radziwill. His plan was simple: seduce Lee, then convince her to dump Stas and marry him. He would then be the brother-in-law of the President of the United States. Jack caught wind of this plan and instructed Lee to tell Onassis to stay out of the United States until after the 1964 election. He also forbade any talk of divorce for a year.

The death of Patrick Bouvier Kennedy gave Onassis the opportunity to strengthen his ties with the Kennedys. Through Lee, Onassis invited Jackie to recuperate on his yacht. He planned an Aegean cruise for the first two weeks of October 1963. Jack insisted that she go. JFK's willingness to ignore public criticism of the trip is a strong indication of how close the tragedy had drawn husband and wife together. Jackie enjoyed the cruise; it pulled her out of her lingering malaise. She relaxed aboard the ship and wrote Jack long, passionate letters. When she returned, she enthusiastically agreed to accompany him on a short campaign trip to Texas the last week in November.

Jackie made a profound connection with Onassis during the cruise, so much so that he came to Washington as her personal guest at the White House the weekend of the assassination. They walked arm in arm through the private family quarters, but few people even knew he was there. He offered Jackie his friendship and any material help within his considerable grasp.

In the years following the assassination, Onassis dropped Lee and set his sights on Jackie. It was irresistible: he was a big-game celebrity hunter, and she was the greatest celebrity of them all. He courted her arduously, and by the spring of 1968 they had discussed marriage. Family loyalty led Jackie to agree not to marry Onassis until after the 1968 presidential election. The Kennedys feared public reaction over such news would harm Bobby's chances, and Jackie's devotion to Bobby took precedence over her own feelings, and those of Onassis.

Bobby's death changed everything. Jackie and Ari wed barely four months later, in a small chapel on Ari's private island. Jackie released a short announcement to the press: "We know you understand that even though people may be well known, they still hold in their hearts the emotions of a simple person for the moments that are the most important of those we know on earth—birth, marriage and death. We wish our wedding to be a private moment among the cypresses of Skorpios with only members of the family present—five of them little children. If you will give us these moments, we will gladly give you all the cooperation possible for you to take the pictures you need."

Jackie sought spiritual advice from Cardinal Cushing, who advised her to follow her heart and chastised those who condemned her. Jackie also spoke to Rose Kennedy, who gave her blessing. Jean Smith and Pat Lawford attended, representing the Kennedys. Ethel, seven months pregnant, sent Ari a telegram: "Are there any more at home like you?" Janet and Hughdie went, as did Lee and Stas, Janet Jr. and her husband, Lewis Rutherfurd. They gathered in a small chapel to watch the Greek Orthodox ceremony, adjourning afterward to a lavish reception on the *Christina*. Jackie posed for photographs with her new husband, wearing an ivory silk and lace Valentino dress she had worn to the wedding of Bunny Mellon's daughter the previous year.

The marriage signaled a huge shift in Jackie's public persona. Mrs.

John F. Kennedy was now Jackie O. This jet-set phase of her life lasted seven years and seemed to the public to be awash in conspicuous and luxurious consumption. There were tales of lavish jewels delivered on the breakfast tray and shopping sprees at couture houses in Paris and Rome. A book, *The $20,000,000 Honeymoon: Jackie and Ari's First Year,* purported to reveal the unimaginable heights of sheer greed that characterized their married life together—Jackie's for his money and Ari's for her status.

It was hard to understand that it wasn't Onassis's fortune that Jackie craved, but the security and freedom that such wealth ensured. If such spending was obscene, well, so were some of the traumas that Jackie witnessed. If one end of the spectrum was the depravity she endured on the streets and in the hospital corridors of Dallas, then balance could be restored to her life by time spent at the opposite end—in an earthly paradise that only great wealth could provide.

There was also an honest attraction, both intellectual and physical, between the couple. Onassis was a vital, alive person, a scoundrel who lived by his own rules, much like Jack Bouvier and Jack Kennedy. Onassis was a man who had invented himself, just as Jackie had invented herself, and he fascinated her. She also enjoyed the physical passion the couple shared, which was very real and something they made little effort to conceal. This was miles away from her relationship with Jack, who rejected public displays of affection and rarely even held Jackie's hand when they were around others. "They are not demonstrative people, period" was close friend Ben Bradlee's observation.

Caroline and John had a better relationship with their stepfather than Ari's two children did with Jackie. John got on better with Ari than Caroline did, but any man would have been in a tough position, for Caroline had stronger memories of her father than did John. Ari and John enjoyed each other's company, and Jackie was grateful that her son had a strong masculine presence in his life. Both Alexander Onassis and his sister, Christina, were openly hostile to Jackie throughout the marriage. They were unwilling to accept her presence in their lives, and their stubbornness would become a source of tension within the marriage. At first, though, Jackie was enchanted with her new husband.

"Don't you think I'm lucky to be married to such a splendid person?" Jackie asked her Bouvier cousin Edie Beale. The first few years of the marriage worked. Her life moved from New York when the children were in school, to Greece in the summers, London for Christmas with the Radziwills, with trips to Paris, Palm Beach, and the Caribbean in between. Jackie's commitment to Caroline and John meant long weeks of separation from her husband, but the couple took it in stride. Onassis, not as reluctant to talk to the press as Jackie was, told a reporter that Jackie was a bird whom he had freed and that she went where she wanted when she wanted with his blessing.

After a few years the marriage turned sour for a variety of reasons. Onassis may have thought Jackie was "a little bird," but she was a woman with an iron will. Despite her true affection and respect for him, she would not readily capitulate to his whims. They were two people used to getting their own way, and after a while they started getting in each other's way. Onassis had not let his marriage interrupt his decade-long affair with opera diva Maria Callas, who, with bitchy disdain, told Gore Vidal that all of the jewels Onassis showered on Jackie were her discards. Onassis began to humiliate Jackie by meeting Callas in public places and being photographed entering her apartment on the chic avenue Foch in Paris. Jackie would retaliate with icy withdrawal, removing herself both physically and emotionally. It was a trick that drove Onassis crazy, as it had JFK, and one that Jackie employed more and more as her marriage began to disintegrate.

By the end of 1972, Onassis had thought enough about divorce to employ the unscrupulous American lawyer Roy Cohn to dig up dirt on Jackie. But tragedy struck in January 1973, when the plane that Alexander Onassis was piloting crashed. Ari's son lay in a coma, suffering from massive head wounds. His family and friends gathered at the hospital. Ari brought a pair of neurosurgeons to Athens, but there was no hope for recovery.

At the hospital Jackie did something as uncharacteristic as it was breathtaking in its audacity. She went to Alexander's fiancée, Fiona von Thyssen, and instead of offering words of condolence or understanding, she asked the grieving young woman if she knew what provisions Ari was prepared to make if he divorced her. Von Thyssen was so shocked that, twenty-five years later, she was unable to talk about the episode. "We only met once," she told Jackie's biographer Sarah Bradford, "and believe me when I say you would not wish to know what was discussed."

Having sat in a hospital room herself when the head of the man she loved was shattered to a bloody pulp, Jackie's insensitivity is hard to understand. She was a woman with a sharply developed sense of courtesy, and such a grotesque lapse is out of character. She had been in the room when both Jack and Bobby died; marriage to Onassis was supposed to free her from such trauma, yet here it was again. Perhaps the nearness to such agonizing pain unleashed some demon deep inside her, the same survival instinct that sent her climbing onto the back of the presidential limousine in Dallas.

The death of his son triggered Onassis's emotional and physical decline. There was a brief period when his grief was so intense that he sought Jackie's comfort, but he soon turned against her. He wondered if marriage to "the widow" had bestowed a curse on the House of Onassis. Christina embarked on a series of unhappy marriages, engineered for spite, not love. His son was dead. His wife was independent and willful. His business suffered losses. His first wife died under suspicious circumstances. By 1974 Ari was diagnosed with myasthenia gravas, a debilitating and incurable disease of the muscular system. Early in 1975 his condition worsened, and Jackie, on the advice of a preeminent heart specialist, arranged to have Ari moved from Athens to the American Hospital in Paris. "He's my husband and I believe this is necessary," she told his family. "Let's not argue about it."

When he died on March 16, 1975, Jackie was not at his side. She was in New York and issued a delicately worded statement to the press. "He meant a lot to me. He brought me into a world where one could find happiness and love. We lived through many beautiful experiences together which cannot be forgotten." She immediately flew to Paris to bring his body back to Skorpios for burial.

Jackie appeared to be in complete control of her emotions at the funeral of her second husband. She wore a sleek black leather coat and the huge dark sunglasses that epitomized the "Jackie O" look. Her face seemed frozen in the big toothy smile so familiar to paparazzi but so incongruous under the circumstances. Perhaps it was her defense mechanism, but it seemed bloodless and cold. Christina, weeping and distraught, stayed as far away from her stepmother as possible, even halting the funeral procession at one point to leave the car she was riding in with Jackie and Ted Kennedy. Jackie had said of Christina, "The same love binds us as when he lived," but it didn't ring true.

Onassis had changed his will to leave Jackie less of his fortune than was hers legally under Greek law. He left her a quarter share in both Skorpios and the *Christina* and an income of between $200,000 and $250,000 a year. After a period of intense negotiations, which included a public statement by Christina repudiating claims that her father had planned to divorce Jackie, a financial settlement was reached. In exchange for forfeiting her interest in his property, Jackie was given more than $26 million dollars.

She was forty-five years old, twice a widow, the mother of two teenage children, and in possession of a substantial fortune. Jackie was ready for her third act.

Saint Tropez, July 1997

"Yes, it's bliss," she told her friend Rosa Monckton.

The summer after Diana's divorce *had* been bliss; her work with the Red Cross land-mine campaign gave her a sense of real accomplishment and underscored the positive use of her celebrity power. She was independent from the royal family and wealthy, having acquired a sum almost identical to the one Jackie had received from the Onassis estate. Like Jackie, too, Diana's second act started on a yacht in the Mediterranean surrounded by wealth and luxury. Sadly, her summer fling with Dodi Fayed ensured that there would be no third act for Diana Spencer.

She first met Dodi at a polo match in July 1986. The playboy son of wealthy Egyptian businessman Mohammed al-Fayed, he dabbled in the world of Hollywood movies. He was the executive producer of the 1981 Academy Award–winning film *Chariots of Fire* (he received the credit after convincing his father to invest in the production). *Hook, F/X*, and *F/X2* were among his other film credits. Forty-one years old that summer, Dodi had the soft good looks of a pampered child of the rich; friends described him as sweet-natured and affectionate.

Dodi came to the Riviera that summer at his father's insistence. Mohammed al-Fayed had invited Diana to bring her two sons to France for a short holiday in mid-July. A fly in the ointment of the British establishment he so persistently wooed, al-Fayed delighted in the thought of entertaining the future king. His four youngest children were around the same age as William and Harry and would be good company for the two princes. Al-Fayed thought Dodi would be good company for Diana. Dodi had been seeing an American model named Kelly Fisher, who joined him in Saint-Tropez but was kept away from the royal party. Dodi would stay with Diana all day and go back to Kelly at night, using his father as an excuse for her exclusion. "I was livid," Kelly said. "They basically kept me hidden."

Diana was front and center throughout the trip, diving off of al-Fayed's yacht, roaring around the surf on a Jet Ski, and ensuring that photographers got dozens of pictures of her in alluring swimsuits. "She leaned forward, revealing a breathtaking cleavage, and preened herself on Mohammed's beach," wrote her old "friend" James Whitaker in *The Mirror*. The pictures went to good use back in England, where on July 18 Charles gave Camilla a fiftieth-birthday party at Highgrove. Tall, tanned, and fit, Diana didn't appear to have a care in the world.

The press, most of whom thought he was a member of the ship's crew, largely ignored Dodi's presence. Diana didn't spend an inordinate amount of time with him, but they had several pleasant conversations, talking about Hollywood and movie stars. When she and the boys returned to London on July 21, Dodi sent pink roses and an $11,000 Cartier watch to Kensington Palace. A week later, after she had traveled to Milan to attend the funeral of her friend the Italian designer Gianni Versace, Diana spent the weekend in Paris with Dodi. After flying from London in one of his father's helicopters, they stayed in the four-room Imperial Suite at the Ritz. The visit went undetected by the press, which Diana found both surprising and delightful.

William and Harry were spending all of August with Charles and the rest of the royal family at Balmoral, so Diana's time was her own. She joined Dodi for a six-day cruise off Sardinia and Corsica, where their love affair started in earnest. They listened to Frank Sinatra and George Michael, swam, read, and soaked up the sun. They had a week's privacy before the *Mirror* published a front-page story, DI'S NEW MAN IS AL-FAYED'S SON. Then the hunt was on. A photograph of Diana kissing another man would be easily worth a million dollars to the photographer lucky, or aggressive, enough to snap it. The fact that her new lover was the son of the controversial al-Fayed made it all the more valuable.

Mohammed al-Fayed was known for his contentious business practices and rough edges. He often spoke without thinking and ran afoul of the British government. After a protracted battle, he had purchased the flagship British store Harrods (where he installed Raine Spencer on the board of directors). That led to a government investigation; when the report revealed several jarring inaccuracies, al-Fayed was denied the British citizenship he fervently desired. Angered, he revealed that he had paid several members of Parliament to lobby on his behalf, bringing shame and scorn to Prime Minister John Major's Conservative Party. None of this unsavory behavior stopped him from becoming close to Diana. He manipulated her, telling her that they were similar because they were both outsiders sharing the same enemies.

Al-Fayed had been accused of racism and sexual harassment in his business dealings, and was quick to cry racism over his treatment by the British establishment. Promoting a romance between his son and the divorced wife of the Prince of Wales was a way for him to infuriate the establishment that treated him with scorn. The future king of England with a Muslim stepfather—the thought brought a wicked smile to the Egyptian's face.

Diana was in Bosnia, on another Red Cross–sponsored trip, when the first photographs of her and Dodi were published. Diana's patronage of the anti-land-mine campaign was effective on both a global scale—it brought real public awareness to the issue for the first time—and a more personal level. Earlier in the year she had visited Huambo, Angola, where London *Sunday Times* war reporter Christina Lamb was sent to report on her trip. "I was very cynical about Diana," she remembered. "I just saw it as a big publicity stunt, another chance for her to be photographed in front of victims, looking beautiful."

But what she saw surprised and moved her. Diana, in jeans and a T-shirt, visited a makeshift hospital, moving effortlessly from patient to patient, with Lamb acting as her Portuguese translator. "We went into one particular ward with children. And there was a little girl who was clearly in a terrible condition. She'd gone to fetch water and had stepped on a mine and basically had her entire insides blown out, and everything was sort of hanging out. It was horrific. And the hospital said that she wouldn't survive—they were just making her as comfortable as possible.... After Diana moved on, I stayed and [the little girl] said to me, 'Who was that?' And it was quite hard to explain Princess Diana to someone who didn't know. And I said, 'She's a princess from England, from far away.' And she said to me, 'Is she an angel?' And I found that really moving. This little girl probably died a few hours after that—I know she died—and it somehow seemed nice that that was the last thing she saw, this beautiful lady she thought was an angel."

Diana didn't mind the press coverage of her new romance, telling a friend, "I really can't sit at home and watch the four walls of Kensington Palace." She went off for a short cruise with her friend Rosa Monckton, the head of Tiffany's London office. She spoke of being made to feel welcome by the whole al-Fayed family and of how Dodi showered her with jewelry; she seemed in love, Monckton said, but made no mention of marriage. Back in London on the twenty-first, Diana told a doctor that she "had never felt so physically well in all her life." When a previously scheduled trip to Italy was canceled because of the death of a friend's father, Dodi asked her to go back to the South of France with him, and she happily agreed.

Diana stirred up more controversy that last week of August, and not just for her choice in male companionship. She had given an interview to the French newspaper *Le Monde* in which she roundly criticized the Conservative Party's "absolutely hopeless" policy on the land-mine issue. "The Labour Party's position has always been clear," she said. "It's going to do terrific work." She wasn't a member of the royal family anymore, but the restrictions against making public political statements seemed to be intact. The reaction from Tory politicians was loud and angry. It was a reminder of how difficult Diana's position was in England; exiled from the royal family and stripped of her title, she was still expected to live by their code of behavior. Little wonder, then, that the passionate attention of a handsome man, a millionaire's yacht, and diamond jewelry appealed to her.

For most of that last week, the pair was openly affectionate. Diana reveled in this display of sensual pleasure. Charles was a man who asked his mother's permission before kissing Diana on their wedding day. Dodi may have been as much a papa's boy as Charles was a mama's boy, but he gave Diana much and demanded little. The Fayeds' wealth gave Diana some breathing room. Private jets and large estates could keep the press at bay, and they were a family who enjoyed the pursuit of pleasure.

There have been many claims made, but no one knows what was in Diana's heart those last days of summer. Her summer had been "bliss," she had found a harmony between her public work and her private life in the year after her divorce, and she had a new life waiting for her back in London.

Chapter Nineteen

Touched by the Sun

Death lies on her like an untimely frost
Upon the sweetest flower of all the field.
> —William Shakespeare, *Romeo and Juliet*

One death was shocking, the other sad, but both came as a cruel surprise. It was unfair that they were taken from us before we were ready to say good-bye. Both deaths touched us in a fundamental way, forcing us to take a look at who we had become as a people. The writer Peggy Noonan said of Jackie's death that it was a last link to a certain kind of past, "a connection to a time, to an old America in which standards were higher and clearer and elegance meant something, a time when elegance was a kind of statement, a way of dressing up the world, and so a generous act."

There was nothing generous or elegant in Diana's violent death. We had veered so far away from that kind of life by the summer of 1997 that it came as no surprise when she was hounded into a tunnel, chased like prey by a pack of aggressive photographers. Our culture of celebrity had grown so out of control that it devoured the greatest celebrity of all.

Diana's death was fast, like a comet racing across the sky. Her death forced the most staid institution on earth, the British monarchy, to change. For the first time in its long history, Britain was in touch with its emotions, the stiff upper lip quivering. The establishment listened, and the monarchy changed the way it went about its business. That is part of Diana's legacy.

The Diana, Princess of Wales, Memorial Fund is a more tangible part of her legacy. Gifts, grants, and earnings totaling more than $150 million have been raised since her death. The beneficiaries of the fund's grants are those interests that were closest to Diana's heart: displaced people, people at the margins of society, survivors of conflict and those requiring conflict mediation, and dying and bereaved people. To date, more than $65 million has been distributed.

Jackie's death did not evoke such a passionate response, but left America longing for its past. Her discretion and sense of privacy had left her frozen in time for thirty years—we remembered the young Jackie, the queen of Camelot, and mourned her passing. There was a sense of regret for the past, a sense echoed in the words of Tennessee Williams—"gone, gone, all vestiges of gracious living."

New York, May 1994

We knew. We knew when she left the hospital that she was going home to die. It was fitting, for she had managed to live her life her way and now she wanted her life to come to its conclusion her way—surrounded by the people she loved in the home where she had lived longer than any other place. We were told that she was "facing just another phase of her illness with great fortitude." But we knew.

With her unerring sense of the rightness of things, Jackie had even managed to bid the world farewell in the most natural of ways—by taking a walk in Central Park. The park had been her playground sixty years earlier, and on that Sunday, five days before her death, she returned one last time with Maurice Tempelsman, Caroline, and her youngest grandchild, one-year-old Jack. She looked as elegant as ever, in tan slacks, pink sweater, and Hermés scarf, but her steps were halting and slow. She knew that photographers would be there, as they had been for the past three decades, but they kept a respectful distance. The photographs they took presented the image that Jackie wanted us to remember her by—an elegant woman of a certain age, content with her life and surrounded by her family. Leaning on Maurice's arm for support, with Caroline walking ahead of her, pushing a stroller, Jackie crossed Fifth Avenue and entered 1040.

Maurice Tempelsman had been an important part of Jackie's life for the past fifteen years. There's a society adage that a woman marries her first husband for love, her second for wealth, and her third for companionship. In Maurice she found "a decent man with an abundance of common sense." He also adored her in a manner that neither of her husbands had been able or willing to. An Orthodox Jew born in Belgium, Tempelsman had made his fortune in the diamond trade. He had known Jackie since the 1950s, when he had helped Jack meet representatives of the South African Diamond Syndicate. Aileen Mehle, the society writer "Suzy," found Maurice to be "erudite, charming, worldly, [a] man who had the brains and the taste and the insight to appreciate the wondrous creature Jackie was. He gave her the love, the support, the refuge and the strength that other men had denied her."

Jackie and Maurice had been in the Caribbean during the Christmas holidays when she first noticed a slight swelling in her neck and a persistent pain in her groin. They returned to New York, and a series of tests revealed that Jackie was suffering from non-Hodgkin's lymphoma, a cancer of the lymph system. Chemotherapy was the recommended treatment, and to protect her privacy, Maurice sought out consultations with preeminent specialists.

To avoid speculation and rumors, Jackie had Nancy Tuckerman make an official announcement. "She's doing very well. She's maintaining her schedule," Tuckerman said. "There is an excellent prognosis. The doctors are very optimistic." It was disturbing news but not alarming; it seemed inconceivable that Jackie could be seriously ill. Too much had happened to her; fate certainly could not be that cruel.

Jackie went back to her normal routine as much as possible and began making plans for the future. She created a living will and between January and March drew up a list of bequests that centered on Caroline and John but included other members of her family

(Lee's children, Tony and Tina Radziwill; Yusha Auchincloss; her niece Alexandra Rutherfurd; her cousin Michel Bouvier) and close friends (Maurice, Nancy Tuckerman, Bunny Mellon, Alexander Forger) and those of her staff who had maintained their loyalty (Marta Sgubin, Provi Parades, her butler Efgenio Pinheiro). Her two surviving blood siblings were excluded; Lee because "I have already done so during my lifetime," and half brother Jamie, who had been exiled for cooperating with a Kitty Kelly biography in the late 1970s.

She saw her close friends, arranging lunches with Carly Simon, publisher Joe Armstrong, and Tiffany executive John Loring. They found themselves in the unusual position of being cheered up by her, and her notes to friends made enthusiastic plans for summer on the Vineyard and foxhunting in the fall. Her treatment caused an ulcer, and Jackie was hospitalized in mid-April for surgery. But by the middle of May, she was back in the hospital, where she was told that the cancer had spread to her brain and liver and that the prognosis was now poor. It was then, Wednesday, May 18, that she left the hospital and returned home for the last time.

Ten-forty Fifth Avenue became, for the next few days, the center of the nation's focus. There had been crowds and press there before—in 1964, when she first moved in, and in 1968, just before her second marriage—but nothing like this. Hundreds of people crowded the streets around her apartment, watching as her children and grandchildren came to say good-bye. Her family came, Lee and Yusha ("I should have felt sad," he later said, "but she made me feel very happy and proud"). She would receive guests in her bedroom, with John, Caroline, and Maurice sitting nearby. Ted Kennedy, whom she adored, traveled up from Washington to sit with her, the way she had sat with him the night Joe Kennedy died. Ethel Kennedy and her children, Sargent and Eunice Shriver, Maria Shriver and Arnold Schwarzenegger, many members of the Kennedy family came to say good-bye to the woman who had done the most to create the Kennedy myth that encompassed them all.

Jacqueline Bouvier Kennedy Onassis died at 10:15 on Thursday evening, May 19. Her son came out to the street the next morning and announced that she had died "surrounded by her friends and her family and her books and the people and things that she loved. And she did it in her own way and on her own terms, and we feel lucky for that, and now she's in God's hands."

Caroline and John invited close friends and family to a private memorial service on Sunday afternoon, the day before the funeral. Mindful that there could be grotesque curiosity about the matter, the family made arrangements for her body to be prepared for burial in her apartment. Her coffin was the same Marsellus model as JFK's, made of hand-rubbed five-hundred-year-old African mahogany. It stood, covered by an antique silk quilt, in the wood-paneled living room as more than a hundred guests came to pay respects. The apartment was crowded as people shared stories and happy memories with those who knew Jackie best. "She was so wonderfully lucky to have had you for those years," a friend told Maurice. "No," he replied, "I was so wonderfully lucky to have had her."

In the midst of the quiet conversation and gentle laughter there was an explosion of emotion. A middle-aged woman broke into sobs, wailing and carrying on in a manner out of sync with the tenor of the gathering. No one could quite place her; was she a Bouvier cousin? A publishing colleague? With a sense of dread, it became apparent that she was an outsider who had somehow made it through the tight security downstairs and had crashed the wake.

With remarkable poise, John Kennedy took the woman into the elevator vestibule and gently but firmly said, "Madam, you do not belong here." John had inherited from his mother the rare ability to do exactly the right thing under the most excruciating of circumstances. That gift was only part of her legacy.

Ted would speak of her greater legacy during his moving eulogy: "She made a rare and noble contribution to the American spirit. But for us, most of all she was a magnificent wife, mother, grandmother, sister, aunt, and friend. She graced our history. And for those of us who knew and loved her—she graced our lives."

Paris, August 31, 1997

Diana once wistfully longed to be free of royal stricture, saying, "It would be quite nice to do things like a weekend in Paris." Sadly, she got her wish that last weekend in August. What was meant to be a romantic evening in the City of Lights became an event that literally stopped the world as nothing had since the death of John Kennedy thirty-four years earlier.

Diana's summer romance with Dodi Fayed was invigorating. It gave her an absence of tension for the first time in years. She could frolic, she could play, she could do what she wanted, with little fear of repercussion. The idyll was "heaven," she said, but it was coming to an end. She was due in London to see her beloved boys that Sunday. They were in Balmoral with Charles and due to spend the last part of their summer vacation with her. When Dodi suggested an overnight stay in Paris, she was thrilled with the romantic spontaneity of his gesture and happily agreed. Paris at the end of the summer is a quiet city; most of the shops are closed, and much of the population is away on vacation. It would be nice to spend a romantic evening in the nearly deserted city.

They flew up on Saturday afternoon and, upon their arrival in Paris, went to the Second Empire mansion on the edge of the Bois de Boulogne that had been the longtime home of the duke and duchess of Windsor. Diana had replaced the duchess as the most notorious woman in the Windsor family; it's ironic that her last hours on earth were spent in the ghostly rooms where the "romance of the century" had played itself out. The rooms were empty, the contents shipped to America, where Mohammed al-Fayed had sent them to be auctioned off. As Diana walked through the house, she may have impishly imagined herself as its new mistress—wouldn't *that* send the royal establishment into a tizzy.

A small pack of photographers had been waiting at Le Bourget airport for Diana and Dodi to arrive. As they moved through Paris, first to the Villa Windsor, then onto the Ritz and Dodi's apartment off the Champs-Elysées, the pack grew larger until it was a small mob, armed with strobe lights and telephoto lenses. They followed

Diana on motorbikes, which were more effective for weaving through traffic. Their aggressive tactics rattled Dodi enough that he impulsively changed his dinner plans and headed back to the Ritz. Privacy there was ensured since his father owned the hotel. The pack of photographers was left waiting in front of the hotel in the place Vendôme.

As the world knows, Diana and Dodi hoped to escape the press by leaving through the hotel's back entrance on the rue Cambon. But even there privacy eluded the couple; a few crafty photographers lay in wait. A guest at the Ritz who was entering the hotel just as Diana was leaving said you could see only a flash of blond hair as she whisked out the door, and then a blaze of photographers' flashguns. Those last photographs of Diana show her at her most radiant—tall, tanned, healthy, dressed simply in white jeans and a black jacket. She got into the Mercedes and slipped away into the night.

She died in the moment of her perfection.

Like the heroine in a Wagnerian opera, Diana was freed from all the traumas of earth. She died at the height of her happiness, happiness she had waited so long to find. Just as she found that happiness, found balance in her life, found a focus for her future, just at the moment that everything came together, she died. In that regard her death was very similar to that of Kick Kennedy, who also died tragically while traveling in France with her lover. Whereas Kick's death saddened everyone who knew her, Diana's death shocked the entire world.

The response to her death was extraordinary. People were caught up in an archetypal seizure, the largest the world had ever seen. People who had never cared about Diana, never understood her appeal, couldn't understand the depth of their feelings—"Why I am crying?" It was jarring to our psyche, something with a global reach that was happening outside of our personal ego control. Few events before or since have matched it.

It was also extraordinary that no moral questions were raised about her death. Here she was with some playboy, an Arab man, with expensive jewelry and the Ritz Hotel and all the elements of a tawdry novel. There were no questions, asked or unasked, about why she wasn't with her children or what she was doing in Paris in the middle of the night. No great public moralist asking, "If she wasn't with her children, why at least wasn't she thinking about them, or pining away outside the gates of Balmoral for them? What was she doing on the Riviera?"

This is a very real part of Diana's legacy to the world. She was a self-confessed adulterer, a bulimic who had sought psychiatric care. Her husband loved another woman, and her in-laws banished her from their lives. She had been rejected. She felt a commonality with the disenfranchised that set her apart from women coming from a similar privileged background.

The writer Carol Gillian was waiting in a bus station in the working-class city of Springfield, Massachusetts, a few days after Diana's death. With nothing to do but stare at the stationary television set, Gillian watched with amazement to see her fellow travelers riveted to the screen. "There was a woman from Diana's village, and she was being interviewed and she said, 'She is one of us and she is coming home.' And I thought, This is extraordinary. We divide women in this society and here's this woman, plain, ordinary, not privileged, not beautiful, and she feels as one with Diana." Diana broke the barriers in society that separate women, and when she spoke publicly and without shame about the truths in her life, people embraced her. She had smashed the icon.

And the destruction of icons leads to revolution.

Diana's death triggered seven days that rocked the British royal family. From the queen's initial refusal to allow a royal plane to bring Diana's body home to England on Sunday to her act of obeisance to her former daughter-in-law on the day of her funeral, it was a week unlike any other in British history. By their own failure to act in a respectful manner, the Windsors faced the biggest crisis the monarchy had seen since Edward VIII's abdication in 1936. From her first tepid public comment, that she was "deeply distressed" by the news, up through her return to Buckingham Palace the afternoon before the funeral, it seemed that Elizabeth could do nothing right. The people of Britain were first shocked, then saddened, then angered by the disrespect the royal family displayed to Diana. From the Sunday-morning church service at Balmoral, where at the queen's insistence there was no mention of Diana, one bad decision after another came from the castle. Finally the newspapers started pleading WHERE IS OUR QUEEN? and SPEAK TO US, MA'AM. The queen was warned that she would be booed or even assaulted by garbage when she returned to London for the funeral.

It was the intervention of Tony Blair, the Labour Party prime minister, that put the queen on the right track. He instinctively understood the larger meaning of Diana's death and the effect it would have on the British public. Blair hailed Diana as "the people's princess" and, working through Prince Charles, ensured that her funeral would pay proper homage to the woman who had changed the face of the British monarchy.

Diana's death was the cause of immense grief, unlike anything Britain had ever witnessed. People placed flowers in front of Diana's home, and as the week progressed, the offerings grew and grew until Kensington Palace was engulfed in acres of flowers. Mourners stood in line for ten or twelve hours to sign one of the books of remembrance. Those who couldn't get to London sat riveted to their television screens. Regular programming was preempted, and every network ran specials as the story unfolded.

Point by point the queen caved in to public sentiment. Diana's body rested in the Chapel Royal at St. James's Palace, where Queen Victoria had been married. She was given as close to a state funeral as possible, with the processional route to Westminster Abbey doubled in length in order to accommodate the mourners who flooded into the city. Elizabeth and Philip, who had planned on flying down to London on Saturday morning to attend the funeral, instead came a day earlier so the queen could make a televised address from Buckingham Palace. Except for her annual Christmas broadcast, it was only the second time in her reign that she had addressed the nation (the Gulf War had been the first). Buckingham Palace submitted her speech to Tony Blair, who felt it read too cold and impersonal. He had an aide insert phrases that provided a human element—"as a grandmother" and "I say from my heart," among others. Elizabeth paid tribute to her former daughter-in-law as an "exceptional and gifted human being" who inspired others "with her warmth and kindness." Elizabeth claimed to have admired and respected Diana, "for her energy and commitment to others, and especially for her devotion to her two boys." She vowed to "cherish her memory." Her last words were a thinly veiled plea for a show of civility toward the royal family, stating that the funeral was "a chance to show to the whole world the British nation united in grief and respect."

Only one last point remained, and on Saturday morning, as the queen left Buckingham Palace for the funeral, the royal standard, which is the queen's personal flag, was lowered. All week long there had been fierce argument that there was no Union Jack flying at half-mast from Buckingham Palace. By long-standing tradition, the only flag that flew above the palace was the monarch's standard when she was in residence. The queen had resisted until the very last moment altering this tradition to honor Diana, whom she felt had showered the monarchy with disrespect. But Elizabeth capitulated on that point, too, and for the first time in history, the British flag was raised atop Buckingham Palace and lowered to half-staff in the universally recognized gesture of mourning.

The previous day, when the queen's standard was being raised, it caught on a snag halfway up the pole and momentarily stopped at the halfway point. A television commentator, reporting live, summed up the situation nicely. "The queen may not want the flag to rest at half-staff," he said, "but God does."

Two Funerals

Give rest, O Lord, to your handmaid who has fallen asleep.
—John Tavener, *Song for Athene*

She had been waked at home, in the manner of the Irish families of Boston, the coffin set proudly in front of the fireplace in the living room so close friends and family could come to pay their respects. The house was quiet with mourning; her two children were preparing themselves for the funeral, with the small tasks that thankfully take one's mind off the sadness, if only for a moment. The family was arguing over the press, how much to allow, how much to restrict, for underlying all of the sorrow was the knowledge that this most painful of ceremonies would be conducted under intense public scrutiny.

There was no way to avoid the prying eyes of the press and public. All week long there had been relentless media coverage and curious onlookers crowding on the streets outside her home. Her children, especially her eldest, understood the needs of the press yet resented the intrusion, especially at this dreadful time. At the last moment a compromise was reached, and the public would have media access to the funeral, but the family's privacy would be protected; their tears could be shed away from the cameras.

The dreaded hour approached; it was time for the funeral to start, time for them to say good-bye to the mother who had loved and protected them all of their lives. The world was waiting outside the door, the glare of the hot sun nearly matched by the television cameras and the photographers' long lenses. As her coffin was gently borne to the street, the waiting crowds got their first glimpse of it and a plaintive wail echoed through the quiet streets.

"Dianaaaaa."

As the horse-drawn caisson left the gates of Kensington Palace on the start of its two-mile journey to Westminster Abbey, the words Ted Kennedy had used to eulogize his sister-in-law four years earlier would have been equally apt. Just as we felt Jackie was "too young to die now," so too was Diana. When Ted spoke of Jackie, his tone was rueful and sad, but calm. Jackie's death had been preceded by months of illness and speculation. When, a few days before her death, she checked herself out of the hospital and returned home, we knew, as surely as she did herself, that she was going home to die. Diana's death, whether we learned of it late at night or first thing upon waking up that Sunday morning, was a shock that pierced our hearts.

They had lived separate lives, joined together in the public consciousness as women admired for their style more than their substance, but each made significant contributions to her country and the world. Their deaths brought a clearer understanding of those contributions, and their funerals were a way for us to express our appreciation.

Their funerals were like the magic looking glass in a fairy tale—in which their lives were reflected and the inner woman revealed. Jackie's funeral was elegant, dignified, and stoic, like Jackie herself. Diana's throbbed with emotion and raged with controversy. It was an intoxicating blend of formal ritual, spontaneity, and glamour, much like the princess.

Both the Kennedys and the Windsors debated strenuously over the amount of media coverage that would be allowed at the funerals. Both families would have welcomed the opportunity to grieve in private, yet they knew that it was not possible. Some members of the Kennedy family tried hard to persuade Caroline to make Jackie's funeral a grand public event, as close to a state funeral as possible for a private person. They argued that it was a fitting honor in light of Jackie's contributions to the nation. The bright spotlight that would shine on such a funeral would tap into the hidden reserves of warm regard that once embraced the entire family. In the end, though, Caroline's wishes prevailed; there would be no cameras in the church. She did relent enough to allow an audio broadcast of the service, which was carried live by all of the major television networks, save ABC.

Cameras were allowed at Arlington National Cemetery, where President Clinton would join the mourners and speak of the very great gifts that God had bestowed on Jackie, and of the equally great burdens he had imposed. He praised her dignity and her "uncommon common sense." We watched as her two children returned to the hillside gravesite of their father and knelt before their mother's coffin to wish her godspeed.

The debate in the Windsor family over Diana's funeral was rancorous and ultimately required the intervention of Prime Minister Tony Blair. Far from wanting any public ritual, the Windsor establishment wanted a private funeral, embellished with as little honor as possible. Their attitude did not take into account public opinion, and it took some very frank conversations between Tony Blair and Prince Charles before the Windsors displayed some flexibility and allowed for what was ultimately described as "a unique service for a unique person." The wishes of the public prevailed, with one exception. The queen allowed television cameras into Westminster Abbey, but she forbade them from turning their lenses on Diana's two sons or on any other member of the Windsor or Spencer families during the service.

That action was a sensitive one, shielding both Will and Harry and giving them a tiny island of privacy. But the queen and her advisers had shown little sensitivity to the memory of Diana during that week between her death and her burial. In shock, his emotions still raw, Diana's brother, Charles, sat down on the morning of Wednesday, September 3, to write a tribute to his sister. It would not only honor her memory but also, in stinging language, pay back some of the hurt and humiliation that Diana had suffered at the hands of her in-laws. Spencer's address was the most piercing rebuke ever personally delivered to the royal family.

Diana and Jackie each revolutionized a dynasty. Jackie's funeral was an occasion to celebrate the genteel revolution she had orchestrated thirty years earlier. One of Jackie's legacies is that she was the first First Lady who, in the words of Washington observer Sally Quinn, "established an identity for herself that was completely different from the President." She had elevated the cultural aspirations of her country and made us proud of our past. She had smashed the archetype. So had Diana. Just as there would never again be a First Lady who would not be compared with Jackie, there would never again be a princess who would not be compared with Diana. Diana's funeral brought the royal family closer to revolution than any event since the Boston Tea Party. The will of the people was heard, and the Windsors were forced to listen and forced to adapt. Diana, a child of the 1960s, the decade of social revolution, was the instrument of revolution at the turn of the millennium. Like it or not, and they surely did not, the Windsors will forever be affected by the changes Diana brought to the monarchy.

New York City, May 1994

Planning Jackie's funeral was a struggle to capture her essence, her son told the congregation assembled at St. Ignatius Loyola. "Three things came to mind over and over again," he said. "Her love of words, the bonds of home and family, and her spirit of adventure." With the help of their family and close friends, John and Caroline were able to create a funeral that was as elegant and poetic as the mother they honored that Monday morning.

The funeral was an exquisite tribute to the remarkable life of an extraordinary woman. Each detail was perfect, each passage of Scripture resonated with meaning, and each personal touch inserted into the formal Catholic ritual offered an appreciation of Jackie's spirit, from the lilies of the valley, her favorite flower, that Bunny Mellon lovingly arranged on her casket, to the navy hymn sung at her burial as it had been sung for JFK thirty-one years earlier. Even the decision to allow an audio broadcast of the service was in keeping with Jackie's essence. It was the lesson Black Jack had taught her so many years earlier: give them something, yes, but, more important, hold something back.

The guest list drew from every chapter of her life. First Ladies Hillary Clinton and Lady Bird Johnson went to honor a member of their elite sorority. Senator John Glenn, the shining symbol of JFK's space program, went, as did the society writer Aileen "Suzy" Mehle. Authors and musicians, elected officials and government appointees, society ladies and publishing executives—they all gathered under the marble dome of St. Ignatius Loyola.

The choice of St. Ignatius was a necessary convenience. Jackie's parish church of St. Thomas More was too small for the number of people that had to be invited, and St. Patrick's Cathedral, despite its connection to the Bouvier family, was not only too big, it also carried painful memories of Bobby's funeral Mass in 1968. But the church of Saint Ignatius, the Spanish nobleman who founded the Jesuit order in the sixteenth century, was a supremely appropriate choice. Jackie had been welcomed into the Catholic faith at St. Ignatius in 1929, attended Sunday Mass there throughout her childhood, and, taking the name Mary, had been confirmed there in 1941.

Jackie was, in effect, returning to her spiritual home, and as the cortege bearing her coffin made its way from 1040 Fifth Avenue, the seven hundred guests listened to Fauré's Requiem and Rachmaninoff's "Blessed Is the Man Who Lives Rightly." Jackie's love of words was reflected in the booklet presented to each guest, which was later published privately by Doubleday as a slim volume clad in periwinkle blue linen. An open seashell, the design that adorned her informal stationery and note cards, was used to decorate the pages, and its symbolic reference to Jackie's soul was underscored in an introductory poem by Sir Walter Raleigh:

> Give me my scallop-shell of quiet,
> My staff of faith to walk upon,

My scrip of joy, immortal diet.
My bottle of salvation,
My gown of glory, hope's true gage;
And thus I'll take my pilgrimage.

For Jackie's final pilgrimage, her children opened their arms and embraced the extended Kennedy, Bouvier, and Auchincloss families, as well as some of their mother's closest friends. Close to thirty family members and friends participated in the service. The eight honorary pallbearers included a representative from each branch of the Kennedy family, her godson Anthony Radziwill, an Auchincloss nephew, and John F. M. Walsh, her longtime Secret Service agent who had once saved her from drowning off the coast of Ireland.

The seven ushers included Kennedy and Auchincloss nieces and nephews, as well as Gustavo Parades, the son of Jackie's White House maid. Gustavo was a lifelong friend of John's; he had portrayed one of the three wise men in a Kennedy family Christmas pageant in 1962.

His mother, Providencia Parades, joined Jackie's cook, butler, and maid in the offertory procession. It was into Provi's arms that Jackie had finally collapsed the night after the assassination, and the two women had remained close. She had spoken to no reporters or biographers, revealing no details of the intimate relationship she shared with Jackie for almost ten years. Jackie valued that unwavering loyalty: Provi and her family used Jackie's house in Hyannis Port for a month every summer, and Provi was left a handsome bequest in Jackie's will.

The readings were chosen with tenderness and insight, and were taken from both the King James Version and the New American Bible so that each thought was articulated with subtlety and nuance. Though she had been raised Roman Catholic, she had studied the King James Bible at Vassar and loved its language. John gave the first reading, from Isaiah 25, which says, in part, "The Lord God will wipe away the tears from all the faces. . . . This is the Lord for whom we looked; let us rejoice and be glad that he has saved us."

Mike Nichols, the Academy Award–winning director who had been Jackie's frequent escort when she moved back to New York in the mid-1960s ("Going out with you," he told her, "is like taking out a national monument." "Yes," she replied, "but isn't it fun!"), delivered the second reading, from Revelation 2:1. Close friends Nancy Tuckerman and Jane Hitchcock; her son-in-law, Edwin Schlossberg; her goddaughter Sydney Lawford McKelvey; and JFK's goddaughter Tina Radziwill read passages and prayers.

Caroline chose Edna St. Vincent Millay's poem "Memory of Cape Cod," which she found in a book that Jackie kept in her bedroom, a book she had won as an outstanding scholar at Miss Porter's School. The poem spoke of Jackie's love of the outdoors: "Let me listen to the wind in the ash . . . It sounds like the surf on the shore."

Two men who had been closest to Jackie in different ways offered the most touching moments in the eighty-minute service. Maurice Tempelsman brought the rich imagery of ancient Greece and the warm sensuality of the Mediterranean into the Park Avenue church as he read C. P. Cavafy's "Ithaka":

May there be many summer mornings when,
with what pleasure, what joy,
you enter harbors you're seeing for the first time;
may you stop at Phoenician trading stations
to buy fine things,
mother of pearl and coral, amber and ebony,
sensual perfume of every kind—
as many sensual perfumes as you can . . .

The poem, about a journey to a Greek island, a spiritual adventure filled with imagery of jewelry and riches, was an oblique, and perhaps unintended, reference to the Onassis years; indeed, it was the closest to any mention of that part of Jackie's life in the entire service. It was a selfless and loving tribute from the man with whom Jackie had found such contentment in the last part of her life, and Tempelsman added a personal coda:

And now the journey is over,
too short, alas, too short.

It was filled with
adventure and wisdom
laughter and love
gallantry and grace.
So farewell, farewell.

As Maurice brought warmth to the soul, Ted Kennedy offered a gentle laugh and a warm embrace. After Communion, during which the great soprano Jesse Norman sang Schubert's "Ave Maria," he walked up to the altar and delivered the eulogy. Jackie adored Ted, whom she had first met when he was a Harvard student in the early 1950s. They had shared so many memories, both happy and sad. It was Ted and his first wife, Joan, to whom Jackie granted custody of her daughter in a 1960 will. It was Jackie who joined Ted in an all-night vigil at the deathbed of Joe Kennedy in 1969, sitting with him as the patriarch's life moved peacefully to its close. It was Ted who walked next to Jackie in JFK's funeral procession to St. Matthew's Cathedral in 1963 and, twelve years later, accompanied her to Greece to help bury her second husband. It was Ted whom Jackie turned to when Caroline was married, asking him to take Jack's place escorting the bride. It was Ted who toasted Jackie that night, calling her "that extraordinary woman, Jack's only love." And it was Ted called upon once more to deliver a eulogy for a woman he loved like a sister and who, as so sadly happens in the Kennedy family, had died before her time.

His spoke of her generosity of spirit, of her contributions to history, and of her devotion to her children. He spoke of her courage in 1963: "She lifted us up, and in the doubts and darkness, she gave her fellow citizens back their pride as Americans." He praised both the private and the public Jackie, telling funny stories and offering sobering insight. "She never wanted public notice," he said, "because it brought back painful memories of an unbearable sorrow." He spoke of how he cherished "those wonderful notes in her distinctive hand on her powder blue stationery." It was a graceful eulogy, and like every element of the funeral, it was supremely appropriate to the person being honored.

The funeral drew to a close with the same prayer that Cardinal Cushing had so movingly invoked in 1963: "May the angels take you into paradise . . ." The congregation paid tribute to both Jackie's role in history and her deeply felt patriotism, singing "America the Beautiful" as her coffin was borne up the aisle and carried out into the noonday sun.

And then there were two.

When Caroline had married, John had toasted his new brother-in-law by saying that "all my life there has just been the three of us . . ." And now, standing on the street in front of the church, it was just the two of them. With Ed Schlossberg and Maurice Tempelsman standing behind them, John wrapped his arm protectively around his elder sister as they watched their mother's coffin being prepared for transport to La Guardia Airport. They would accompany the coffin to Washington, just as their mother had done for their father, and bring their parents together for eternity on the gentle slope below the Custis-Lee Mansion, overlooking the city that they had once dazzled.

London, September 1997

There are times in public life when people rise to the occasion. In times of trial, or great happiness, or great sorrow, there are those few who can step up and do exactly what is necessary at that specific moment in time. Winston Churchill during World War II is one example; another, more contemporary, is New York mayor Rudolph Giuliani in the weeks after the World Trade Center tragedy. By virtue of the global reach of television, Jacqueline Kennedy became the most visible illustration of such a person those four days in November.

In eight and one half minutes on the morning of September 6, 1997, Charles Spencer joined their ranks. He was the center of the world's attention as he spoke of his sister, her extraordinary life, and shocking death, with a searing, impassioned oration.

Spencer said exactly what needed to be said, describing Diana's life with honesty and clarity—not so much attacking the royal family, the "establishment," and the press as holding them accountable for the part they played in her life. It was a loving gesture for Spencer, becoming the protector of the elder sister who had protected him as a child. A loving gesture, and a brave move. The queen, after all, was his godmother; his family had long been part of the aristocratic establishment, and he himself had once served as her page of honor. And yet his first thrust came but a hundred and fifty words into his speech when he rightly claimed that Diana "needed no royal title to continue to generate her particular brand of magic." Those sitting in the abbey caught their breath, for one does not speak like that in front of the queen, and all eyes discreetly turned toward the monarch to gauge her reaction. But Elizabeth, with over sixty years' experience of holding back her emotions in public, sat impassively, her eyes focused straight on the coffin of the woman she had once characterized as "that troublesome girl."

"That troublesome girl" had blossomed into a complex woman, and her funeral incorporated many of the different essences that made her both admired and reviled. She had taken a moribund institution and infused it with glamour and compassion. To every person who claimed she trivialized the monarchy, there were those who believed she made it more relevant. For every film star she met at a premiere, there were a dozen AIDS patients or elderly invalids whose sickbed she had sat on. She was, as Charles said, "a very British girl who transcended nationality" and "someone with a natural nobility who was classless."

Diana's funeral was a remarkable event in English history, truly unique as it wove elements from all the disparate aspects of her life. It was the climax of a week that had seen a public outpouring of emotion never before seen in the land of the "stiff upper lip." The people of Britain had surprised themselves with the depth of their feeling. They wept without shame, mourned without guilt, and turned hostile to those who wouldn't follow suit. All Britain turned to London to mourn her. Gathered in the nave of the great medieval abbey were royalty and movie stars, aristocrats and servants, corporate executives and celebrity dressmakers, pop stars and charity workers.

All these elements came together that morning in Westminster Abbey. The service was a blend of old and new, formal and casual, classical and pop. There were the traditional hymns: "I Vow to Thee, My Country," which uses music from Gustav Holst's *The Planets*. It had been sung so movingly at the funeral of Lord Mountbatten in 1979. Diana had heard it then, and asked for it to be sung at her wedding. The prayer of St. Francis of Assisi contained Diana's credo—"Where there's despair in life, let me bring hope." The Westminster Boys Choir sang "An Air from County Derry," the melody familiar to most as the Irish song "Danny Boy."

The Spencer family had asked Luciano Pavarotti to sing, but the Italian tenor feared that he would not be able to control his emotions and begged off. Elton John was Prince William's suggestion. He and Diana had been close for many years; a recent fissure in their relationship had been repaired earlier in the summer at the funeral of the designer Gianni Versace. John, with his partner, Bernie Taupin, reworked the lyrics to one of his most haunting songs, "Candle in the Wind." The song was an elegy to Marilyn Monroe, who, like Diana, had died at the age of thirty-six. In calling her "England's rose," John elevated Diana into the pantheon of pop iconography (and earned himself the scorn of Rolling Stone Keith Richards, who sneered at "another song about a dead blonde").

Earl Spencer's address followed John, but both of Diana's sisters participated in the service. Sarah read a stanza by A. Price Hughes that was traditionally read at Spencer family memorial services. Jane, her voice eerily reminiscent of Diana's, chose another Spencer family favorite, Henry Van Dyke's "Time."

> Time is too slow for those who wait,
> Too swift for those who fear,

Too long for those who grieve,
Too short for those who rejoice
But for those who love, time is eternity.

Listening in the abbey were family and friends, people from all periods of Diana's life. The Windsors had, for the day, welcomed Sarah Ferguson, the now-nonroyal duchess of York, back into the family, and she sat with her ex-husband and their children in the row behind the queen and Prince Philip. Television cameras showed a weeping Fergie as she entered the church, looking more slender than she had since the day of her wedding, the last major royal event to have taken place in Westminster Abbey. Sarah looked so slim that enrollment in Weight Watchers, whose TV commercials she appeared in, skyrocketed in the weeks following the funeral.

The film director Steven Spielberg came, waiting in line for his place along with actors Tom Cruise, Nicole Kidman, and Tom Hanks. Diana Ross was spotted in the crowd, as was Diana's stepmother Raine, who stopped to admire the floral tributes with a theatrical flourish, ensuring that all the photographers were able to get a shot of her. The designer Karl Lagerfeld attended with *Vogue* editor Anna Wintour and Gianni Versace's sister, Donatella. George Michael came, as did Sting and his wife, Trudie Styler. Luciano Pavarotti arrived and looked slightly abashed as he was led to his seat at the very rear of the abbey. Hillary Clinton came, and sat next to Queen Noor of Jordan in the row to the left of the royal family. French President Jacques Chirac and his wife, who had escorted Charles and the Spencer sisters at the hospital in Paris that sad Sunday afternoon, sat with former prime ministers Margaret Thatcher and John Major and the American statesman Henry Kissinger.

Sitting off to the side in the Northern Transept was Mary Robertson, one of Diana's first employers, who had hired her as an au pair. The two women had maintained their friendship. For Diana it was a touchstone to her former life, and she had had memorable reunions with Mary and her former charge, Patrick, in Washington, D.C., and in London. Patrick's passport had expired, so Mrs. Robertson traveled to London alone to say good-bye to the woman she had known for so many years. As she sat in the abbey, she listened to the congregation sing "God Save the Queen," the national anthem that shares a melody with the American song "My Country 'Tis of Thee." As the song ended, Mrs. Robertson heard a voice behind her mutter, in reference to the queen, "May she drop dead tomorrow," and wondered if she was witnessing treason.

Treason? Perhaps not. But as the ceremony unfolded and Earl Spencer delivered his eulogy, Mrs. Robertson wondered if she was hearing correctly. Certainly in England, in other times, the response to Spencer's oration would have been a swift "Off with his head." But that day in Britain, there was nothing but support for Diana. Mary Robertson listened and watched in amazement as the sound of applause, at first appearing like gentle summer thunder, grew from the crowds watching the service in Hyde Park and listening to it in Parliament Square until it engulfed the abbey. The majority of the nineteen hundred mourners joined in while the queen and her family sat in stunned silence. It was a moment of quiet revolution, and as Elizabeth sat there, the power of the moment must have revealed itself to her.

Diana had revolutionized the monarchy, and no sign was more evident of the royal family's surrender to the power she held over them than an incident that had occurred earlier that morning. As Diana's funeral procession passed Buckingham Palace, the Windsor family, led by the queen and including every member except the ninety-seven-year-old Queen Mother and the quartet of princes who would be joining the procession as it passed St. James's Palace, walked across the forecourt and stood, waiting, at the Monarch's Gate. It was an unprecedented display, as the queen waits for no one—she arrives last and leaves first, and people wait for *her*. There she stood, lined up with her family, two or three deep, waiting for Diana just as her subjects had waited so many times for her to pass by. The American television commentators didn't realize what they were witnessing, but their British counterparts did, and were amazed. What happened next truly astonished them.

As the coffin passed in front of her, the queen bowed her head in honor. It was an extraordinary moment in the history of Elizabeth's reign. As Queen Regnant, Elizabeth outranks everyone. She is the equal of few (other monarchs, a sitting President, the Pope), but second to none. The one other time in her reign when she had shown obeisance to another person was forty-five years earlier when she gave her last curtsy to her father, as his coffin lay in St. George's Chapel, Windsor. George VI had not only been her beloved father, he had been her king and the former emperor of India. It was an extraordinary gesture on the part of the queen to honor Diana, a woman whom Elizabeth neither loved nor respected. Seven days earlier she had reluctantly authorized use of one of her airplanes to retrieve Diana's body ("Would you rather, ma'am," a courtier asked, "that she be taken away in a Harrods van?"); that day Elizabeth bowed before her. At that moment, Diana had bent the will of the queen and altered the course of the monarchy. Elizabeth may be forgiven if she was relieved as the service drew to a close.

For many watching the funeral, the recessional was unbearably moving. The honor guard moved into place, their scarlet coats standing out from the sea of black-dressed mourners. Locking their hands and arms together, they lifted Diana's coffin to their shoulders. The final hymn began. Prince Charles had suggested the music "Song for Athene," a tribute the modern classical composer John Tavener had written for a close friend who had died in a cycling accident. For his lyrics, he took lines from Hamlet—"May flights of angels sing thee to thy rest"—and the orthodox funeral service—"Come, enjoy rewards and crowns I have prepared for you." The melody was based on early Christian chanting, and as the atonal music filled the nave of the Gothic structure, the only other sound one could hear was the rhythmic cadence of the honor guards' boots against the ancient stones as they slowly carried Diana toward the great west door of the abbey.

It was a moment of medieval splendor. The great gray walls of Westminster Abbey, witness to nine hundred years of coronations and weddings and funerals. The sun streaming though the jewel-tone rose windows. The royal standard draped over the coffin, its gold lions and harps, its fields of blue and red, its white border joining the honor guards' coats and bishops cloaks as the only splashes of color as it slowly made its way up the aisle. The quiet sobs and rustling handkerchiefs following the coffin on its slow journey. When the cortege reached the Great West Door, shortly after twelve noon, it came to a halt. There was a minute of silence as the nation stopped to pray in remembrance of Diana.

Then the half-muffled bells of the abbey rang out, their clangers wrapped in leather strips to deaden the sound. Diana's coffin was placed in a hearse, which would drive to Althorp. She was to be buried on an island in the middle of an ornamental lake behind the great house. Only ten mourners were allowed on the island to bid a final farewell—her two sons, her ex-husband, her mother, her brother, her two sisters and their husbands, and the only nonfamily member, her butler, Paul Burrell. The public farewell was over. But the public couldn't let go quite yet. As the hearse drove through London, people stood on the road and tossed flowers at the car. A carpet of blossoms wend its way through the city as the hearse drove through the crowded streets toward the highway. The bouquets piled up on top of the hood, and the driver had to stop and remove them as they blocked his windshield. Our last view of Diana was of the hearse approaching the honey-colored stone gates of Althorp. As the motorcade slowed down to pass through the narrow gates, the cameras clicked for one last time, and Diana slipped away forever.

There is a Native American proverb that says, "When you are born, you cry and the world rejoices. Live your life in such a way that when you die, the world cries and you rejoice." The world cried at the death of Diana Frances Spencer, Princess of Wales; she had earned her right to rejoice.

Afterword

"Fifty years from now, they're not going to be writing books and musicals about Princess Margaret and Princess Anne," the writer Dominick Dunne once said. "They're going to be writing about Diana. She upstaged the British royal family. The aristos hate her. The crowds love her. She's a great character."

The same is true about Jackie. Nobody is writing about Mamie Eisenhower or Bess Truman. Fifty years of newspaper articles, books, plays, and even an opera haven't dampened our interested in her. She remains a unique figure on the American scene.

Jackie enriched our spirit. Diana ennobled our psyche. Jackie's impact let Americans look at their country with renewed pride, knowing that an American dance company or an American designer represented the best in the world. Diana's influence enabled people around the world to look at themselves with more pride—paradoxically, by encouraging them to take an inward look at their flaws, and to feel less shame because Diana spoke out for them. This was Diana's gift.

They became public figures through their relationship with men, through marriage. It has been said that Jackie and Jack had an imperfect perfect marriage—despite their problems, they were well suited to each other temperamentally and on an intellectual plane. If that is the case, then Diana and Charles could be said to have had a perfect imperfect marriage—with nothing in common and widely disparate temperaments. But in surviving their turbulent marriages, both Diana and Jackie emerged as independent women.

If Jackie taught us how to behave in the face of calamity, Diana taught us how to behave in the face of hypocrisy. Jackie successfully rode the tiger that is fame, while Diana spent most of her life being tumbled and tossed about. Just as she was gaining a stronger understanding of her ability to empathize with those in need, she fell victim to her fame, hunted like an animal into a tunnel.

Jackie, too, could empathize with people who were suffering, and she did so in the unobtrusive manner that characterized the last two decades of her life. One example: There were a few select stores on Manhattan's Upper East Side where she felt protected enough to seek refuge if she wanted a brief rest or needed to escape the advances of the public or the press. At one of them, a woman with whom Jackie had cultivated an affectionate acquaintance recalled a heartfelt chat when her marriage was falling apart. Jackie took her hand, looked her in the eye, and said, "You *will* survive this. Remember that." When the initial shock of "Oh my God, Jacqueline Onassis is giving *me* advice about a difficult husband" faded, Jackie's genuine concern helped the woman put her situation into a perspective that made her feel less isolated, less in pain. What Jackie did for a small circle of friends and trusted associates, Diana did for the world.

And yet Diana could approach a crisis with the same sense of calm dignity and steely will that Jackie employed. Her take-charge attitude during the Klosters avalanche disaster in 1988 is one example; another is the funeral of Princess Grace of Monaco in September 1982. She had been a royal princess for little more than a year, a mother for three months, and was battling a combination of postpartum depression and marital woes. With dignity and poise, Diana ably represented the Windsors at the funeral of the glamorous blond princess whose death— following a tragic automobile accident—eerily presaged Diana's own.

Diana and Jackie were complex women and, years after their deaths, remain fascinating characters. Jack Kennedy, of all people, understood the appeal of a strong character moving across the pages of history. Sitting on the brick paved terrace of his Hyannis Port cottage one summer night, he told his friend Ben Bradlee, "What makes journalism so fascinating and biography so interesting [is] the struggle to answer that single question: What's he like?"

As we live in the age of a fervent press, that question—"What was she like?"—is certain to be asked again and again for years. The answer undoubtedly will prove to be as elusive and complex as the two ladies themselves.

Acknowledgments

Jack Kennedy once said, "One of the great myths of American life is that nothing is pleasanter or easier than lying around all day and painting a picture or writing a book and leading a rather easy life. In my opinion, the ultimate in self-discipline is a creative work." A writer himself, he understood the rigors and the hours of isolation that come with the job. Even though the process of writing is a solitary exercise, it is, in fact, a collaborative endeavor and one in which I have been the beneficiary of much largesse.

I have been blessed by the inspiration and support of a contemporary version of the three graces: Linda Frances Lee, Victoria Moran, and Cathy Pratt.

There are family members and friends of both Diana, Princess of Wales, and Jacqueline Kennedy Onassis who gave generously of their time and memories. Those who asked not to be mentioned by name are hereby acknowledged and thanked, unnamed as promised but much appreciated.

Heartfelt thanks to Yusha Auchincloss, Letitia Baldrige, Lesley Ann Beck, Barbara Bejoian, Kathie Berlin, Lois Bradford, Alice Cahn, Paula and Bob Cashin, Cathy Cavender, Bob Colacello, Megan Desnoyers, the duke and duchess of Devonshire, Dominick Dunne, Grada Fischer, Lisa Gamble, Caroline Gervasi, Alan Goodrich, Christopher Harrington, James Hill, Jorge Jaramillo, Joan Bennett Kennedy, Josh Kamerman, Marjorie Kaplan, Sally Kilbridge, Tom Lynch, Vasken Matteosian, Andrea Miller, Deborah Mitchell, Katy Mulvaney, Carol Ostrow, Charles Passler, Barbara Reeder, Richard Robertiello, Mary Salter, Frances Schwartz, Kathrin Seitz, Julie Sogg Seymour, Denise Shapiro, James Spada, Jeff Steele, Elisa Sullivan,

Kathleen and Dek Tillett, Lady Anne Tree, Jim Wagner, Mark West, and to all my unnamed angels in the rooms.

Special thanks go to Tom Eslinger, who knows why.

At St. Martin's Press, I am indebted to Sally Richardson and her team, including Meg Drislane, Karen Gillis, Lisa Herman, Susan Joseph, Amelie Littell, Michael McKenzie, John Murphy, Laura Russo, James Sinclair, and Steve Snider. I want to acknowledge and thank Steve Lamont, whose graceful copy editing of all three of my books has improved them immeasurably. I am grateful for the support from Joe Cleemann, Anderson Bailey, Josh Rivkin, and, above all, my great friend and that able disassembler of my baroque syntax, Charles Spicer.

As always, best love to Meghan Cashin, Colleen Cashin, and Kevin Cashin.

Bibliography

Adler, Bill. *The Uncommon Wisdom of Jacqueline Kennedy Onassis. A Portrait in Her Own Words*. New York: Citadel Press, 1994.

Anderson, Christopher. *Diana's Boys*. New York: William Morrow, 2001.

————. *The Day Diana Died*. New York: William Morrow, 1998.

————. *Jack and Jackie: Portrait of an American Marriage*. New York: William Morrow and Company, 1996.

Anthony, Carl Sferrazza. *As We Remember Her*. New York: HarperCollins Publishers, 1997.

Aronson, Theo. *Royal Family: Years of Transition*. London: John Murray, 1983.

Baldrige, Leticia. *A Lady, First*. New York: Viking, 2001.

Barry, Stephen. *Royal Service: My Twelve Years as Valet to Prince Charles*. New York: Macmillan, 1983.

————. *Royal Secrets: The View from Downstairs*. New York: Villard Books, 1985.

Berry, Wendy. *The Housekeeper's Diary: Charles and Diana Before the Breakup*. New York: Barricade Books, 1995.

Bradford, Sarah. *Elizabeth: A Biography of Britain's Queen*. New York: Farrar, Straus & Giroux, 1996.

————. *America's Queen: The Life of Jacqueline Kennedy Onassis*. New York: Viking, 2000.

Christie's. *Dresses from the Collection of Diana, Princess of Wales*. Sale catalog. New York: Christie's, June 25, 1997.

Clarke, Mary. *Diana: Once upon a Time*. London: Sidgwick & Jackson, 1994.

Clayton, Tim, and Phil Craig. *Diana: Story of a Princess*. London: Pocket Books, 2001.

Curtis, Charlotte. *The First Lady*. New York: Pyramid Books, 1962.

Dallas, Rita, with Jeanira Ratcliffe. *The Kennedy Case*. New York: G. P Putnam's Sons, 1973.

Davis, John H. *The Bouviers: Portrait of an American Family*. New York: Farrar, Straus & Giroux, 1969.

Dimbleby, Jonathan. *The Prince of Wales: A Biography*. New York: Morrow, 1994.

Edwards, Anne. *Ever After: Diana and the Life She Led*. New York: St. Martin's Press, 1999.

Gallagher, Mary Barelli. *My Life with Jacqueline Kennedy*. New York: David McKay Company, 1969.

Goodwin, Doris Kearns. *The Fitzgeralds and the Kennedys: An American Saga*. New York: Simon & Schuster, 1987.

Hall, Unity. *The Private Lives of Britain's Royal Women*. London: Michael O'Mara Books, 1991.

Hewitt, James. *Love and War*. London: Blake, 1999.

Heyman, C. David. *A Woman Named Jackie*. New York: Signet, 1990.

Hoey, Brian. *Her Majesty: Fifty Regal Years*. London: HarperCollins, 2001.

James, Robert Rhodes, editor. *Chips: The Diaries of Sir Henry Channon*. London, Weidenfeld and Nicolson, 1967.

Jephson, P. D. *Shadows of a Princess*. London: HarperCollins, 2000.

Kennedy, Rose Fitzgerald. *Times to Remember*. New York: Doubleday. 1975.

Klein, Edward. *Just Jackie: Her Private Years*. New York: Ballantine, 1998.

———. *All Too Human: The Love Story of Jack and Jackie Kennedy*. New York: Pocket Books, 1996.

Learner, Laurence. *The Kennedy Men: 1901–1963*. New York, William Morrow, 2001.

———. *The Kennedy Women*. New York: Doubleday, 1994.

Levin, Angela. *Raine & Johnnie: The Spencers and the Scandal of Althorp*. London: Weidenfeld and Nicolson, 1993.

Levine, Michael. *The Princess and the Package: Exploring the Love-Hate Relationship Between Diana and the Media*. Los Angeles: Renaissance Books, 1998.

Lowe, Jacques. *Jacqueline Kennedy Onassis: A Tribute by Jacques Lowe*. New York: Jacques Lowe Visual Arts Project, 1995.

Manchester, William. *The Death of a President: November 1963*. New York: Harper & Row, 1967.

Morton, Andrew. *Diana: Her True Story—In Her Own Words*. New York: Simon & Schuster, 1997.

———. *Inside Kensington Palace*: London: Michael O'Mara Books, 1987.

Pottker, Jan. *Janet and Jackie: The Story of a Mother and Her Daughter, Jacqueline Kennedy Onassis*. New York: St. Martin's Press, 2001.

Radziwill, Lee. *Happy Times*. New York: Assouline, 2001.

Robertson, Mary. *The Diana I Knew*. New York: HarperCollins, 1998.

Sgubin, Marta, and Nancy Nicholas. *Cooking for Madam*. New York: A Lisa Drew Book/Scribner, 1998.

Seward, Ingred. *The Queen and Di*. New York: Arcade Publishing, 2001.

———. *Royal Style*. New York: St. Martin's Press, 1988.

Smith, Amanda (editor). *Hostage to Fortune: The Letters of Joseph P. Kennedy*. New York: Viking, 2001.

Smith, Sally Bedell. *Diana in Search of Herself: Portrait of a Troubled Princess*. New York: New American Library, 2000.

Sotheby's. *The Estate of Jacqueline Kennedy Onassis*. Sale catalog. New York: Sotheby's, April 23–26, 1996.

Spencer, Charles. *Althorp: The Story of an English House*. New York: St. Martin's Press, 1998.

Thayer, Mary Van Rensselaer. *Jacqueline Bouvier Kennedy*. New York: Doubleday, 1961.

Whitaker, James. *Charles vs. Diana: Royal Blood Feud*. New York: Dutton, 1993.

York, Sarah, the Duchess of, with Jeff Coplon. *My Story*. New York: Simon & Schuster, 1996.

Index